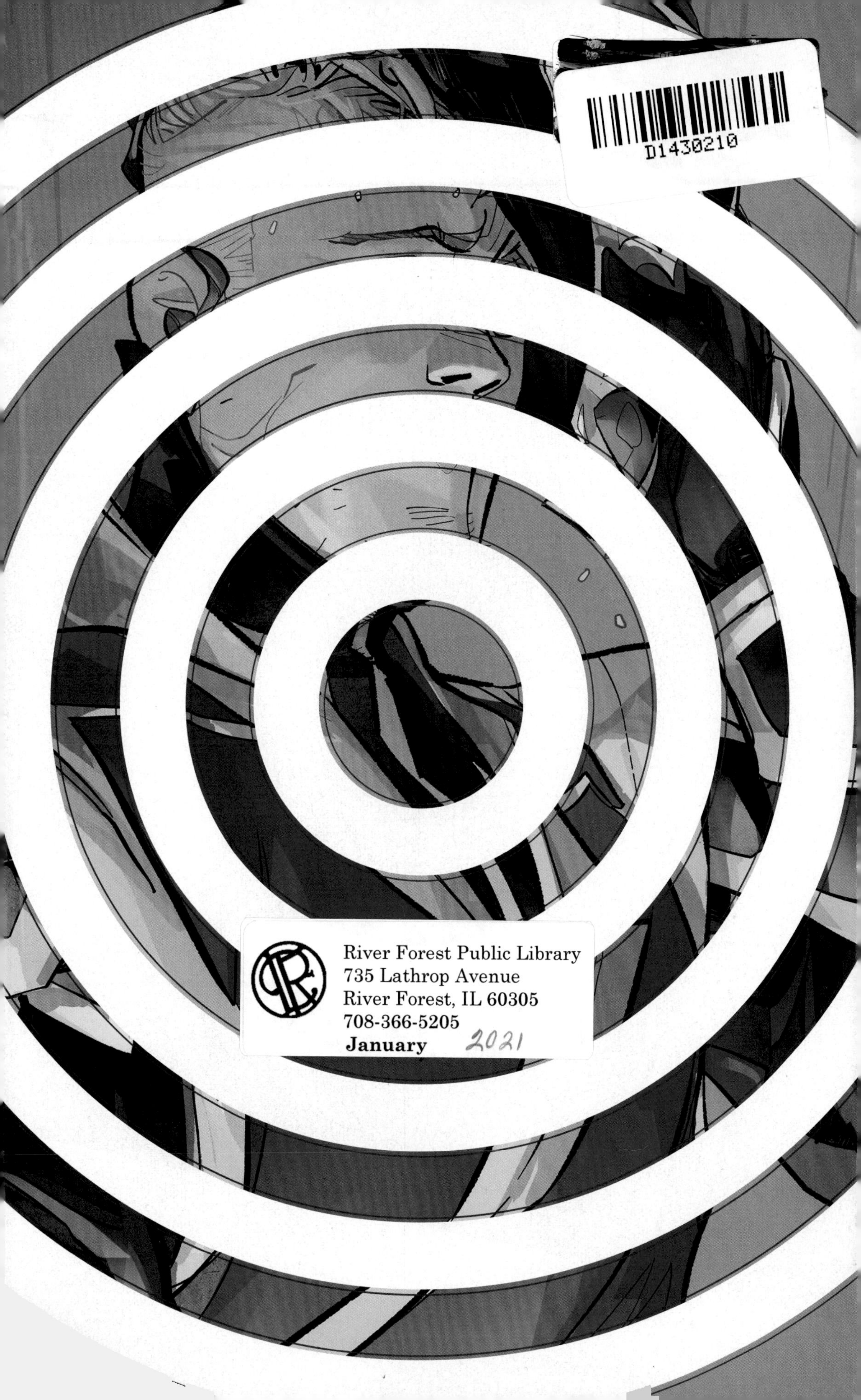

HAWKEYE: FREEFALL. Contains material originally published in magazine form as HAWKEYE: FREEFALL (2020) #1-6. First printing 2020. ISBN 978-1-302-92111-8. Published by MARVEL WORLDWIDE, INC., a subsidiary of MARVEL ENTERTAINMENT. LLC. OFFICE OF PUBLICATION: 1290 Avenue of the Americas, New York, NY 10104. © 2020 MARVEL No similarity between any of the names, characters, persons, and/or institutions in this magazine with those of any living or dead person or institution is intended, and any such similarity which may exist is purely coincidental. **Printed in Canada.** KEVIN FEIGE, Chief Creative Officer; DAN BUCKLEY, President, Marvel Entertainment; JOHN NEE, Publisher; JOE QUESADA, EVP & Creative Director; TOM BREVOORT, SVP of Publishing; DAVID BOGART, Associate Publisher & SVP of Talent Affairs; Publishing & Partnership; DAVID GABRIEL, VP of Print & Digital Publishing; JEFF YOUNGQUIST. VP of Production & Special Projects; DAN CARR, Executive Director of Publishing Technology; ALEX MORALES, Director of Publishing Operations; DAN EDINGTON, Managing Editor; RICKEY PURDIN, Director of Talent Relations; SUSAN CRESPI, Production Manager; STAN LEE, Chairman Emeritus. For information regarding advertising in Marvel Comics or on Marvel.com, please contact Vit DeBellis, Custom Solutions & Integrated Advertising Manager, at vdebellis@marvel.com. For Marvel subscription inquiries, please call 888-511-5480. **Manufactured between 10/30/2020 and 12/1/2020 by SOLISCO PRINTERS, SCOTT, QC, CANADA.**

10 9 8 7 6 5 4 3 2 1

WRITER: **MATTHEW ROSENBERG**
ARTIST: **OTTO SCHMIDT**
LETTERER: **VC's JOE SABINO**

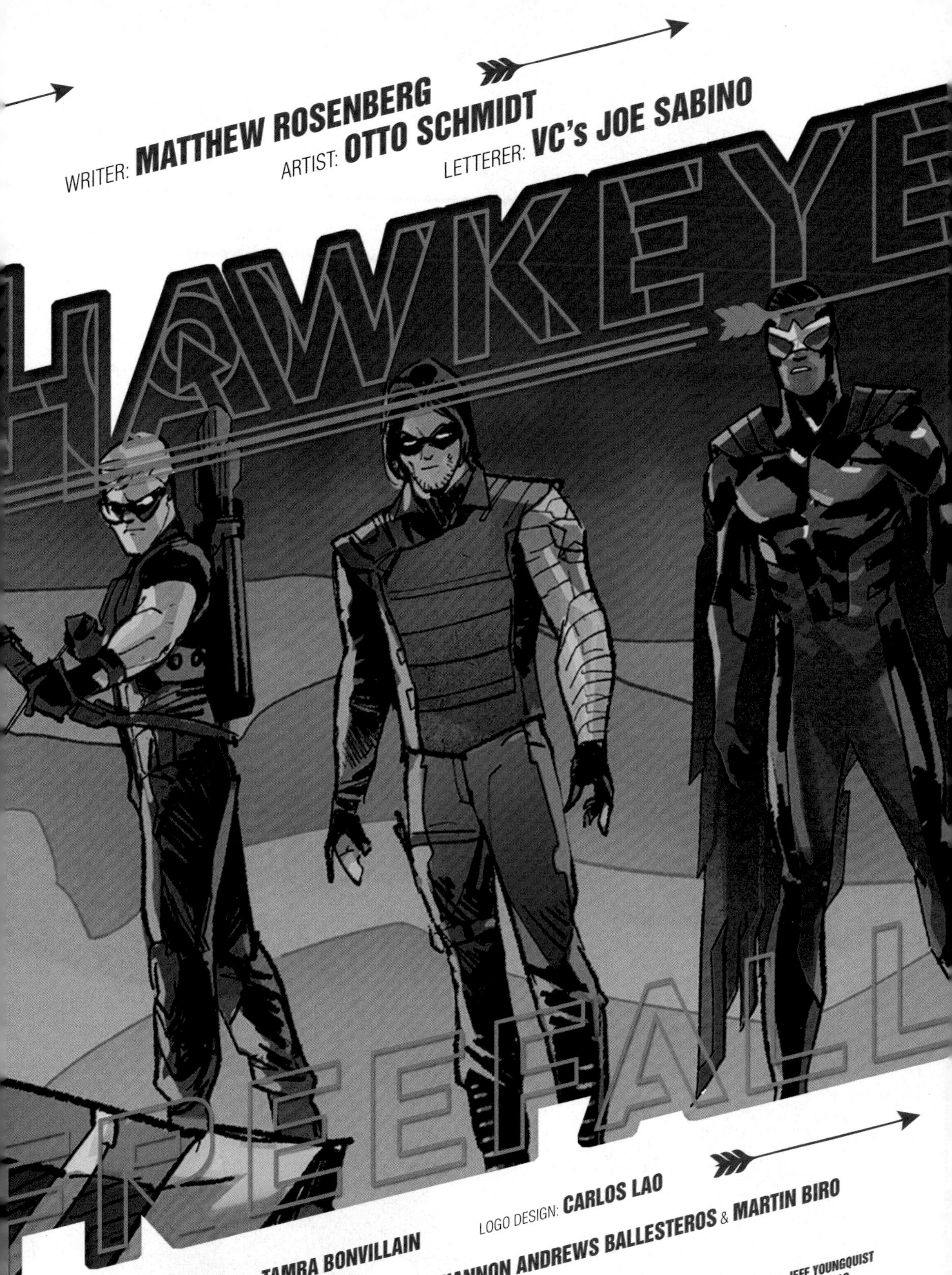

LOGO DESIGN: **CARLOS LAO**
COVER ART: **KIM JACINTO** & **TAMRA BONVILLAIN**
ASSISTANT EDITORS: **SHANNON ANDREWS BALLESTEROS** & **MARTIN BIRO**
EDITOR: **ALANNA SMITH**

COLLECTION EDITOR: **JENNIFER GRÜNWALD**
ASSISTANT MANAGING EDITOR: **MAIA LOY**
ASSISTANT MANAGING EDITOR: **LISA MONTALBANO**

VP PRODUCTION & SPECIAL PROJECTS: **JEFF YOUNGQUIST**
BOOK DESIGNER: **ADAM DEL RE** WITH **CARLOS LAO**
SVP PRINT, SALES & MARKETING: **DAVID GABRIEL**
EDITOR IN CHIEF: **C.B. CEBULSKI**

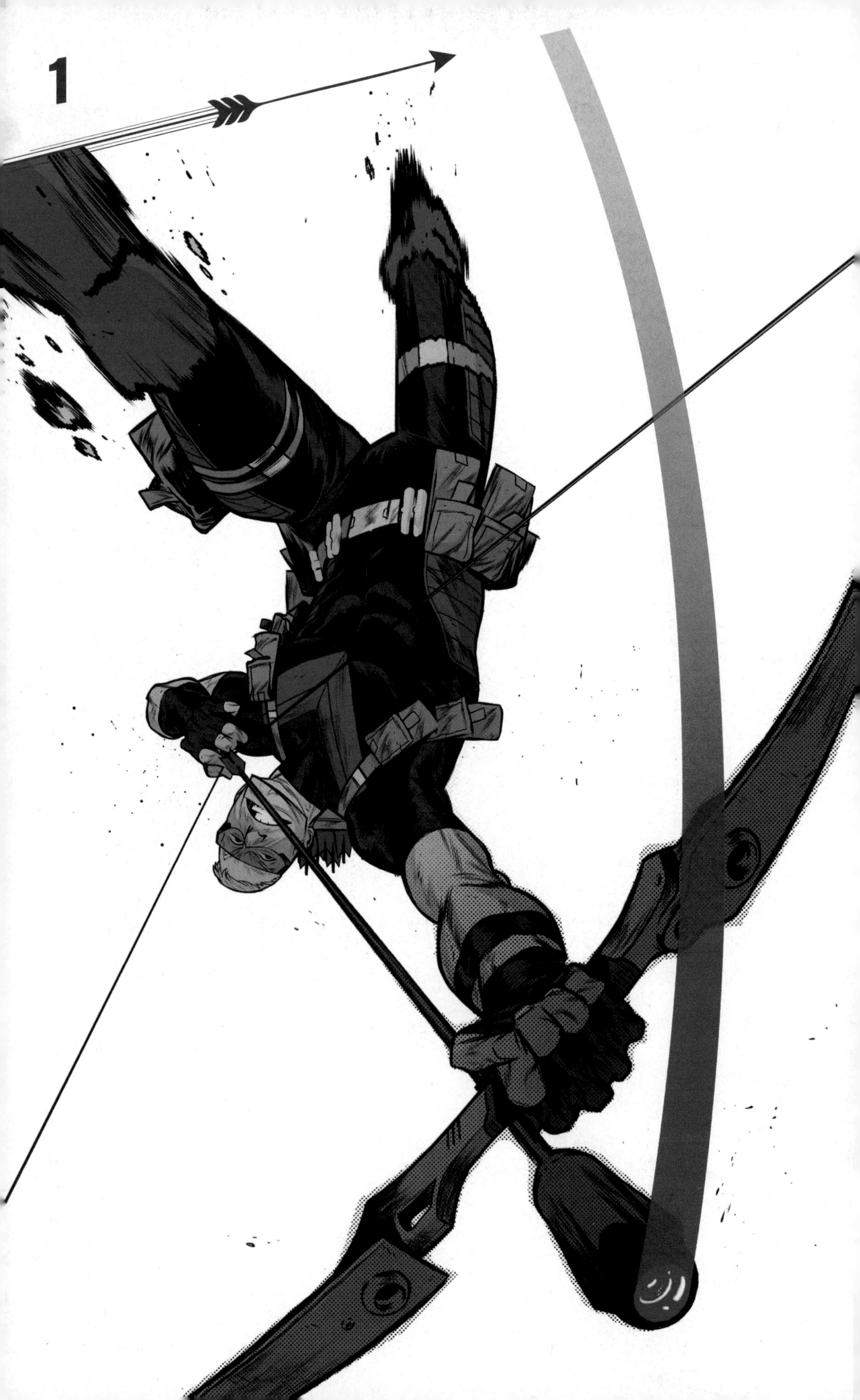
1

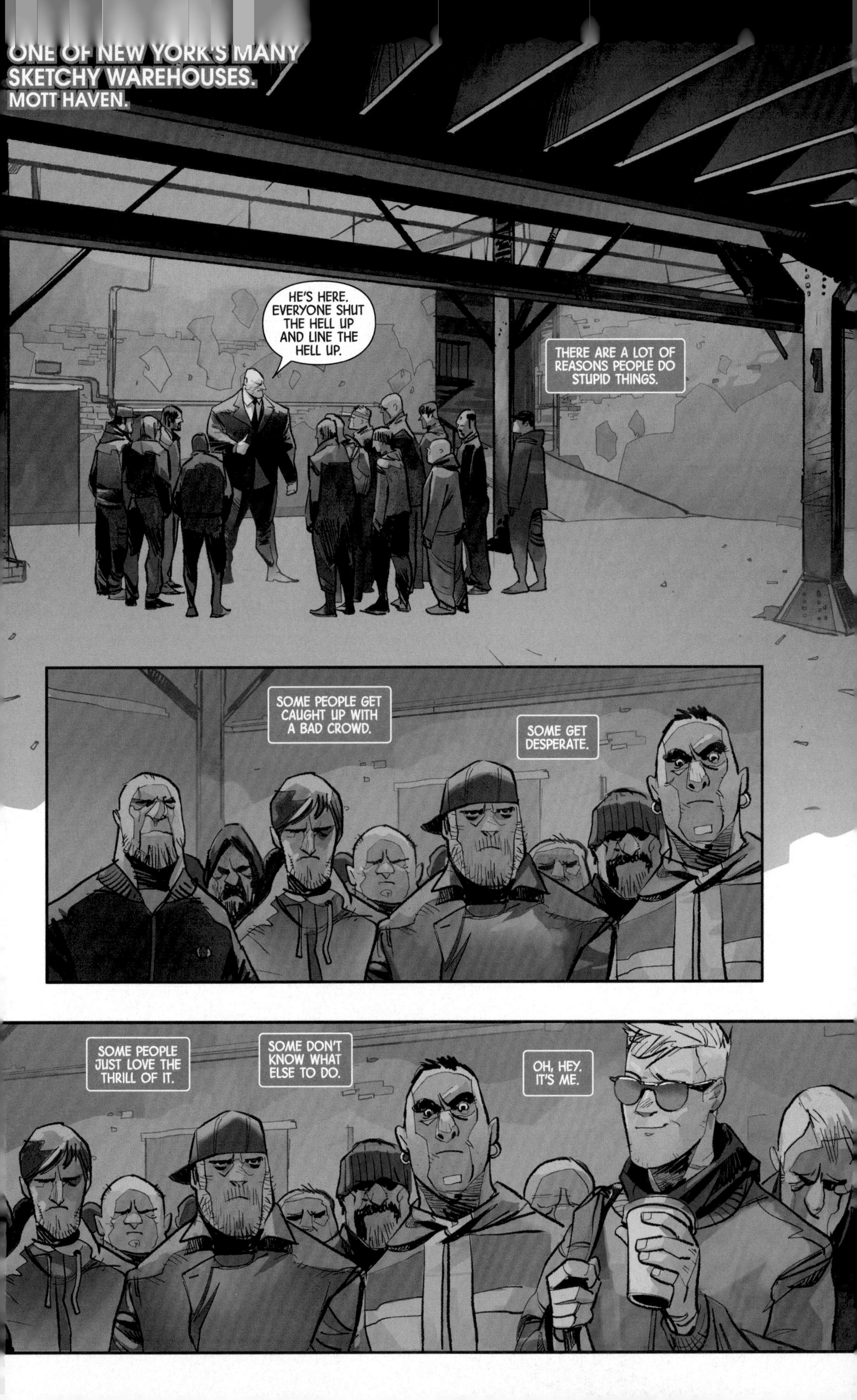
ONE OF NEW YORK'S MANY SKETCHY WAREHOUSES.
MOTT HAVEN.
HE'S HERE. EVERYONE SHUT THE HELL UP AND LINE THE HELL UP.
THERE ARE A LOT OF REASONS PEOPLE DO STUPID THINGS.
SOME PEOPLE GET CAUGHT UP WITH A BAD CROWD.
SOME GET DESPERATE.
SOME PEOPLE JUST LOVE THE THRILL OF IT.
SOME DON'T KNOW WHAT ELSE TO DO.
OH, HEY. IT'S ME.

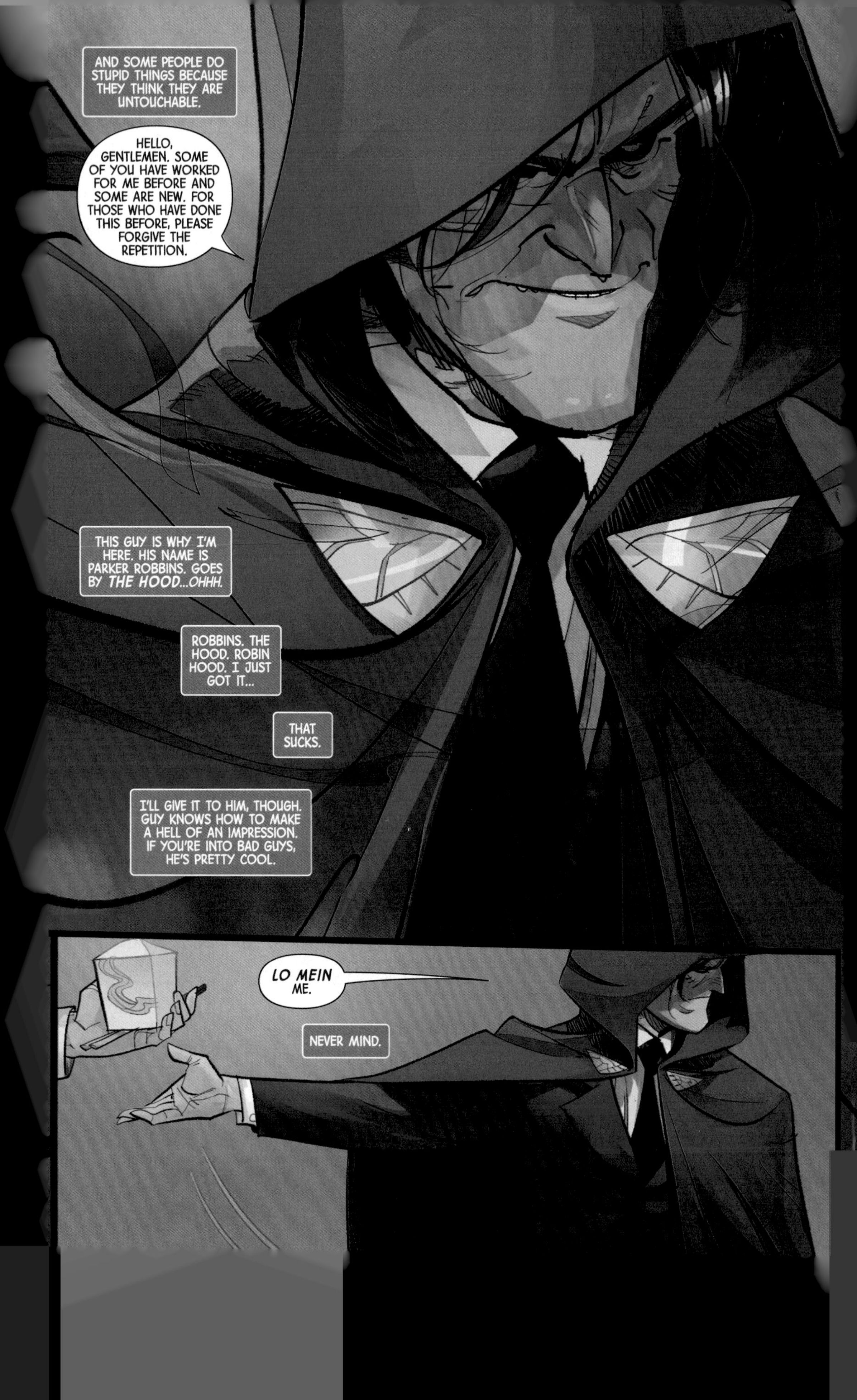
AND SOME PEOPLE DO STUPID THINGS BECAUSE THEY THINK THEY ARE UNTOUCHABLE.
HELLO, GENTLEMEN. SOME OF YOU HAVE WORKED FOR ME BEFORE AND SOME ARE NEW. FOR THOSE WHO HAVE DONE THIS BEFORE, PLEASE FORGIVE THE REPETITION.
THIS GUY IS WHY I'M HERE. HIS NAME IS PARKER ROBBINS. GOES BY THE HOOD...OHHH.
ROBBINS. THE HOOD. ROBIN HOOD. I JUST GOT IT...
THAT SUCKS.
I'LL GIVE IT TO HIM, THOUGH. GUY KNOWS HOW TO MAKE A HELL OF AN IMPRESSION. IF YOU'RE INTO BAD GUYS, HE'S PRETTY COOL.
LO MEIN ME.
NEVER MIND.

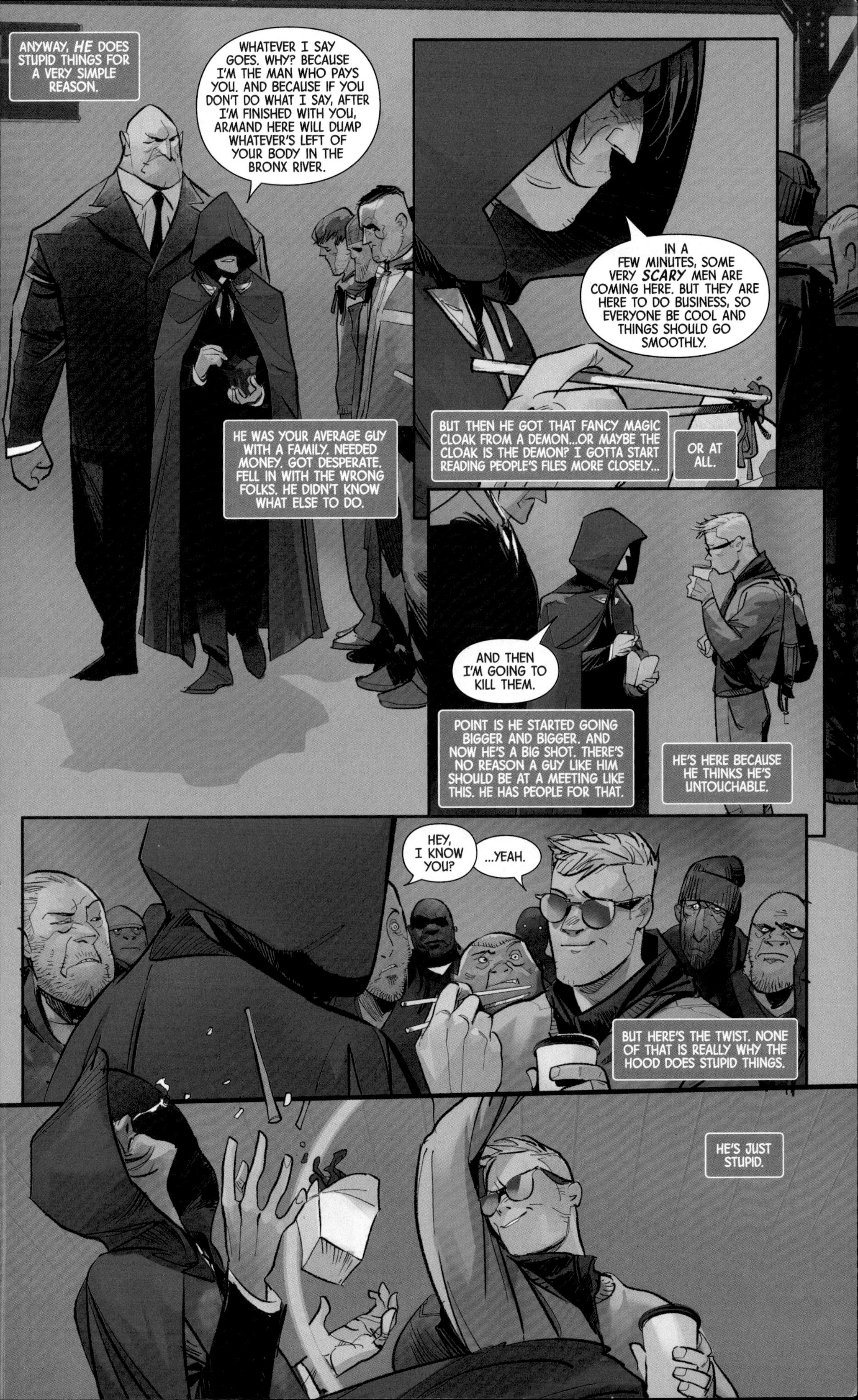

ANYWAY, HE DOES STUPID THINGS FOR A VERY SIMPLE REASON.
WHATEVER I SAY GOES. WHY? BECAUSE I'M THE MAN WHO PAYS YOU. AND BECAUSE IF YOU DON'T DO WHAT I SAY, AFTER I'M FINISHED WITH YOU, ARMAND HERE WILL DUMP WHATEVER'S LEFT OF YOUR BODY IN THE BRONX RIVER.
HE WAS YOUR AVERAGE GUY WITH A FAMILY. NEEDED MONEY. GOT DESPERATE. FELL IN WITH THE WRONG FOLKS. HE DIDN'T KNOW WHAT ELSE TO DO.
IN A FEW MINUTES, SOME VERY SCARY MEN ARE COMING HERE. BUT THEY ARE HERE TO DO BUSINESS, SO EVERYONE BE COOL AND THINGS SHOULD GO SMOOTHLY.
BUT THEN HE GOT THAT FANCY MAGIC CLOAK FROM A DEMON...OR MAYBE THE CLOAK IS THE DEMON? I GOTTA START READING PEOPLE'S FILES MORE CLOSELY...
OR AT ALL.
AND THEN I'M GOING TO KILL THEM.
POINT IS HE STARTED GOING BIGGER AND BIGGER. AND NOW HE'S A BIG SHOT. THERE'S NO REASON A GUY LIKE HIM SHOULD BE AT A MEETING LIKE THIS. HE HAS PEOPLE FOR THAT.
HE'S HERE BECAUSE HE THINKS HE'S UNTOUCHABLE.
HEY, I KNOW YOU?
...YEAH.
BUT HERE'S THE TWIST. NONE OF THAT IS REALLY WHY THE HOOD DOES STUPID THINGS.
HE'S JUST STUPID.

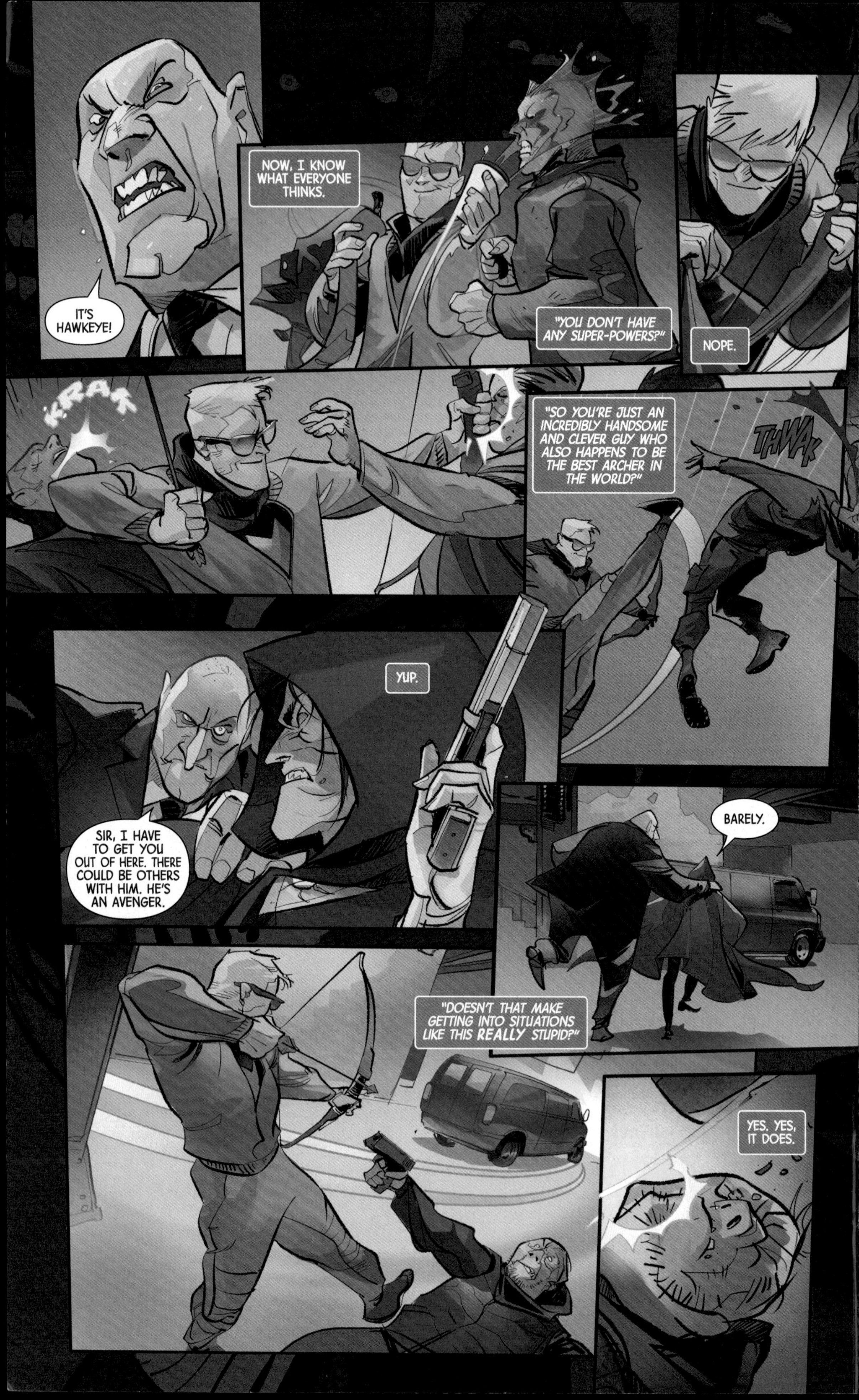
IT'S HAWKEYE!
NOW, I KNOW WHAT EVERYONE THINKS.
"YOU DON'T HAVE ANY SUPER-POWERS?"
NOPE.
KRAK
"SO YOU'RE JUST AN INCREDIBLY HANDSOME AND CLEVER GUY WHO ALSO HAPPENS TO BE THE BEST ARCHER IN THE WORLD?"
THWAK
YUP.
SIR, I HAVE TO GET YOU OUT OF HERE. THERE COULD BE OTHERS WITH HIM. HE'S AN AVENGER.
BARELY.
"DOESN'T THAT MAKE GETTING INTO SITUATIONS LIKE THIS REALLY STUPID?"
YES. YES, IT DOES.

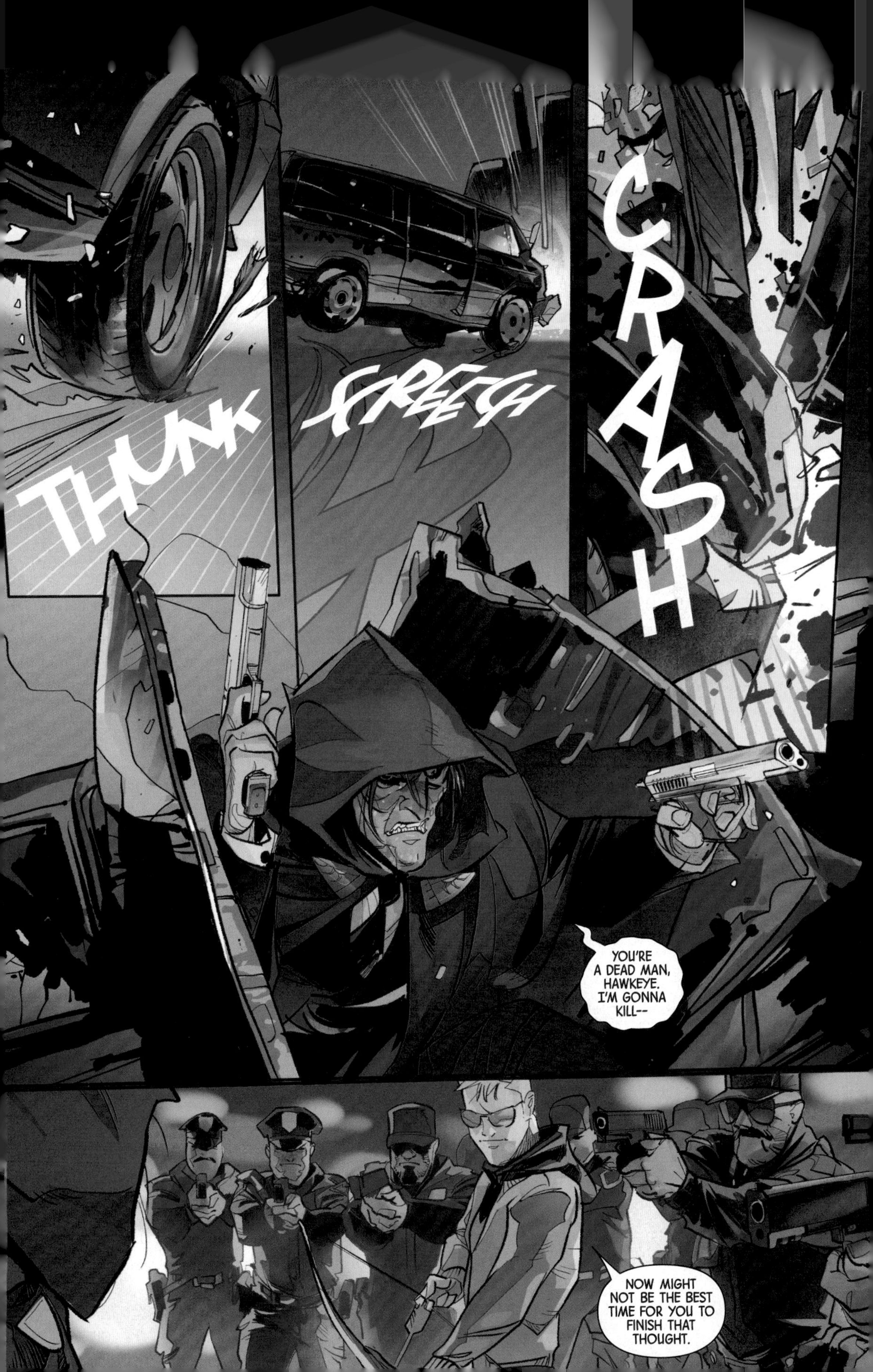
THUNK
SCREECH
CRASH
YOU'RE A DEAD MAN, HAWKEYE. I'M GONNA KILL--
NOW MIGHT NOT BE THE BEST TIME FOR YOU TO FINISH THAT THOUGHT.

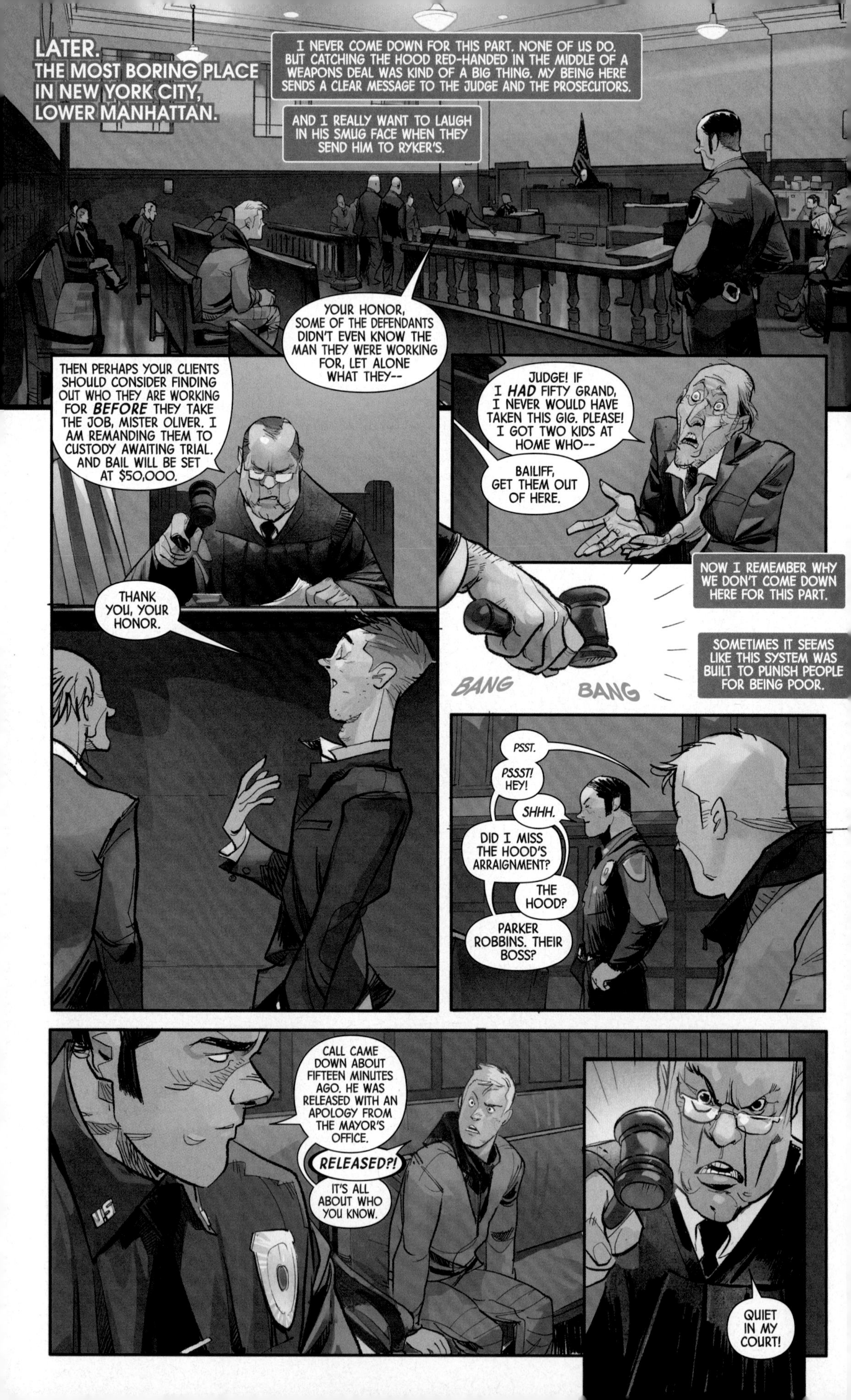
LATER.
THE MOST BORING PLACE IN NEW YORK CITY, LOWER MANHATTAN.
I NEVER COME DOWN FOR THIS PART. NONE OF US DO. BUT CATCHING THE HOOD RED-HANDED IN THE MIDDLE OF A WEAPONS DEAL WAS KIND OF A BIG THING. MY BEING HERE SENDS A CLEAR MESSAGE TO THE JUDGE AND THE PROSECUTORS.
AND I REALLY WANT TO LAUGH IN HIS SMUG FACE WHEN THEY SEND HIM TO RYKER'S.
YOUR HONOR, SOME OF THE DEFENDANTS DIDN'T EVEN KNOW THE MAN THEY WERE WORKING FOR, LET ALONE WHAT THEY--
THEN PERHAPS YOUR CLIENTS SHOULD CONSIDER FINDING OUT WHO THEY ARE WORKING FOR BEFORE THEY TAKE THE JOB, MISTER OLIVER. I AM REMANDING THEM TO CUSTODY AWAITING TRIAL. AND BAIL WILL BE SET AT $50,000.
JUDGE! IF I HAD FIFTY GRAND, I NEVER WOULD HAVE TAKEN THIS GIG, PLEASE! I GOT TWO KIDS AT HOME WHO--
BAILIFF, GET THEM OUT OF HERE.
THANK YOU, YOUR HONOR.
BANG
BANG
NOW I REMEMBER WHY WE DON'T COME DOWN HERE FOR THIS PART.
SOMETIMES IT SEEMS LIKE THIS SYSTEM WAS BUILT TO PUNISH PEOPLE FOR BEING POOR.
PSST.
PSSST! HEY!
SHHH.
DID I MISS THE HOOD'S ARRAIGNMENT?
THE HOOD?
PARKER ROBBINS. THEIR BOSS?
CALL CAME DOWN ABOUT FIFTEEN MINUTES AGO. HE WAS RELEASED WITH AN APOLOGY FROM THE MAYOR'S OFFICE.
RELEASED?!
IT'S ALL ABOUT WHO YOU KNOW.
QUIET IN MY COURT!

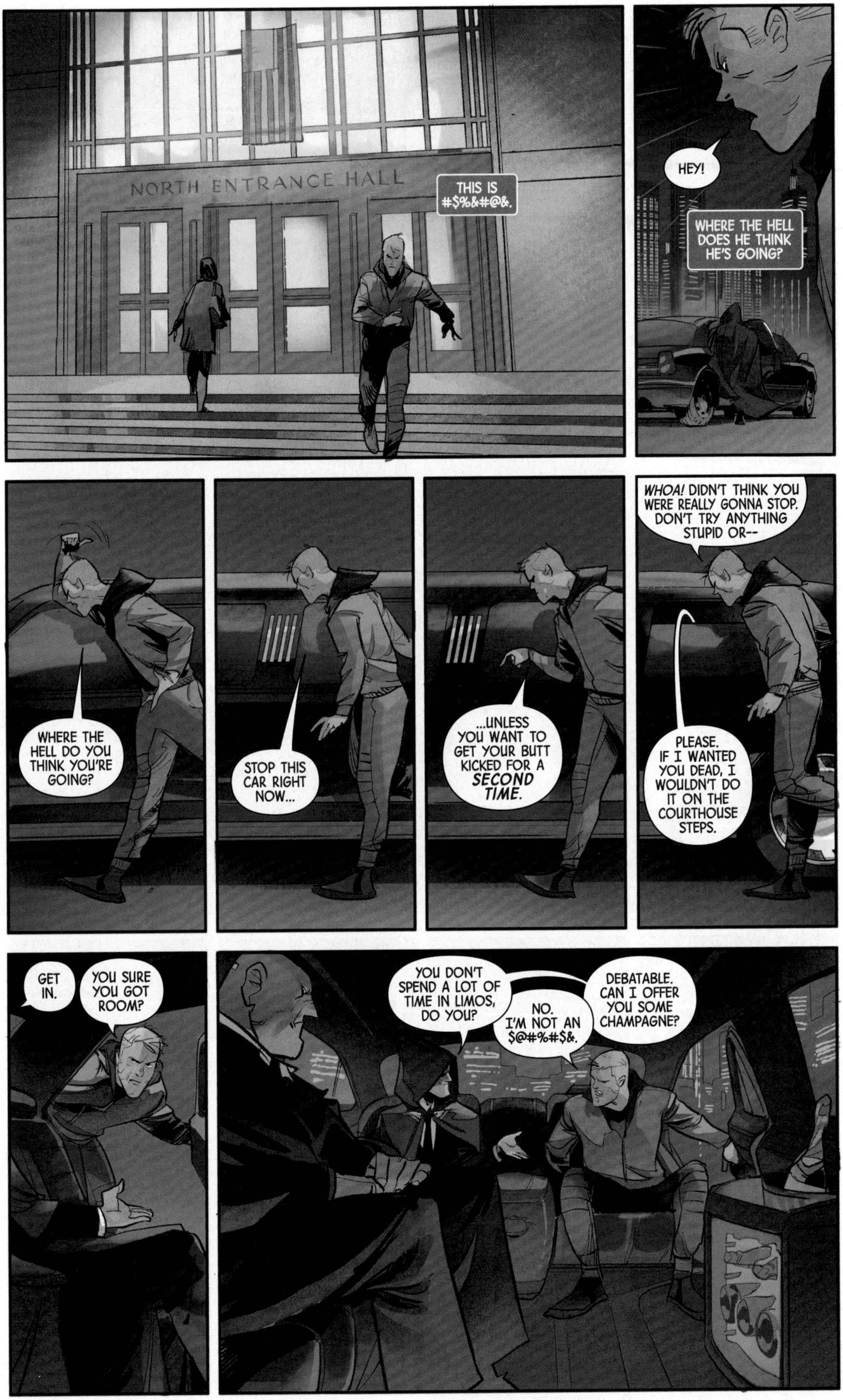
NORTH ENTRANCE HALL
THIS IS #$%&#@&.
HEY!
WHERE THE HELL DOES HE THINK HE'S GOING?
WHERE THE HELL DO YOU THINK YOU'RE GOING?
STOP THIS CAR RIGHT NOW...
...UNLESS YOU WANT TO GET YOUR BUTT KICKED FOR A *SECOND TIME*.
WHOA! DIDN'T THINK YOU WERE REALLY GONNA STOP. DON'T TRY ANYTHING STUPID OR--
PLEASE. IF I WANTED YOU DEAD, I WOULDN'T DO IT ON THE COURTHOUSE STEPS.
GET IN.
YOU SURE YOU GOT ROOM?
YOU DON'T SPEND A LOT OF TIME IN LIMOS, DO YOU?
NO. I'M NOT AN $@#%#$&.
DEBATABLE. CAN I OFFER YOU SOME CHAMPAGNE?

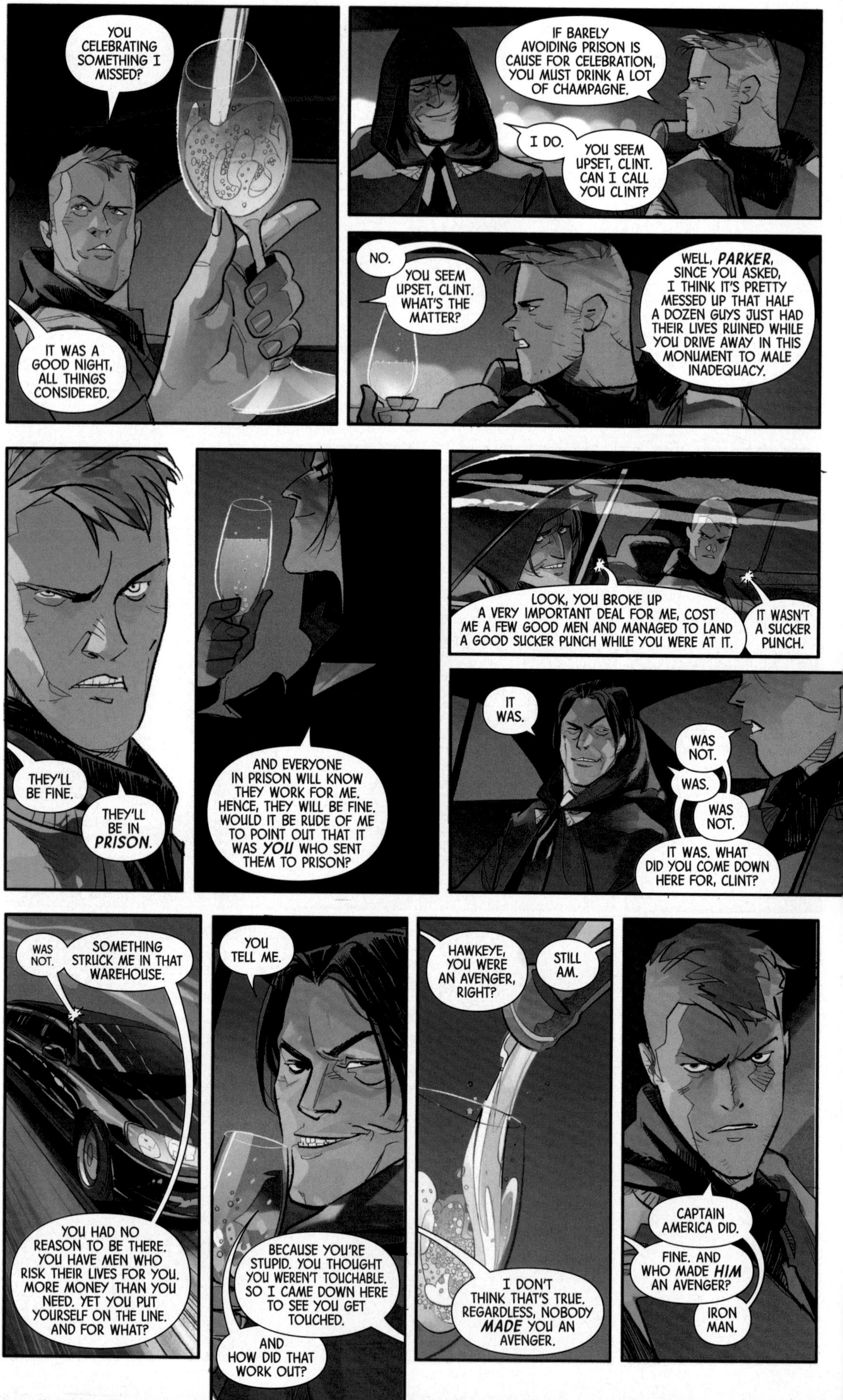

YOU CELEBRATING SOMETHING I MISSED?
IT WAS A GOOD NIGHT, ALL THINGS CONSIDERED.
IF BARELY AVOIDING PRISON IS CAUSE FOR CELEBRATION, YOU MUST DRINK A LOT OF CHAMPAGNE.
I DO.
YOU SEEM UPSET, CLINT. CAN I CALL YOU CLINT?
NO.
YOU SEEM UPSET, CLINT. WHAT'S THE MATTER?
WELL, PARKER, SINCE YOU ASKED, I THINK IT'S PRETTY MESSED UP THAT HALF A DOZEN GUYS JUST HAD THEIR LIVES RUINED WHILE YOU DRIVE AWAY IN THIS MONUMENT TO MALE INADEQUACY.
THEY'LL BE FINE.
THEY'LL BE IN PRISON.
AND EVERYONE IN PRISON WILL KNOW THEY WORK FOR ME. HENCE, THEY WILL BE FINE. WOULD IT BE RUDE OF ME TO POINT OUT THAT IT WAS YOU WHO SENT THEM TO PRISON?
LOOK, YOU BROKE UP A VERY IMPORTANT DEAL FOR ME, COST ME A FEW GOOD MEN AND MANAGED TO LAND A GOOD SUCKER PUNCH WHILE YOU WERE AT IT.
IT WASN'T A SUCKER PUNCH.
IT WAS.
WAS NOT.
WAS.
WAS NOT.
IT WAS. WHAT DID YOU COME DOWN HERE FOR, CLINT?
WAS NOT.
SOMETHING STRUCK ME IN THAT WAREHOUSE.
YOU HAD NO REASON TO BE THERE. YOU HAVE MEN WHO RISK THEIR LIVES FOR YOU. MORE MONEY THAN YOU NEED. YET YOU PUT YOURSELF ON THE LINE. AND FOR WHAT?
YOU TELL ME.
BECAUSE YOU'RE STUPID. YOU THOUGHT YOU WEREN'T TOUCHABLE. SO I CAME DOWN HERE TO SEE YOU GET TOUCHED.
AND HOW DID THAT WORK OUT?
HAWKEYE, YOU WERE AN AVENGER, RIGHT?
STILL AM.
I DON'T THINK THAT'S TRUE. REGARDLESS, NOBODY MADE YOU AN AVENGER.
CAPTAIN AMERICA DID.
FINE. AND WHO MADE HIM AN AVENGER?
IRON MAN.

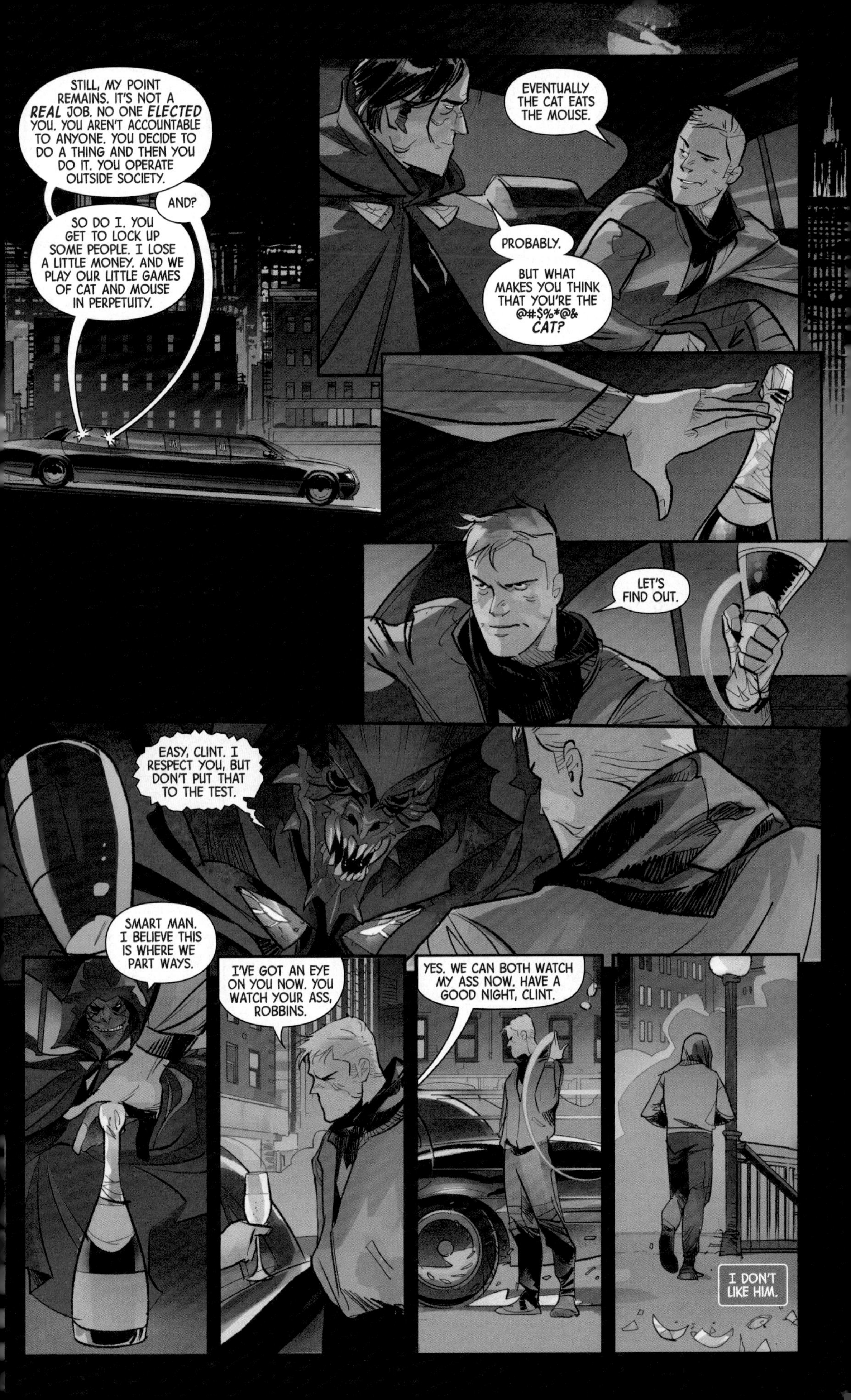
STILL, MY POINT REMAINS. IT'S NOT A *REAL* JOB. NO ONE *ELECTED* YOU. YOU AREN'T ACCOUNTABLE TO ANYONE. YOU DECIDE TO DO A THING AND THEN YOU DO IT. YOU OPERATE OUTSIDE SOCIETY.
AND?
SO DO I. YOU GET TO LOCK UP SOME PEOPLE. I LOSE A LITTLE MONEY. AND WE PLAY OUR LITTLE GAMES OF CAT AND MOUSE IN PERPETUITY.
EVENTUALLY THE CAT EATS THE MOUSE.
PROBABLY.
BUT WHAT MAKES YOU THINK THAT YOU'RE THE @#$%*@& *CAT?*
LET'S FIND OUT.
EASY, CLINT. I RESPECT YOU, BUT DON'T PUT THAT TO THE TEST.
SMART MAN. I BELIEVE THIS IS WHERE WE PART WAYS.
I'VE GOT AN EYE ON YOU NOW. YOU WATCH YOUR ASS, ROBBINS.
YES. WE CAN BOTH WATCH MY ASS NOW. HAVE A GOOD NIGHT, CLINT.
I DON'T LIKE HIM.

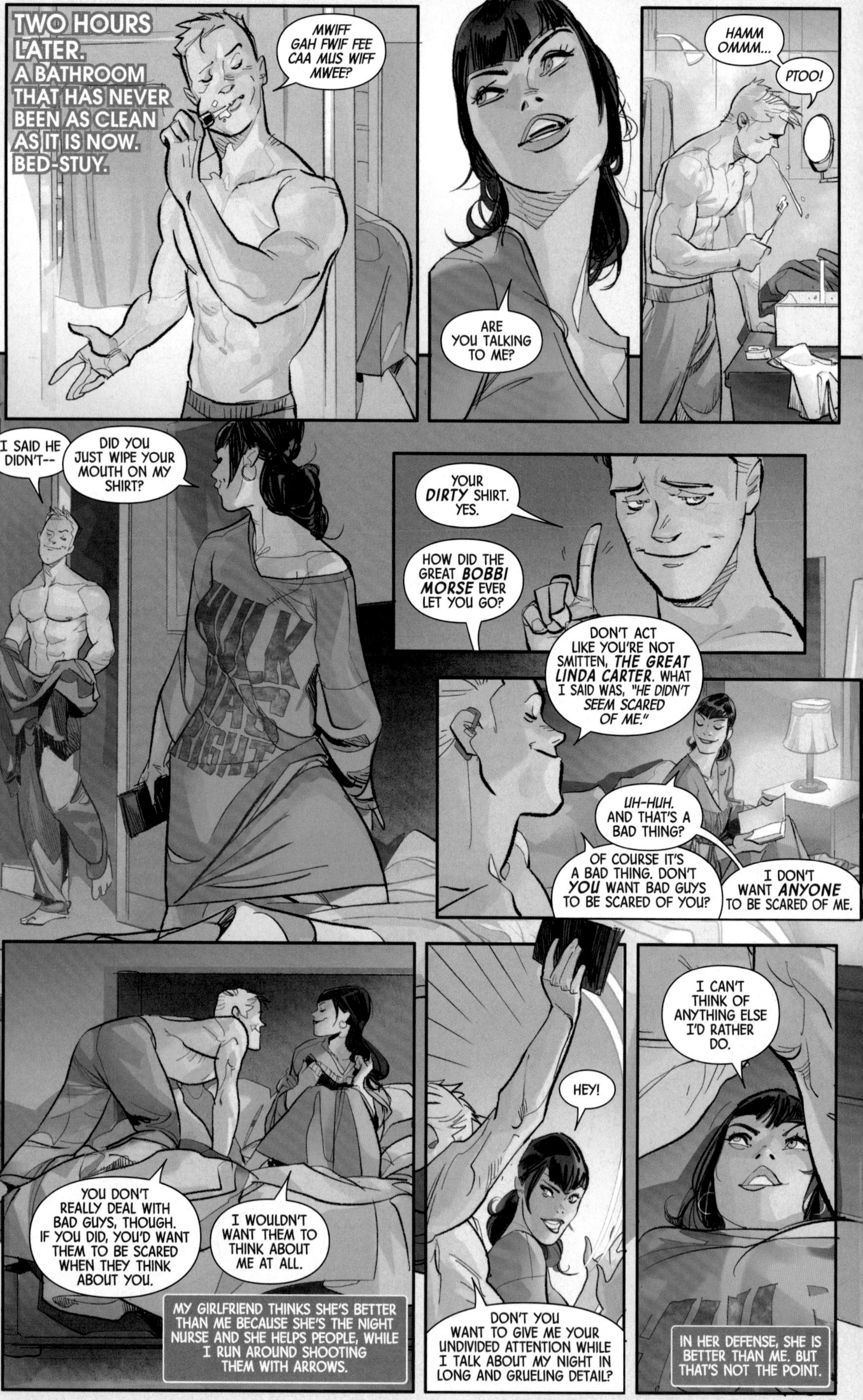
TWO HOURS LATER. A BATHROOM THAT HAS NEVER BEEN AS CLEAN AS IT IS NOW. BED-STUY.
MWIFF GAH FWIF FEE CAA MUS WIFF MWEE?
ARE YOU TALKING TO ME?
HAMM OMMM...
PTOO!
I SAID HE DIDN'T--
DID YOU JUST WIPE YOUR MOUTH ON MY SHIRT?
YOUR DIRTY SHIRT. YES.
HOW DID THE GREAT BOBBI MORSE EVER LET YOU GO?
DON'T ACT LIKE YOU'RE NOT SMITTEN, THE GREAT LINDA CARTER. WHAT I SAID WAS, "HE DIDN'T SEEM SCARED OF ME."
UH-HUH. AND THAT'S A BAD THING?
OF COURSE IT'S A BAD THING. DON'T YOU WANT BAD GUYS TO BE SCARED OF YOU?
I DON'T WANT ANYONE TO BE SCARED OF ME.
YOU DON'T REALLY DEAL WITH BAD GUYS, THOUGH. IF YOU DID, YOU'D WANT THEM TO BE SCARED WHEN THEY THINK ABOUT YOU.
I WOULDN'T WANT THEM TO THINK ABOUT ME AT ALL.
MY GIRLFRIEND THINKS SHE'S BETTER THAN ME BECAUSE SHE'S THE NIGHT NURSE AND SHE HELPS PEOPLE, WHILE I RUN AROUND SHOOTING THEM WITH ARROWS.
HEY!
DON'T YOU WANT TO GIVE ME YOUR UNDIVIDED ATTENTION WHILE I TALK ABOUT MY NIGHT IN LONG AND GRUELING DETAIL?
I CAN'T THINK OF ANYTHING ELSE I'D RATHER DO.
IN HER DEFENSE, SHE IS BETTER THAN ME. BUT THAT'S NOT THE POINT.

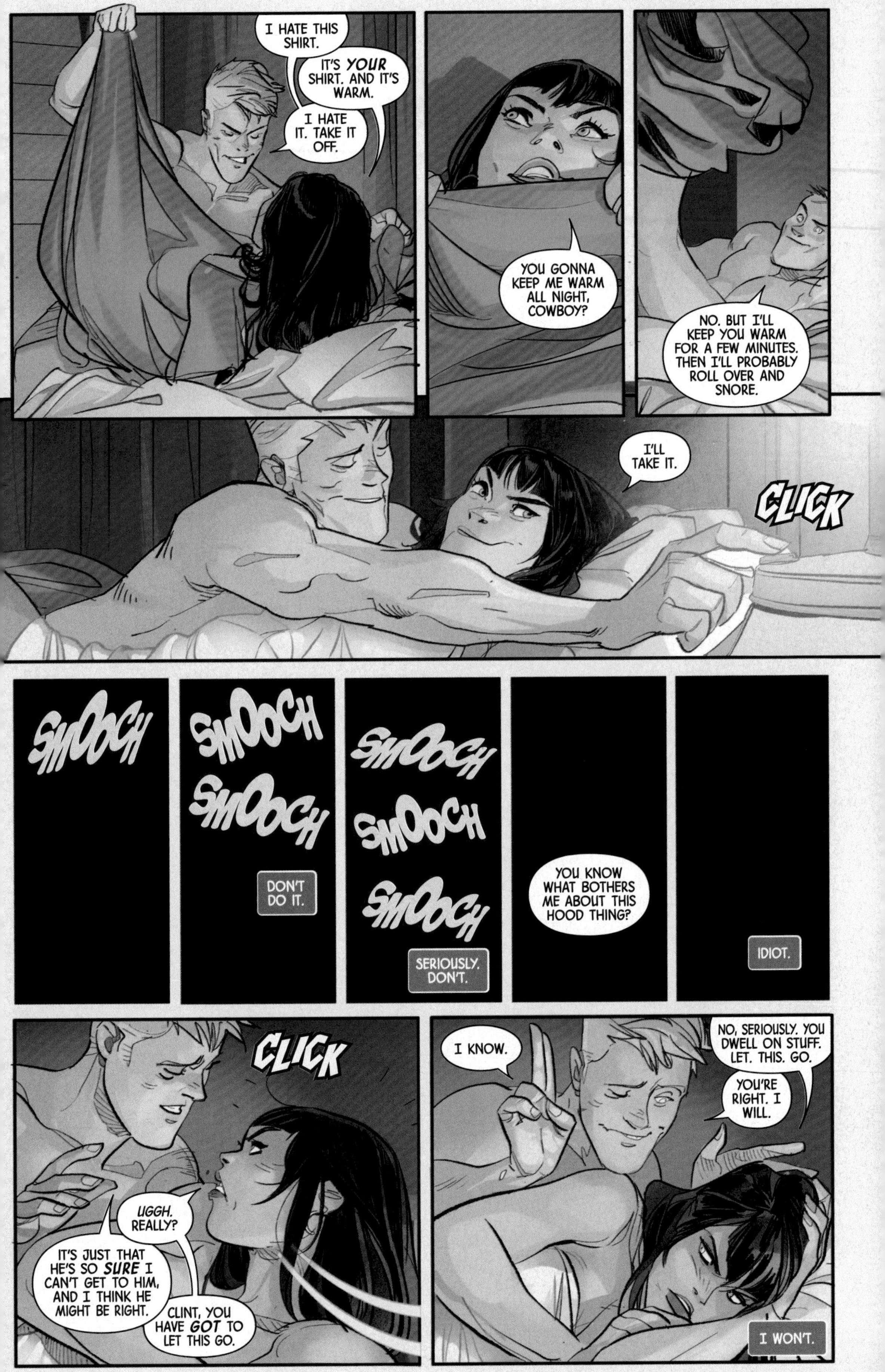

I HATE THIS SHIRT.
IT'S YOUR SHIRT. AND IT'S WARM.
I HATE IT. TAKE IT OFF.
YOU GONNA KEEP ME WARM ALL NIGHT, COWBOY?
NO. BUT I'LL KEEP YOU WARM FOR A FEW MINUTES. THEN I'LL PROBABLY ROLL OVER AND SNORE.
I'LL TAKE IT.
CLICK
SMOOCH
SMOOCH
SMOOCH
DON'T DO IT.
SMOOCH
SMOOCH
SMOOCH
SERIOUSLY. DON'T.
YOU KNOW WHAT BOTHERS ME ABOUT THIS HOOD THING?
IDIOT.
CLICK
UGGH. REALLY?
IT'S JUST THAT HE'S SO SURE I CAN'T GET TO HIM, AND I THINK HE MIGHT BE RIGHT.
CLINT, YOU HAVE GOT TO LET THIS GO.
I KNOW.
NO, SERIOUSLY. YOU DWELL ON STUFF. LET. THIS. GO.
YOU'RE RIGHT. I WILL.
I WON'T.

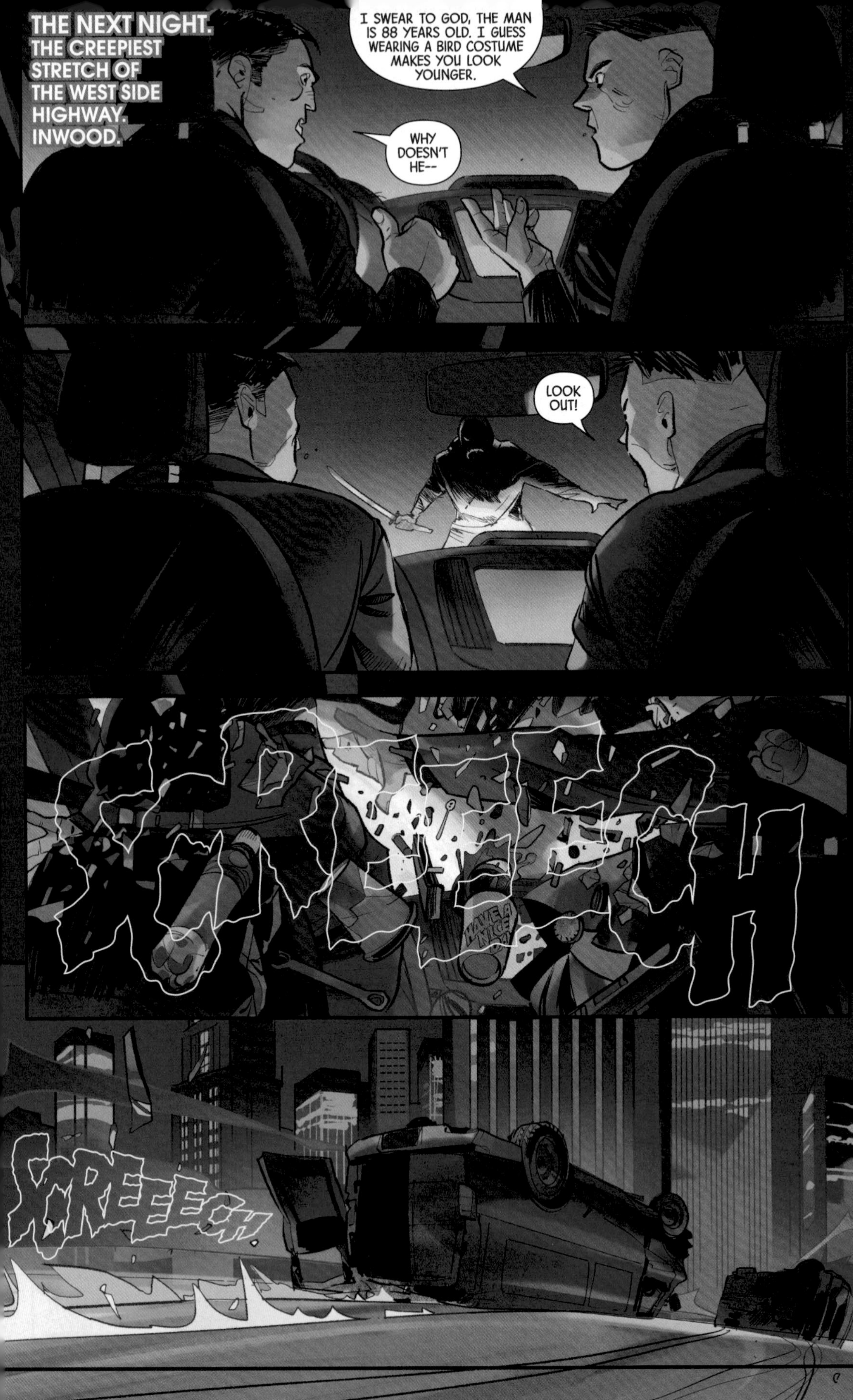
THE NEXT NIGHT. THE CREEPIEST STRETCH OF THE WEST SIDE HIGHWAY. INWOOD.
I SWEAR TO GOD, THE MAN IS 88 YEARS OLD. I GUESS WEARING A BIRD COSTUME MAKES YOU LOOK YOUNGER.
WHY DOESN'T HE--
LOOK OUT!
HAVE A NICE DAY
SCREECH!

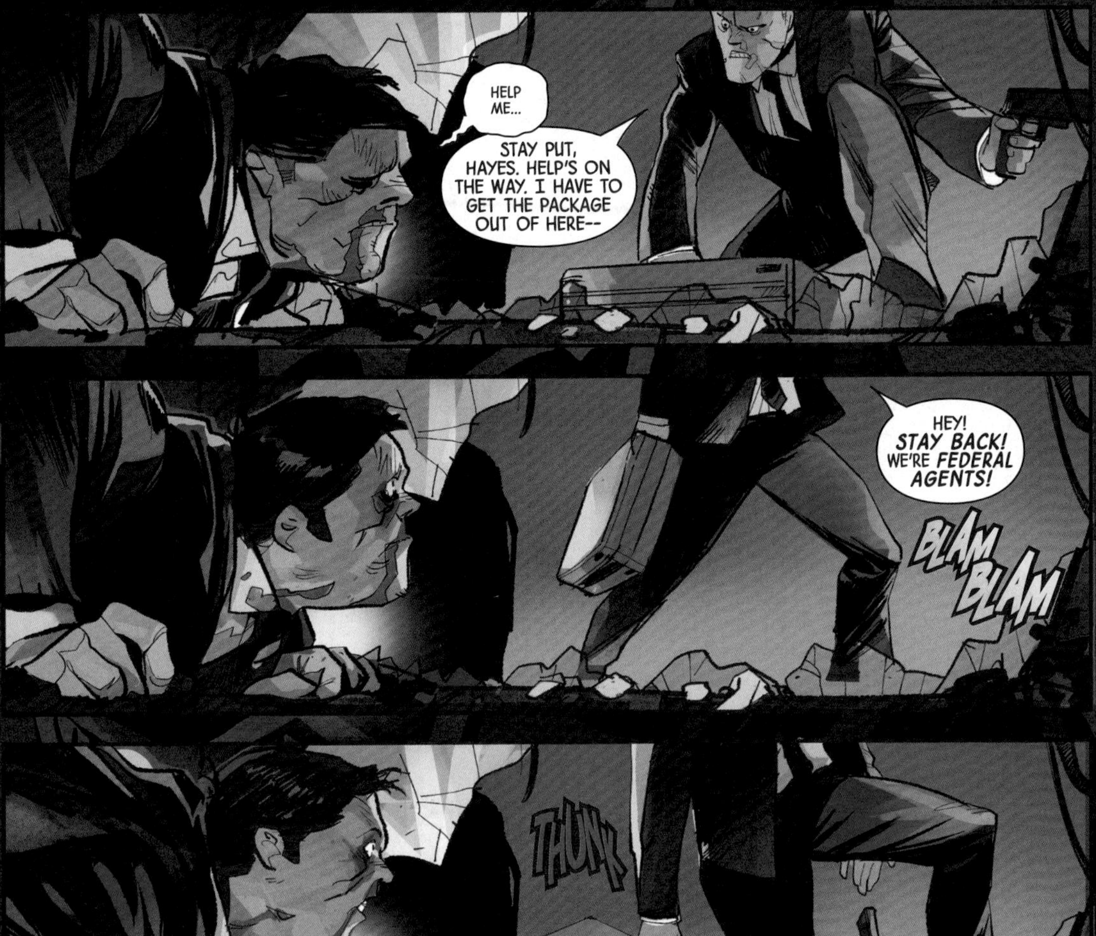
HELP ME...
STAY PUT, HAYES. HELP'S ON THE WAY. I HAVE TO GET THE PACKAGE OUT OF HERE--
HEY! STAY BACK! WE'RE FEDERAL AGENTS!
BLAM BLAM
THUNK
OHGOD OHGODOHGOD OHGOD.
I--I CAN'T LET YOU TAKE THAT CASE.
LET ME?

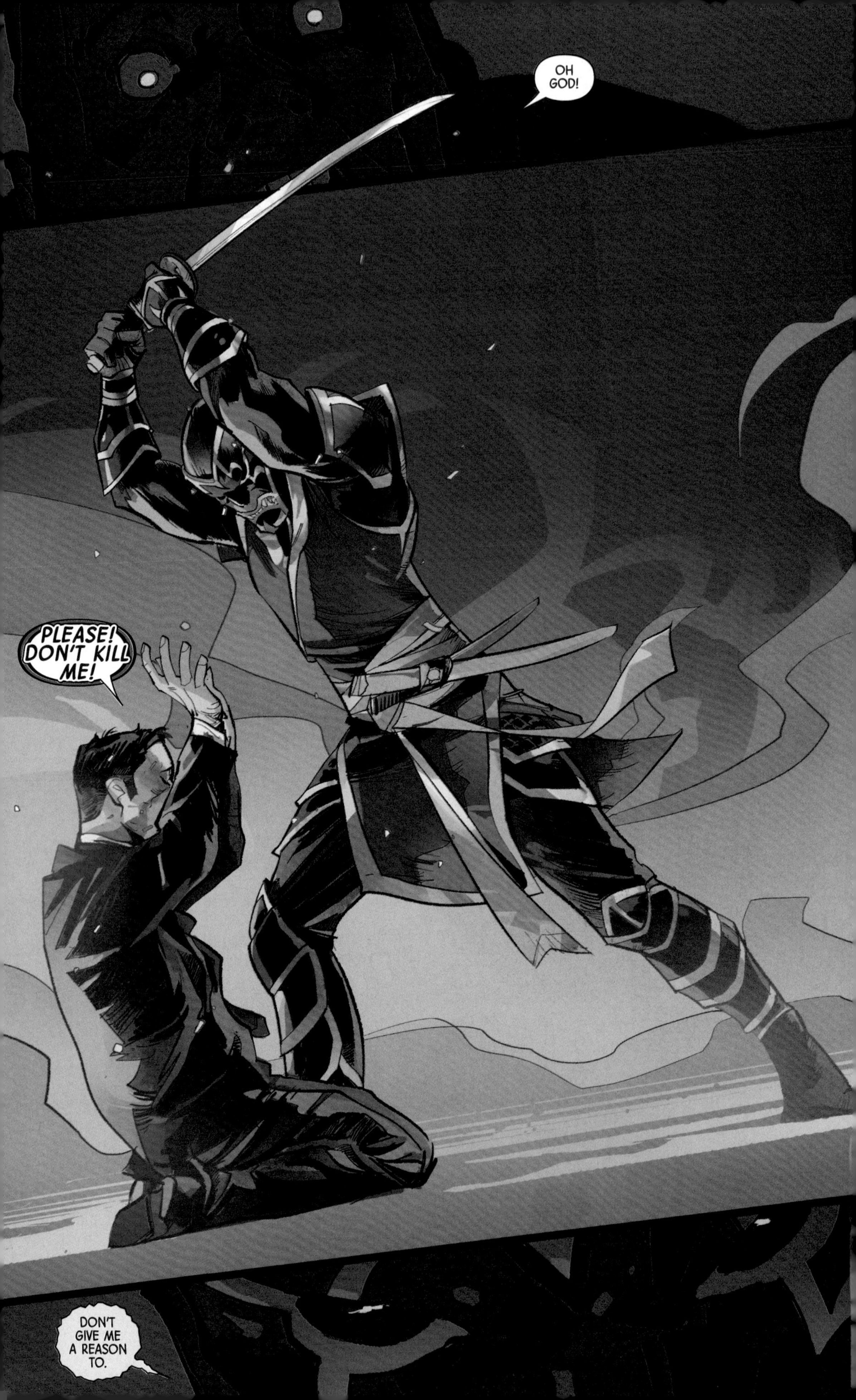
OH GOD!
PLEASE! DON'T KILL ME!
DON'T GIVE ME A REASON TO.

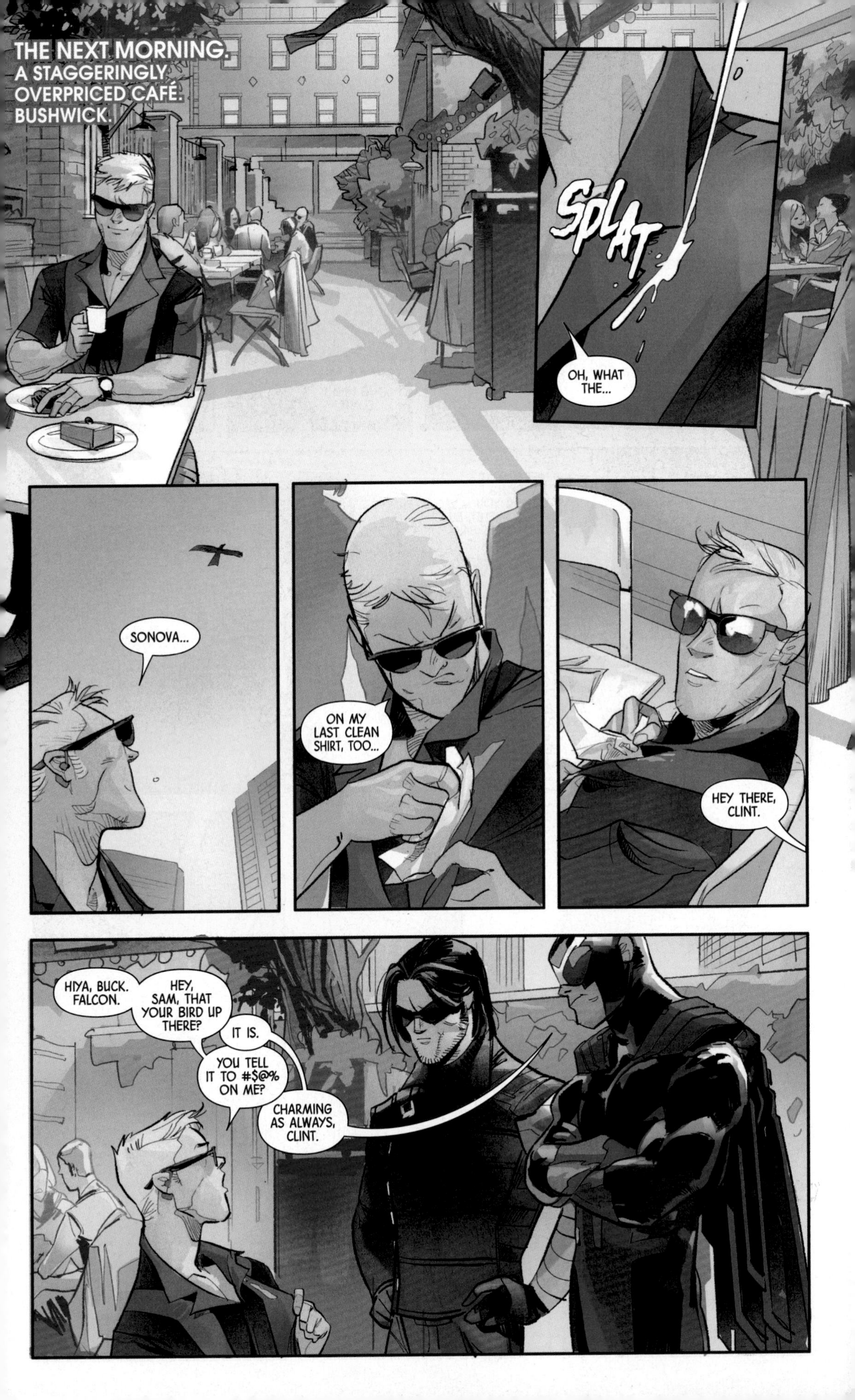
THE NEXT MORNING.
A STAGGERINGLY OVERPRICED CAFÉ.
BUSHWICK.
SPLAT
OH, WHAT THE...
SONOVA...
ON MY LAST CLEAN SHIRT, TOO...
HEY THERE, CLINT.
HIYA, BUCK. FALCON.
HEY, SAM, THAT YOUR BIRD UP THERE?
IT IS.
YOU TELL IT TO #$@% ON ME?
CHARMING AS ALWAYS, CLINT.

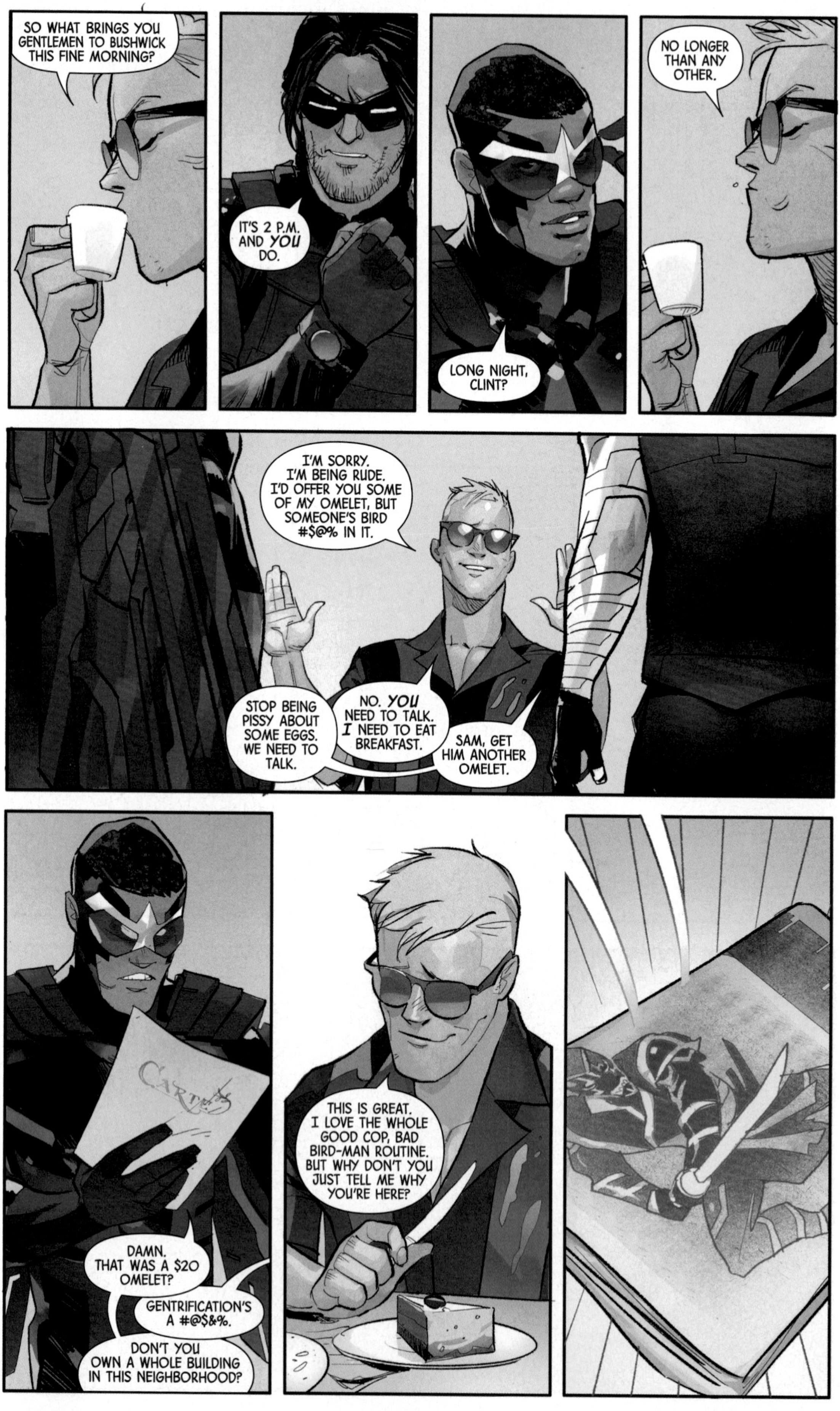

SO WHAT BRINGS YOU GENTLEMEN TO BUSHWICK THIS FINE MORNING?
IT'S 2 P.M. AND *YOU* DO.
LONG NIGHT, CLINT?
NO LONGER THAN ANY OTHER.
I'M SORRY. I'M BEING RUDE. I'D OFFER YOU SOME OF MY OMELET, BUT SOMEONE'S BIRD #$@% IN IT.
STOP BEING PISSY ABOUT SOME EGGS. WE NEED TO TALK.
NO. *YOU* NEED TO TALK. *I* NEED TO EAT BREAKFAST.
SAM, GET HIM ANOTHER OMELET.
DAMN. THAT WAS A $20 OMELET?
GENTRIFICATION'S A #@$&%.
DON'T YOU OWN A WHOLE BUILDING IN THIS NEIGHBORHOOD?
THIS IS GREAT. I LOVE THE WHOLE GOOD COP, BAD BIRD-MAN ROUTINE. BUT WHY DON'T YOU JUST TELL ME WHY YOU'RE HERE?

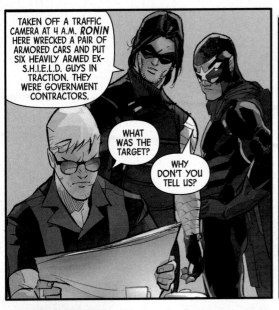

TAKEN OFF A TRAFFIC CAMERA AT 4 A.M. *RONIN* HERE WRECKED A PAIR OF ARMORED CARS AND PUT SIX HEAVILY ARMED EX-S.H.I.E.L.D. GUYS IN TRACTION. THEY WERE GOVERNMENT CONTRACTORS.

WHAT WAS THE TARGET?

WHY DON'T YOU TELL US?

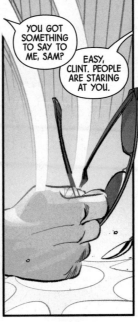

YOU GOT SOMETHING TO SAY TO ME, SAM?

EASY, CLINT. PEOPLE ARE STARING AT YOU.

THEY'RE STARING BECAUSE MY BREAKFAST WAS JUST INTERRUPTED BY A *BIG BIRD* COSPLAYER AND THE WORLD'S GREASIEST CYBORG.

I HOLD MY SADNESS INSIDE. YOU THINK THIS WAS ME?

MAD ABOUT SOME EGGS, BUT YOU DON'T SEEM UPSET THAT SIX OF OUR GUYS ARE IN THE HOSPITAL.

HE'S WEARING YOUR OLD RONIN COSTUME.

WHICH *THREE OTHER PEOPLE* HAVE WORN.

SHOSTAKOV IS OUT OF THE COUNTRY. THESE GUYS WEREN'T VAMPIRES, SO PROBABLY WASN'T *BLADE*. AND THIS DOESN'T LOOK LIKE A WOMAN TO ME, SO I'M GOING TO RULE OUT *ECHO*. I'LL JUST ASK...

WAS IT *YOU?*

SCREW YOU FOR EVEN ASKING ME THAT, BUCK.

THEN YOU WOULDN'T MIND IF WE GO TO YOUR PLACE AND--

SAM, IF HE SAYS IT WASN'T HIM, THAT'S GOOD ENOUGH. BESIDES, THIS DUDE WAS IN WAY BETTER SHAPE THAN CLINT.

NO OFFENSE.

%$#@ YOU.

NONE TAKEN.

LOOK, I'M NOT HAPPY SOME WHACKJOB IS RUNNING AROUND IN MY OLD GEAR EITHER.

I BUTTED HEADS WITH THE HOOD THE OTHER NIGHT. MAYBE THIS IS *HIS* PAYBACK. I HEARD A RUMOR HE HAS SOMETHING GOING DOWN TONIGHT. IF I FIND ANYTHING--

WE'LL GO WITH YOU.

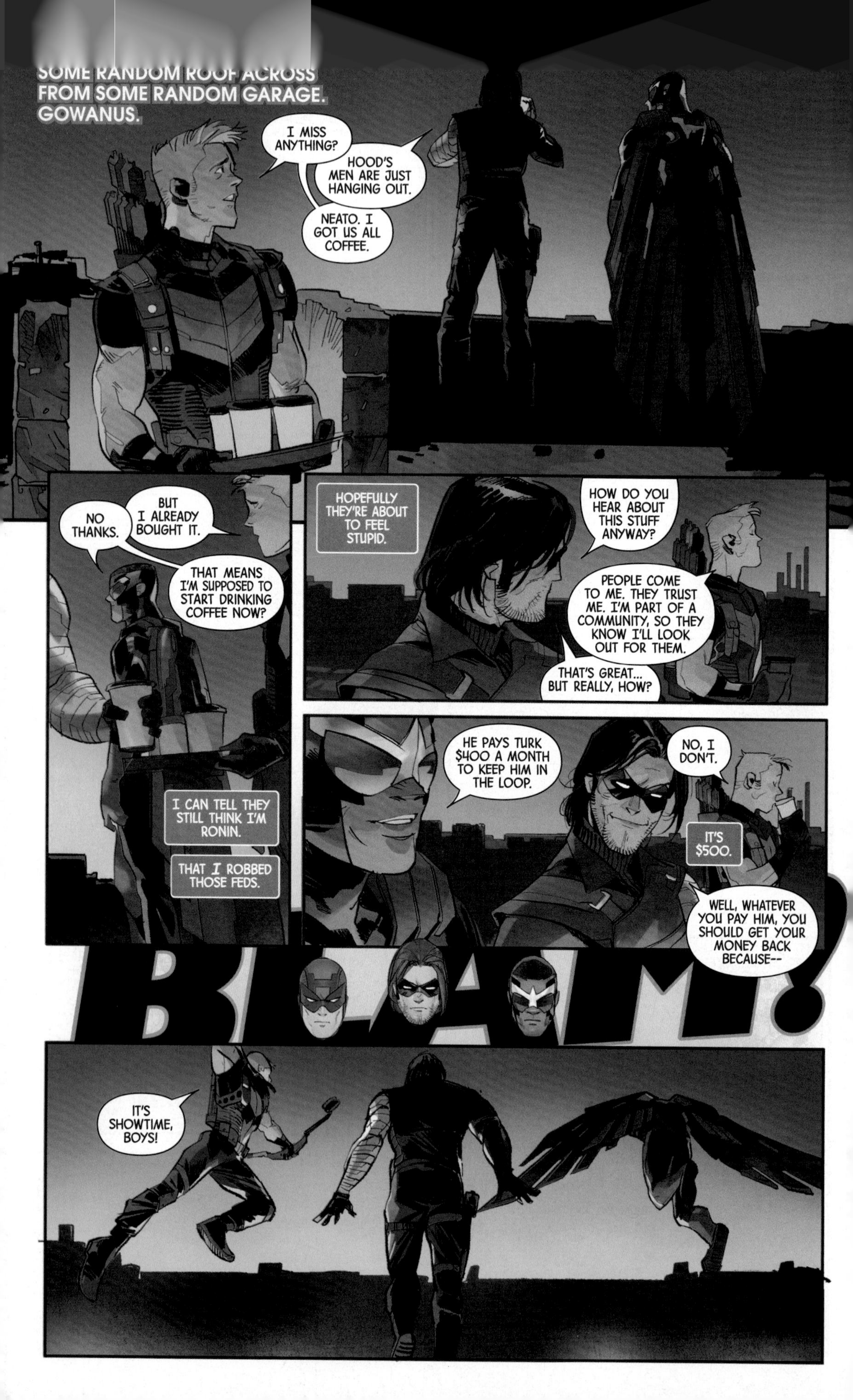
SOME RANDOM ROOF ACROSS FROM SOME RANDOM GARAGE. GOWANUS.
I MISS ANYTHING?
HOOD'S MEN ARE JUST HANGING OUT.
NEATO. I GOT US ALL COFFEE.
NO THANKS.
BUT I ALREADY BOUGHT IT.
THAT MEANS I'M SUPPOSED TO START DRINKING COFFEE NOW?
I CAN TELL THEY STILL THINK I'M RONIN.
THAT I ROBBED THOSE FEDS.
HOPEFULLY THEY'RE ABOUT TO FEEL STUPID.
HOW DO YOU HEAR ABOUT THIS STUFF ANYWAY?
PEOPLE COME TO ME. THEY TRUST ME. I'M PART OF A COMMUNITY, SO THEY KNOW I'LL LOOK OUT FOR THEM.
THAT'S GREAT... BUT REALLY, HOW?
HE PAYS TURK $400 A MONTH TO KEEP HIM IN THE LOOP.
NO, I DON'T.
IT'S $500.
WELL, WHATEVER YOU PAY HIM, YOU SHOULD GET YOUR MONEY BACK BECAUSE--
IT'S SHOWTIME, BOYS!

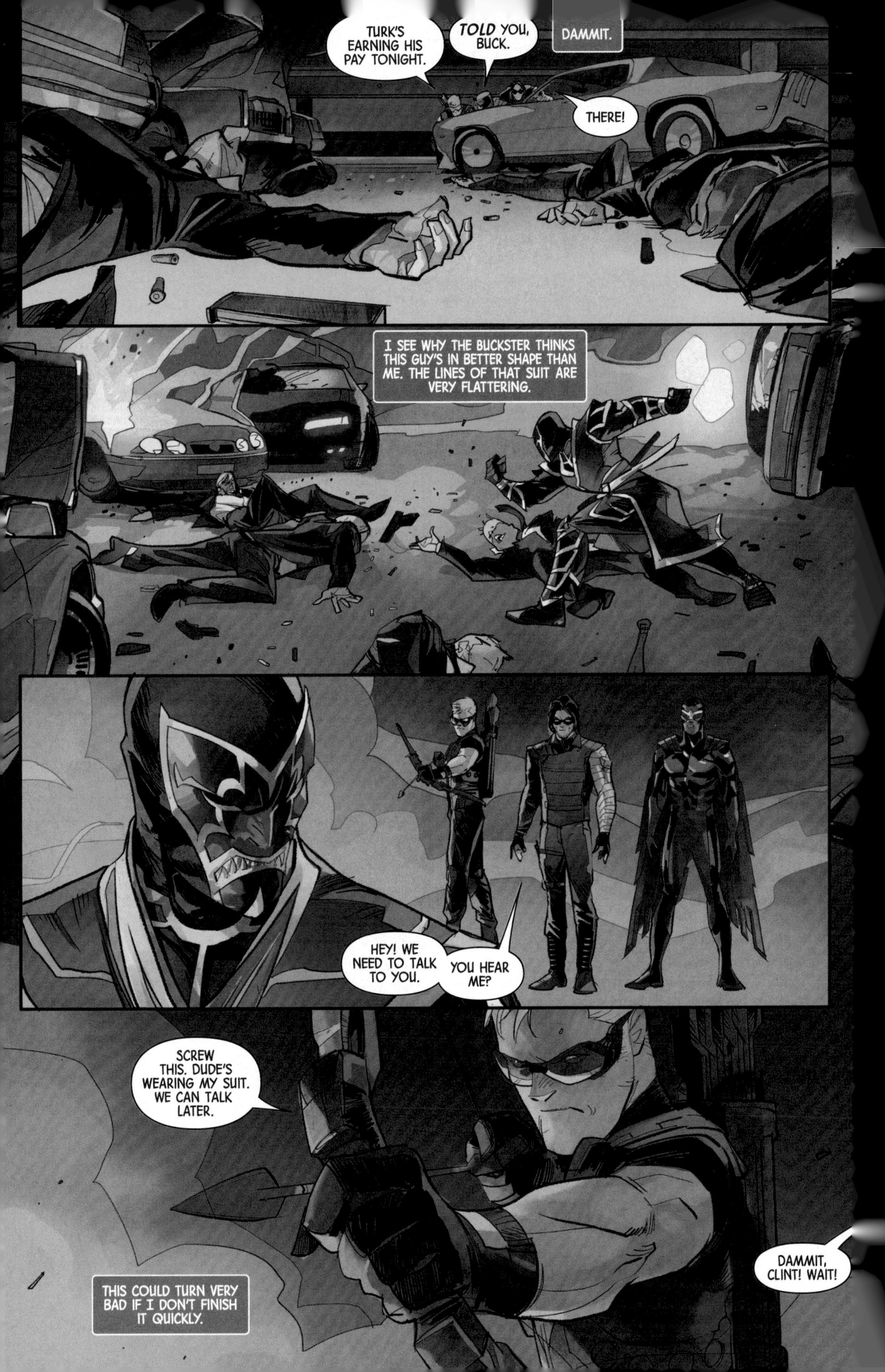
TURK'S EARNING HIS PAY TONIGHT.
TOLD YOU, BUCK.
DAMMIT.
THERE!
I SEE WHY THE BUCKSTER THINKS THIS GUY'S IN BETTER SHAPE THAN ME. THE LINES OF THAT SUIT ARE VERY FLATTERING.
HEY! WE NEED TO TALK TO YOU.
YOU HEAR ME?
SCREW THIS. DUDE'S WEARING MY SUIT. WE CAN TALK LATER.
DAMMIT, CLINT! WAIT!
THIS COULD TURN VERY BAD IF I DON'T FINISH IT QUICKLY.

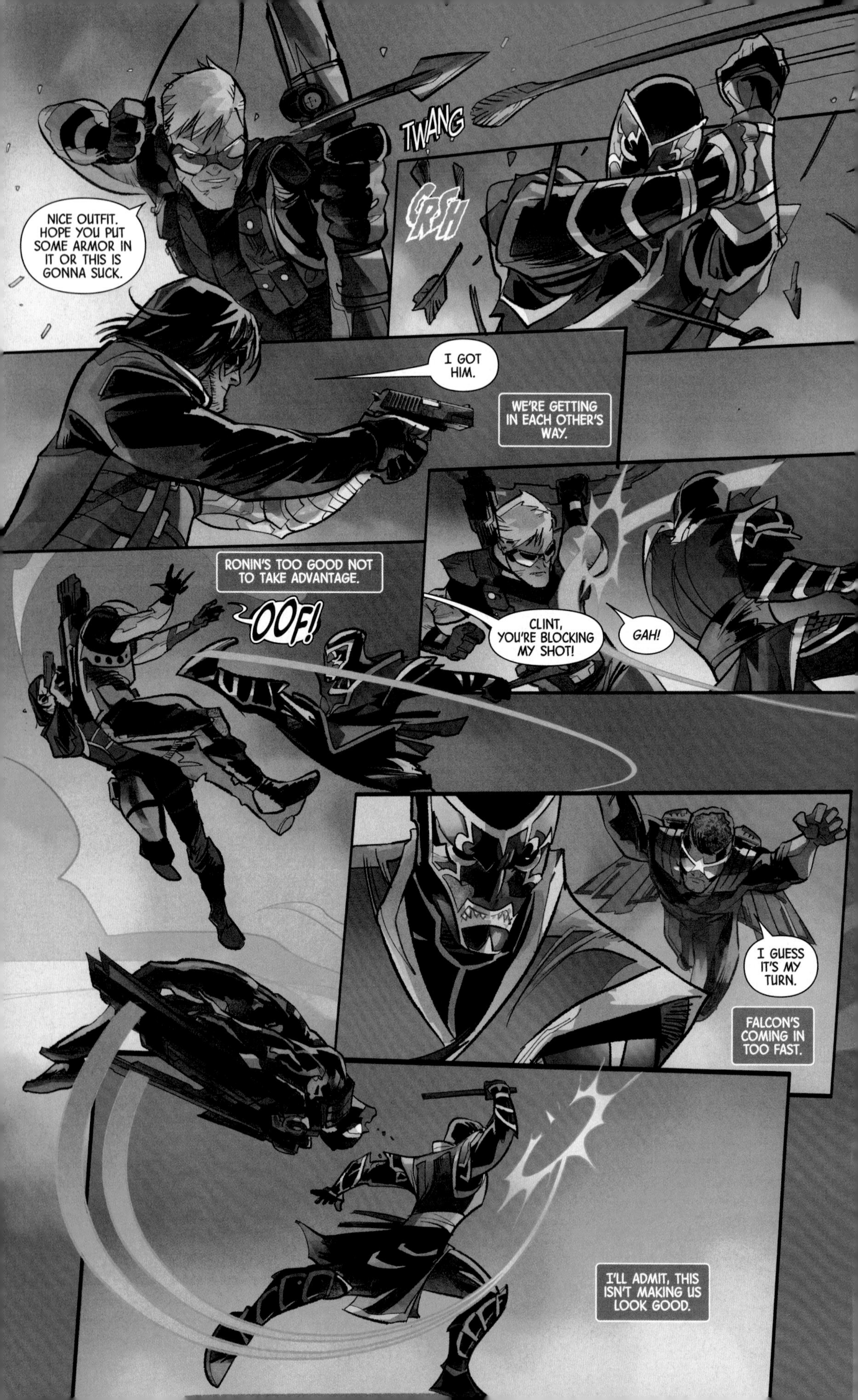
NICE OUTFIT. HOPE YOU PUT SOME ARMOR IN IT OR THIS IS GONNA SUCK.
TWANG
CRSH
I GOT HIM.
WE'RE GETTING IN EACH OTHER'S WAY.
CLINT, YOU'RE BLOCKING MY SHOT!
GAH!
RONIN'S TOO GOOD NOT TO TAKE ADVANTAGE.
OOF!
I GUESS IT'S MY TURN.
FALCON'S COMING IN TOO FAST.
I'LL ADMIT, THIS ISN'T MAKING US LOOK GOOD.

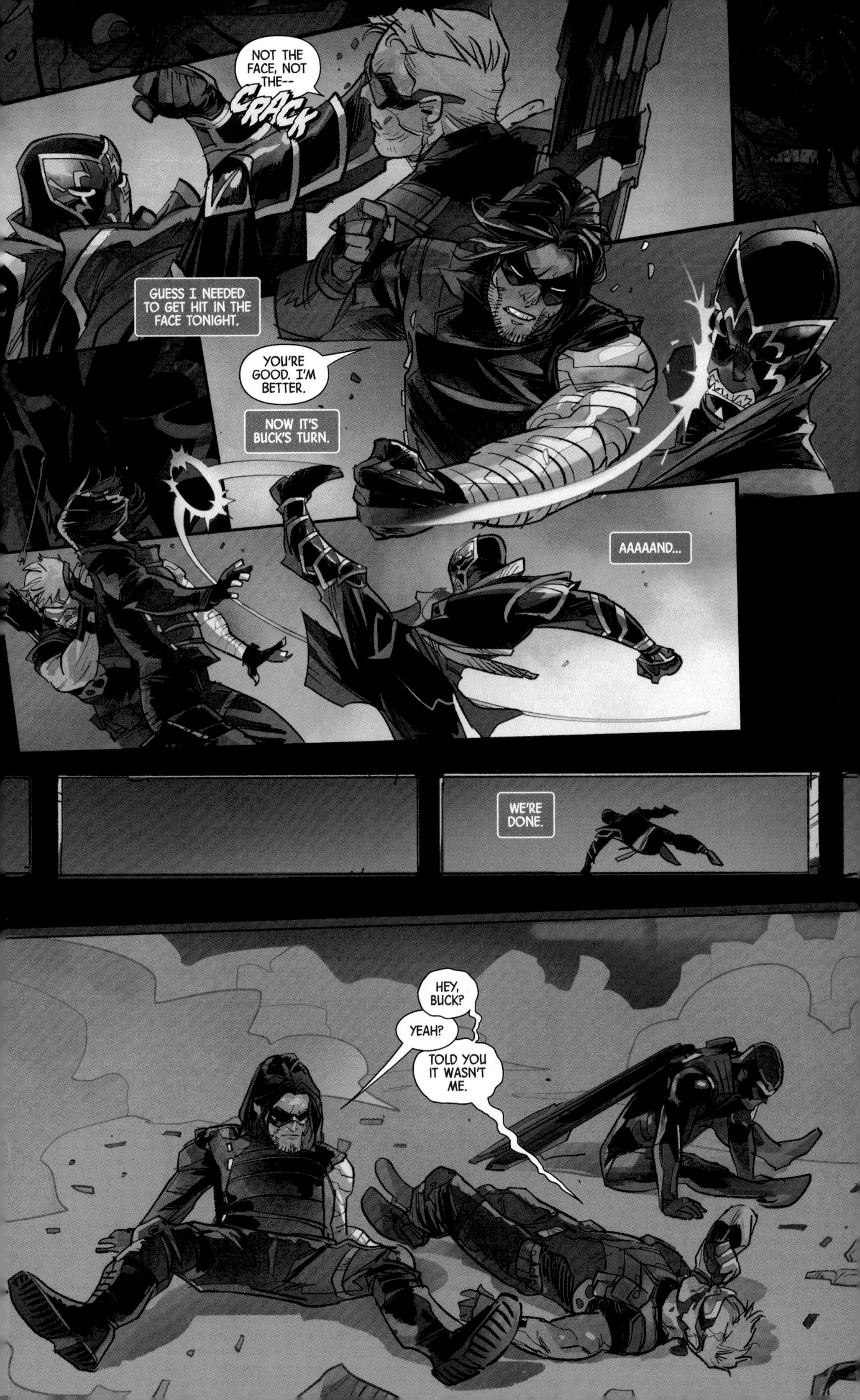
NOT THE FACE, NOT THE--
CRACK
GUESS I NEEDED TO GET HIT IN THE FACE TONIGHT.
YOU'RE GOOD. I'M BETTER.
NOW IT'S BUCK'S TURN.
AAAAAND...
WE'RE DONE.
HEY, BUCK?
YEAH?
TOLD YOU IT WASN'T ME.

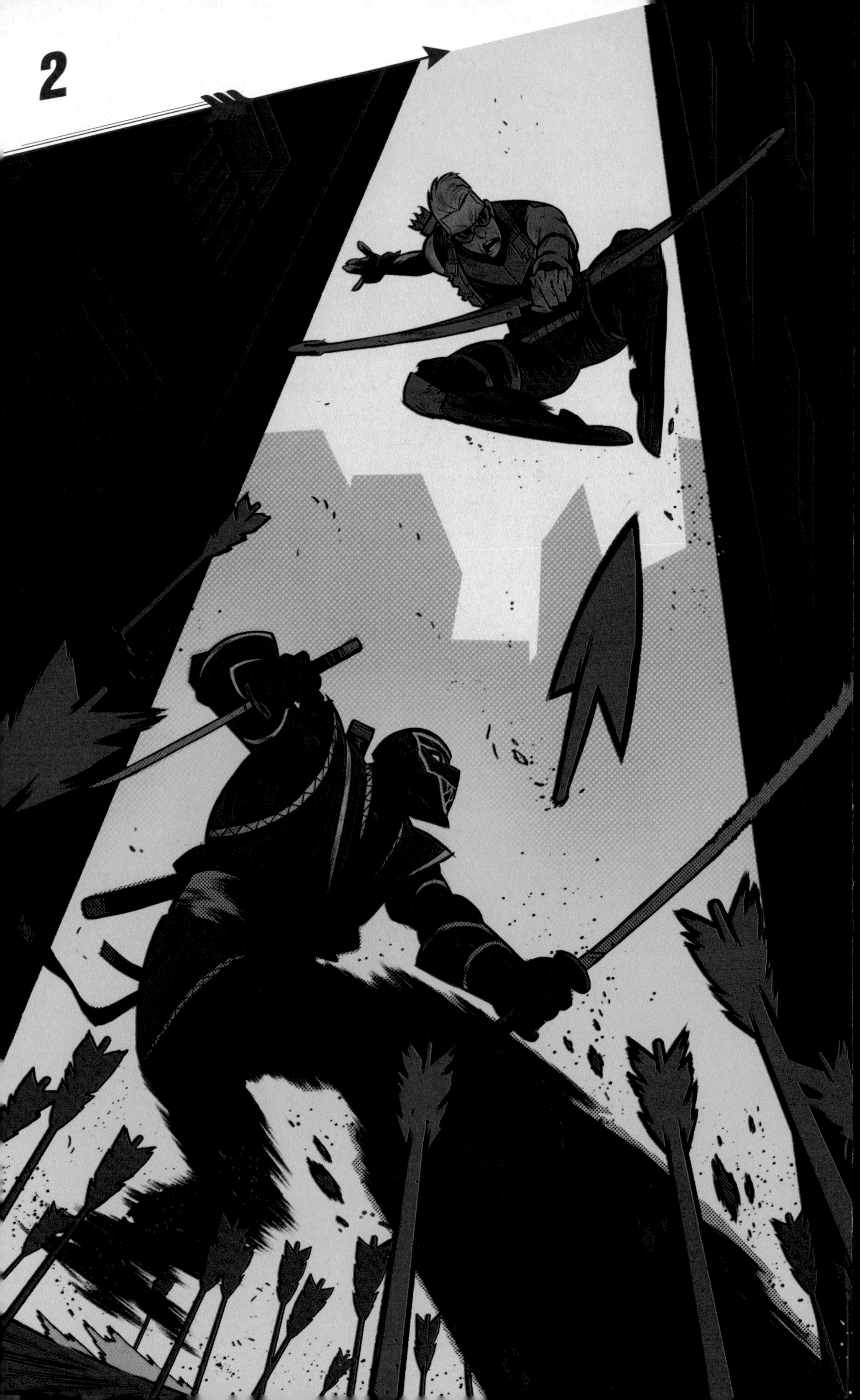

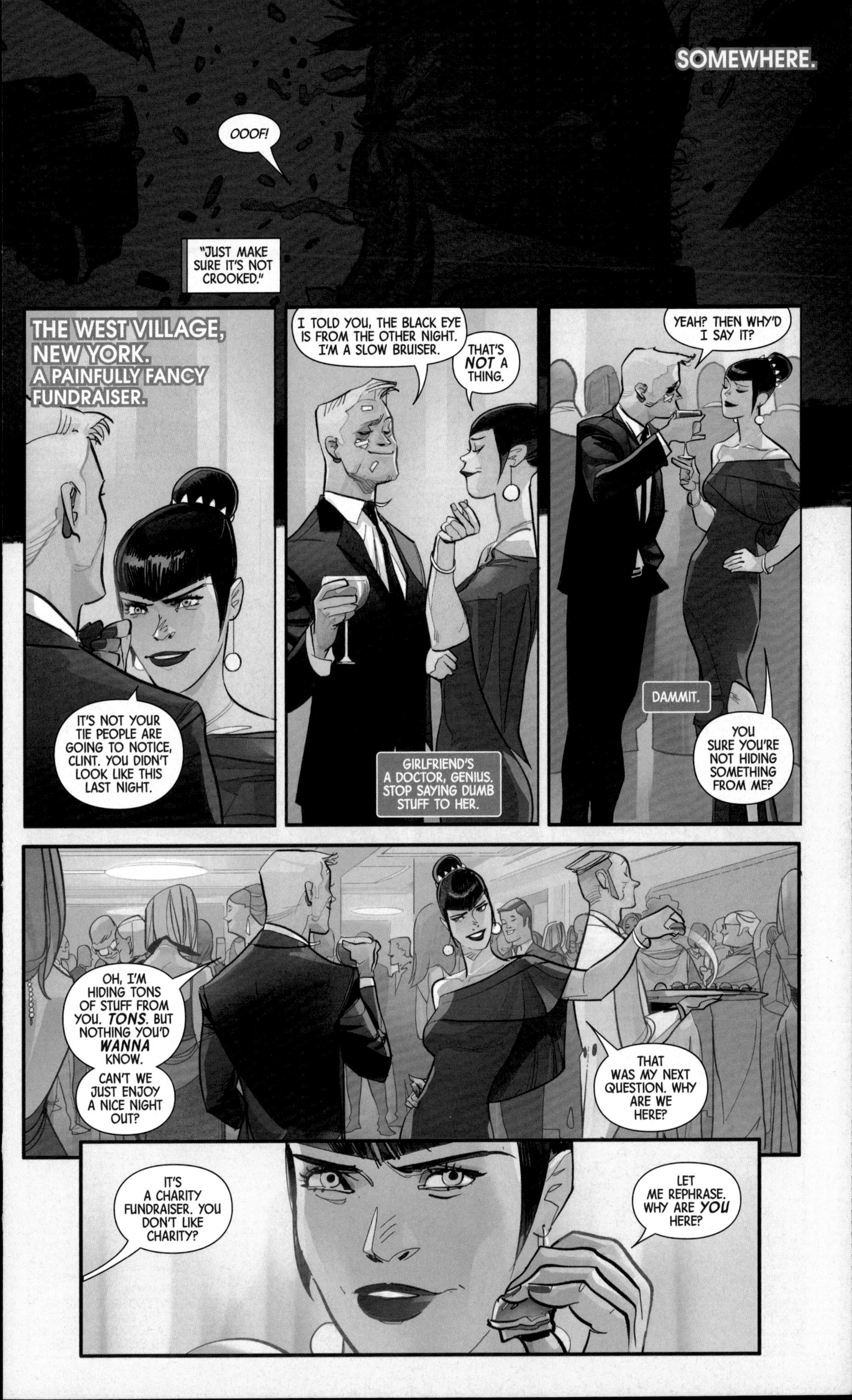
SOMEWHERE.
OOOF!
"JUST MAKE SURE IT'S NOT CROOKED."
THE WEST VILLAGE, NEW YORK. A PAINFULLY FANCY FUNDRAISER.
IT'S NOT YOUR TIE PEOPLE ARE GOING TO NOTICE, CLINT. YOU DIDN'T LOOK LIKE THIS LAST NIGHT.
I TOLD YOU, THE BLACK EYE IS FROM THE OTHER NIGHT. I'M A SLOW BRUISER.
THAT'S ***NOT*** A THING.
GIRLFRIEND'S A DOCTOR, GENIUS. STOP SAYING DUMB STUFF TO HER.
YEAH? THEN WHY'D I SAY IT?
DAMMIT.
YOU SURE YOU'RE NOT HIDING SOMETHING FROM ME?
OH, I'M HIDING TONS OF STUFF FROM YOU. ***TONS***. BUT NOTHING YOU'D ***WANNA*** KNOW.
CAN'T WE JUST ENJOY A NICE NIGHT OUT?
THAT WAS MY NEXT QUESTION. WHY ARE WE HERE?
IT'S A CHARITY FUNDRAISER. YOU DON'T LIKE CHARITY?
LET ME REPHRASE. WHY ARE ***YOU*** HERE?

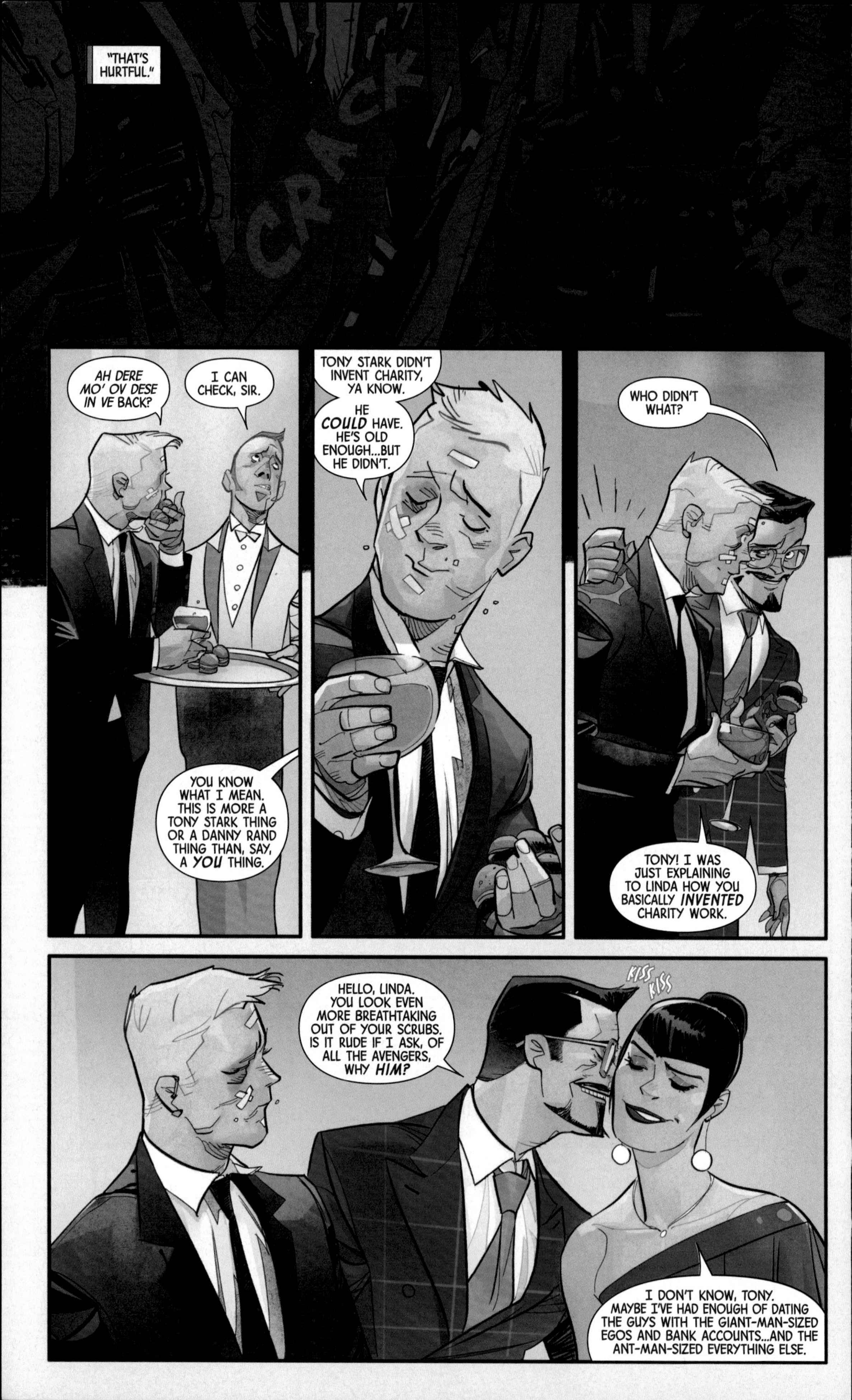
"THAT'S HURTFUL."
CRACK
AH DERE MO' OV DESE IN VE BACK?
I CAN CHECK, SIR.
YOU KNOW WHAT I MEAN. THIS IS MORE A TONY STARK THING OR A DANNY RAND THING THAN, SAY, A YOU THING.
TONY STARK DIDN'T INVENT CHARITY, YA KNOW.
HE COULD HAVE. HE'S OLD ENOUGH...BUT HE DIDN'T.
WHO DIDN'T WHAT?
TONY! I WAS JUST EXPLAINING TO LINDA HOW YOU BASICALLY INVENTED CHARITY WORK.
KISS KISS
HELLO, LINDA. YOU LOOK EVEN MORE BREATHTAKING OUT OF YOUR SCRUBS. IS IT RUDE IF I ASK, OF ALL THE AVENGERS, WHY HIM?
I DON'T KNOW, TONY. MAYBE I'VE HAD ENOUGH OF DATING THE GUYS WITH THE GIANT-MAN-SIZED EGOS AND BANK ACCOUNTS...AND THE ANT-MAN-SIZED EVERYTHING ELSE.

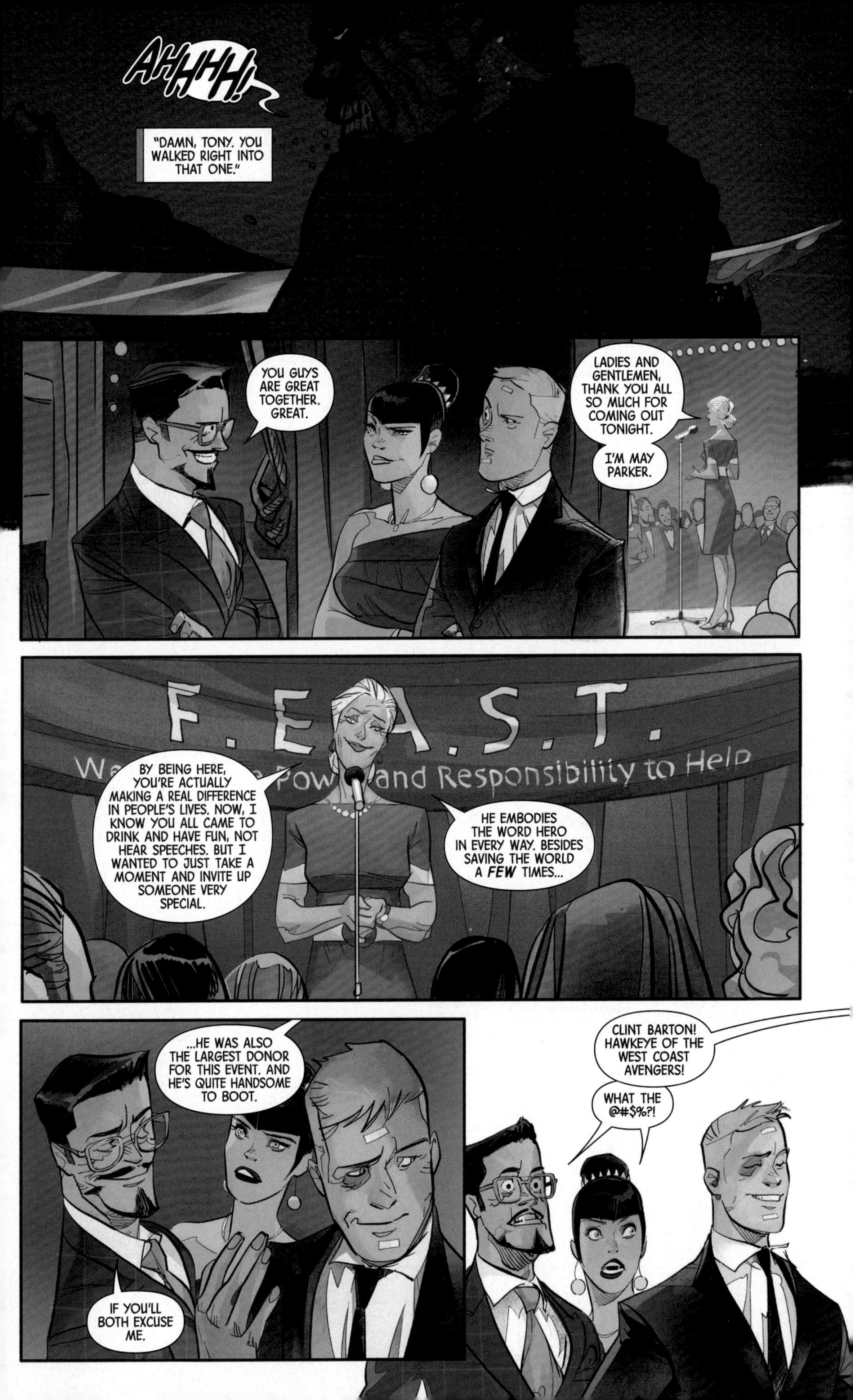
AHHHH!
"DAMN, TONY. YOU WALKED RIGHT INTO THAT ONE."
YOU GUYS ARE GREAT TOGETHER. GREAT.
LADIES AND GENTLEMEN, THANK YOU ALL SO MUCH FOR COMING OUT TONIGHT.
I'M MAY PARKER.
F.E.A.S.T.
and Responsibility to Help
BY BEING HERE, YOU'RE ACTUALLY MAKING A REAL DIFFERENCE IN PEOPLE'S LIVES. NOW, I KNOW YOU ALL CAME TO DRINK AND HAVE FUN, NOT HEAR SPEECHES. BUT I WANTED TO JUST TAKE A MOMENT AND INVITE UP SOMEONE VERY SPECIAL.
HE EMBODIES THE WORD HERO IN EVERY WAY. BESIDES SAVING THE WORLD A FEW TIMES...
...HE WAS ALSO THE LARGEST DONOR FOR THIS EVENT. AND HE'S QUITE HANDSOME TO BOOT.
IF YOU'LL BOTH EXCUSE ME.
CLINT BARTON! HAWKEYE OF THE WEST COAST AVENGERS!
WHAT THE @#$%?!

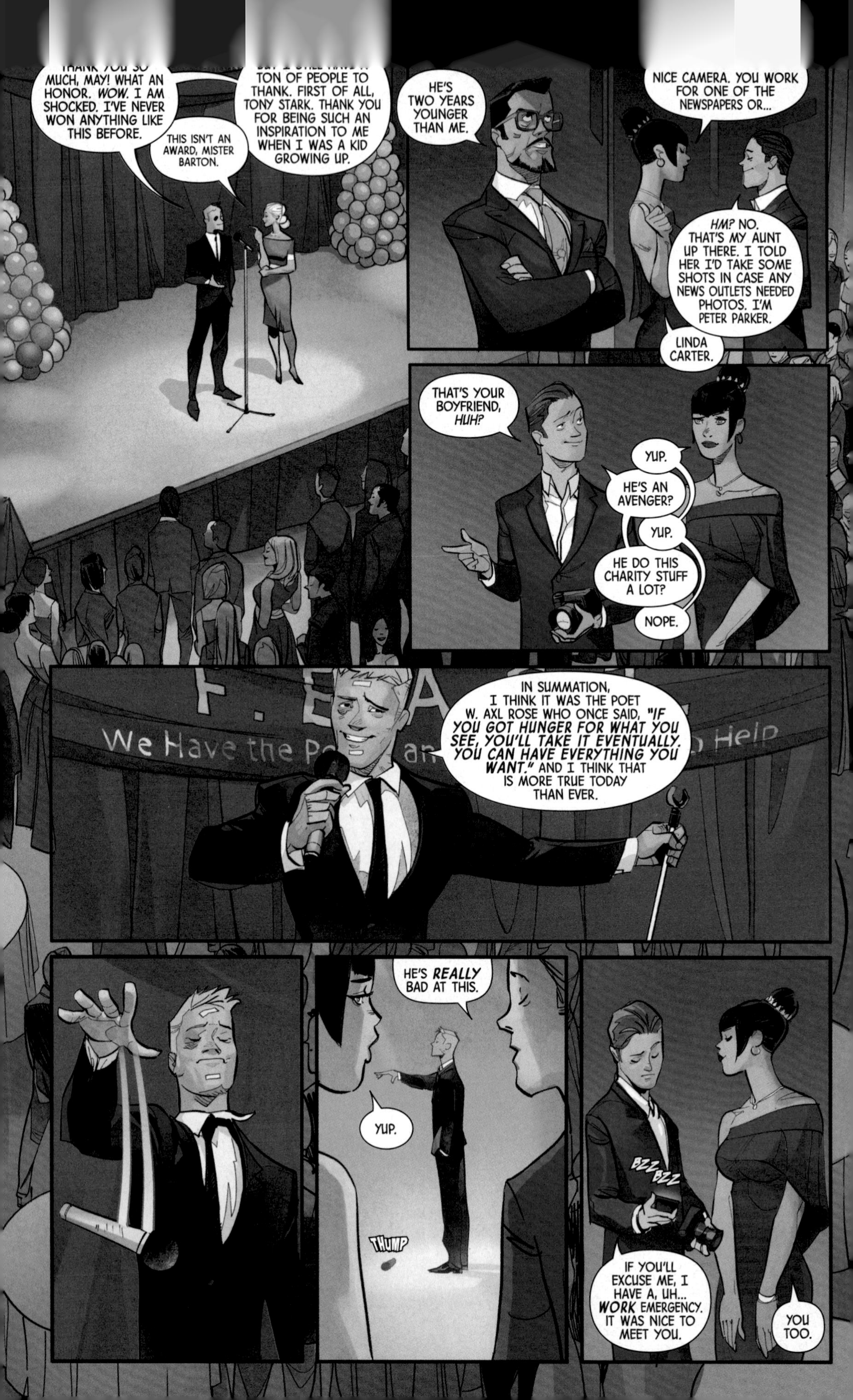
MUCH, MAY! WHAT AN HONOR. WOW. I AM SHOCKED. I'VE NEVER WON ANYTHING LIKE THIS BEFORE.
THIS ISN'T AN AWARD, MISTER BARTON.
TON OF PEOPLE TO THANK. FIRST OF ALL, TONY STARK. THANK YOU FOR BEING SUCH AN INSPIRATION TO ME WHEN I WAS A KID GROWING UP.
HE'S TWO YEARS YOUNGER THAN ME.
NICE CAMERA. YOU WORK FOR ONE OF THE NEWSPAPERS OR...
HM? NO. THAT'S MY AUNT UP THERE. I TOLD HER I'D TAKE SOME SHOTS IN CASE ANY NEWS OUTLETS NEEDED PHOTOS. I'M PETER PARKER.
LINDA CARTER.
THAT'S YOUR BOYFRIEND, HUH?
YUP.
HE'S AN AVENGER?
YUP.
HE DO THIS CHARITY STUFF A LOT?
NOPE.
IN SUMMATION, I THINK IT WAS THE POET W. AXL ROSE WHO ONCE SAID, "IF YOU GOT HUNGER FOR WHAT YOU SEE, YOU'LL TAKE IT EVENTUALLY. YOU CAN HAVE EVERYTHING YOU WANT." AND I THINK THAT IS MORE TRUE TODAY THAN EVER.
HE'S REALLY BAD AT THIS.
YUP.
THUMP
BZZ BZZ
IF YOU'LL EXCUSE ME, I HAVE A, UH... WORK EMERGENCY. IT WAS NICE TO MEET YOU.
YOU TOO.

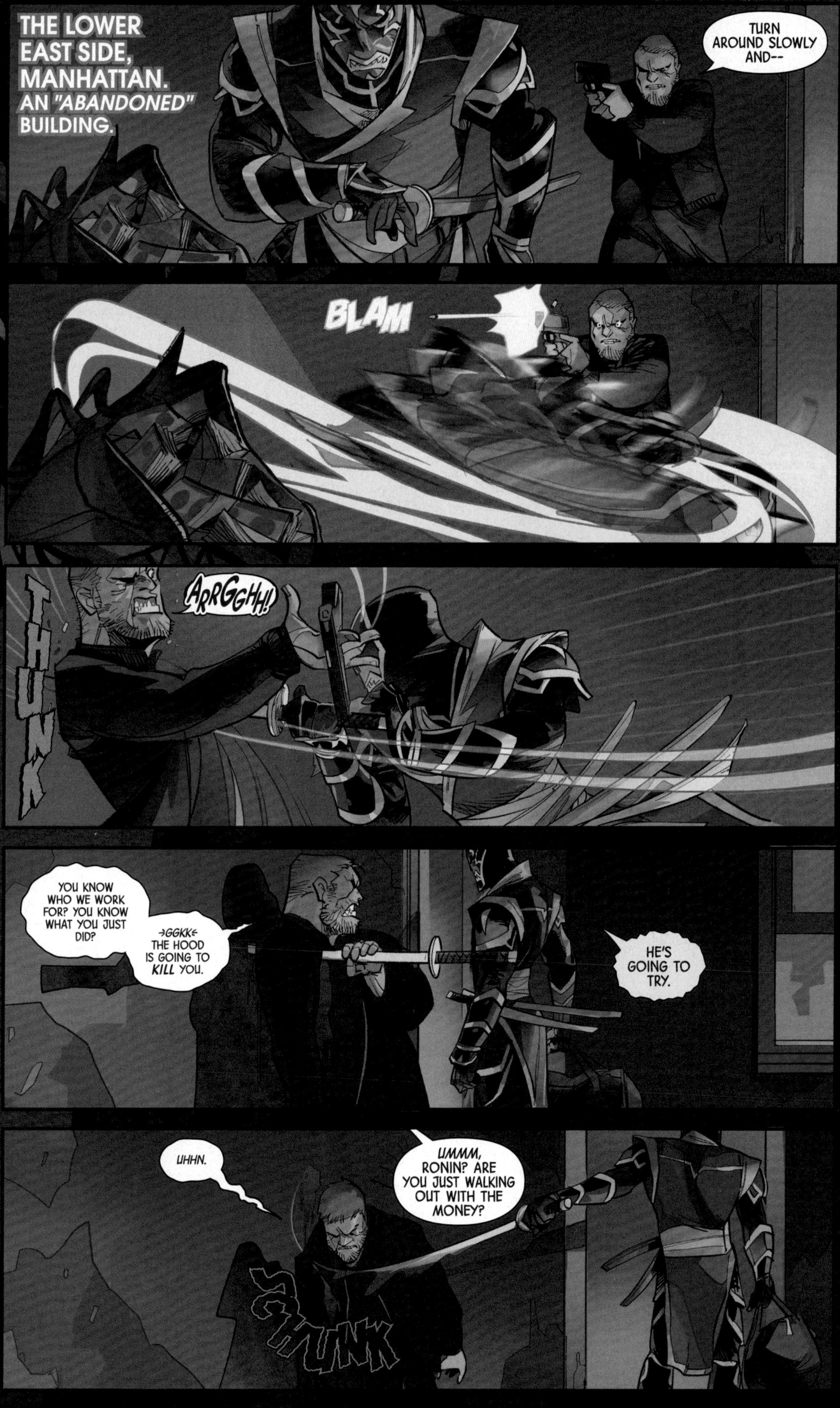
THE LOWER EAST SIDE, MANHATTAN. AN "ABANDONED" BUILDING.
TURN AROUND SLOWLY AND--
BLAM
ARRGGHH!
THUNK
YOU KNOW WHO WE WORK FOR? YOU KNOW WHAT YOU JUST DID?
→GGKK← THE HOOD IS GOING TO KILL YOU.
HE'S GOING TO TRY.
UHHN.
UMMM, RONIN? ARE YOU JUST WALKING OUT WITH THE MONEY?
SCHUNK

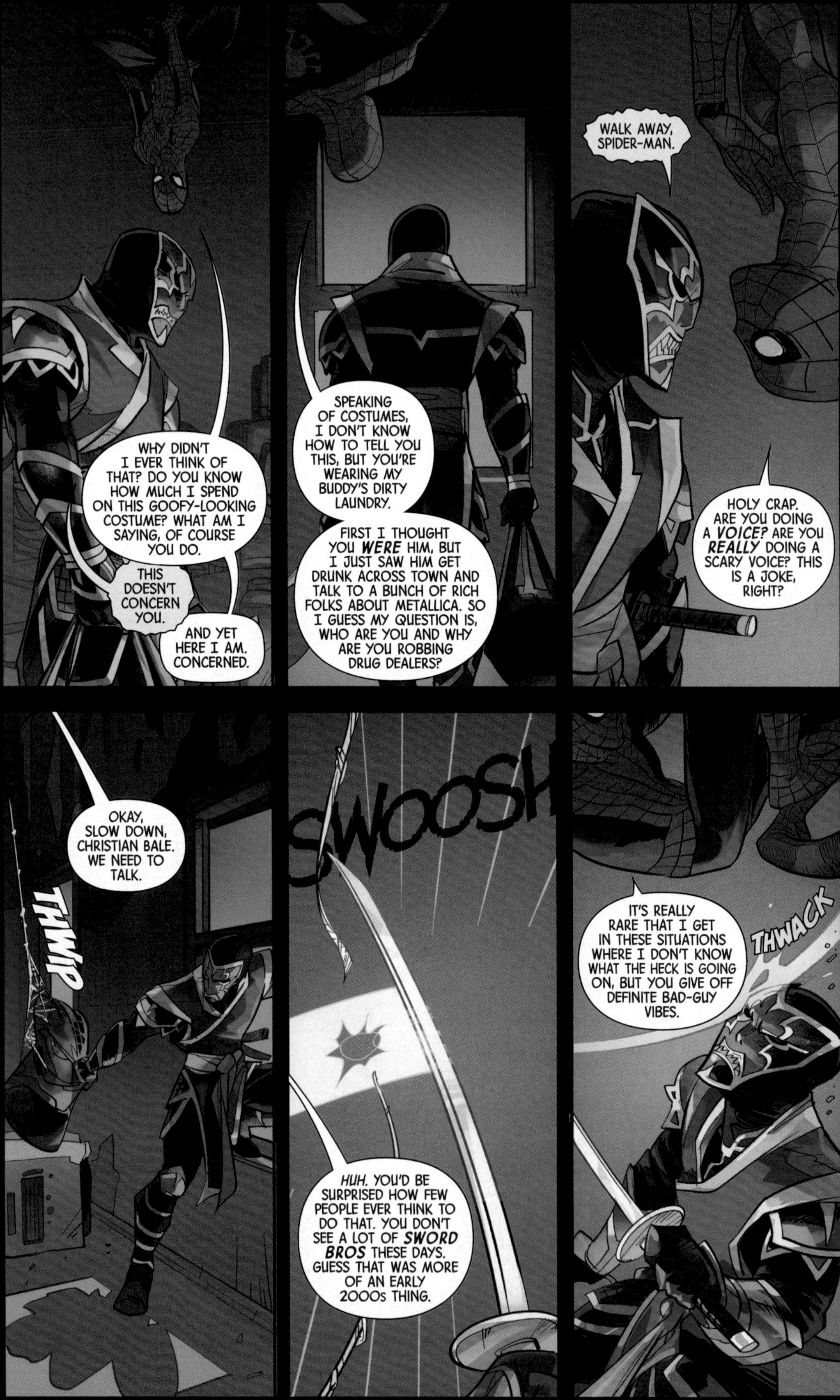

WHY DIDN'T I EVER THINK OF THAT? DO YOU KNOW HOW MUCH I SPEND ON THIS GOOFY-LOOKING COSTUME? WHAT AM I SAYING, OF COURSE YOU DO.
THIS DOESN'T CONCERN YOU.
AND YET HERE I AM. CONCERNED.
SPEAKING OF COSTUMES, I DON'T KNOW HOW TO TELL YOU THIS, BUT YOU'RE WEARING MY BUDDY'S DIRTY LAUNDRY.
FIRST I THOUGHT YOU *WERE* HIM, BUT I JUST SAW HIM GET DRUNK ACROSS TOWN AND TALK TO A BUNCH OF RICH FOLKS ABOUT METALLICA. SO I GUESS MY QUESTION IS, WHO ARE YOU AND WHY ARE YOU ROBBING DRUG DEALERS?
WALK AWAY, SPIDER-MAN.
HOLY CRAP. ARE YOU DOING A *VOICE?* ARE YOU *REALLY* DOING A SCARY VOICE? THIS IS A JOKE, RIGHT?
OKAY, SLOW DOWN, CHRISTIAN BALE. WE NEED TO TALK.
THWIP
SWOOSH
HUH. YOU'D BE SURPRISED HOW FEW PEOPLE EVER THINK TO DO THAT. YOU DON'T SEE A LOT OF ***SWORD BROS*** THESE DAYS. GUESS THAT WAS MORE OF AN EARLY 2000s THING.
IT'S REALLY RARE THAT I GET IN THESE SITUATIONS WHERE I DON'T KNOW WHAT THE HECK IS GOING ON, BUT YOU GIVE OFF DEFINITE BAD-GUY VIBES.
THWACK

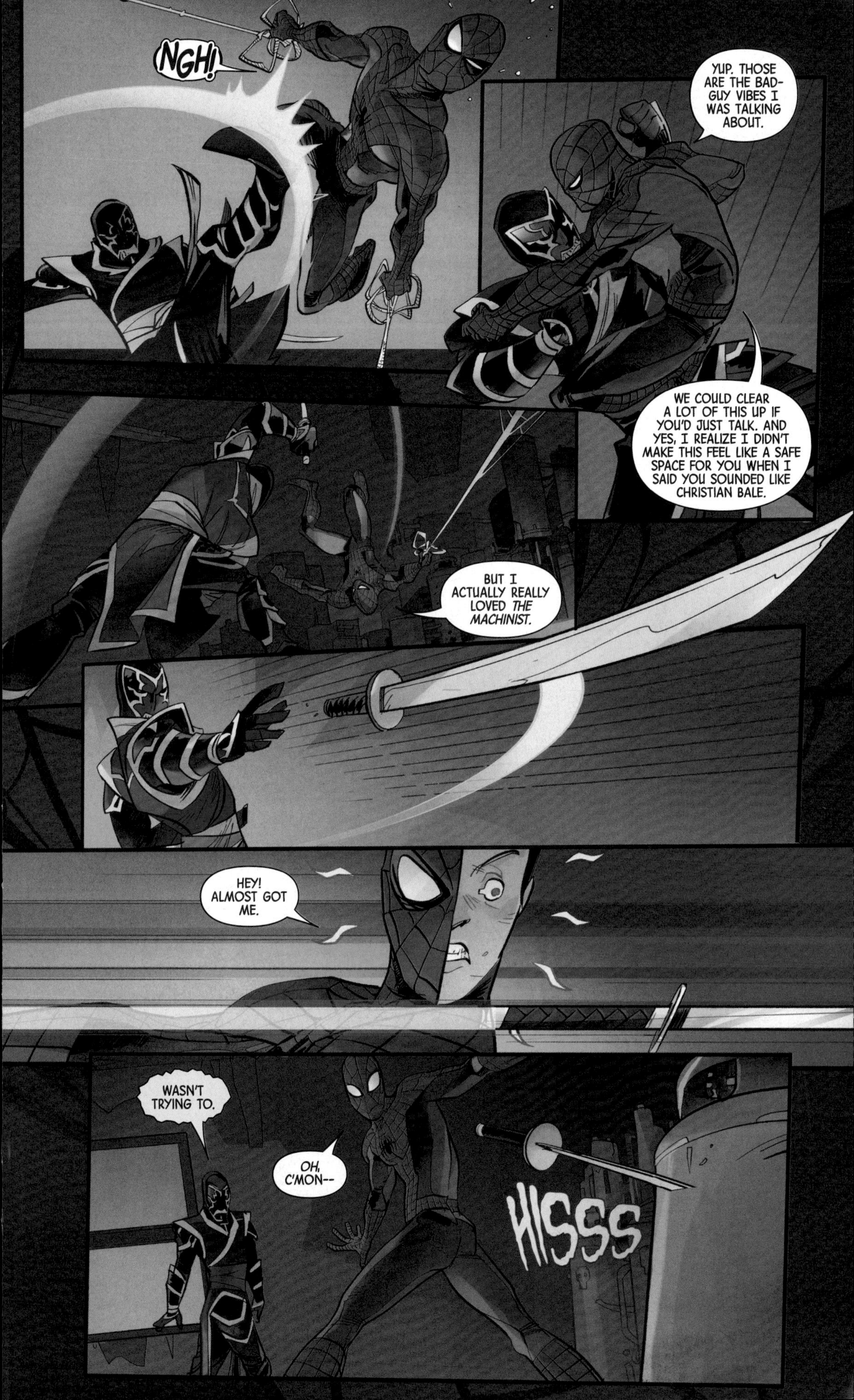
NGH!
YUP. THOSE ARE THE BAD-GUY VIBES I WAS TALKING ABOUT.
WE COULD CLEAR A LOT OF THIS UP IF YOU'D JUST TALK. AND YES, I REALIZE I DIDN'T MAKE THIS FEEL LIKE A SAFE SPACE FOR YOU WHEN I SAID YOU SOUNDED LIKE CHRISTIAN BALE.
BUT I ACTUALLY REALLY LOVED *THE MACHINIST.*
HEY! ALMOST GOT ME.
WASN'T TRYING TO.
OH, C'MON--
HISSS

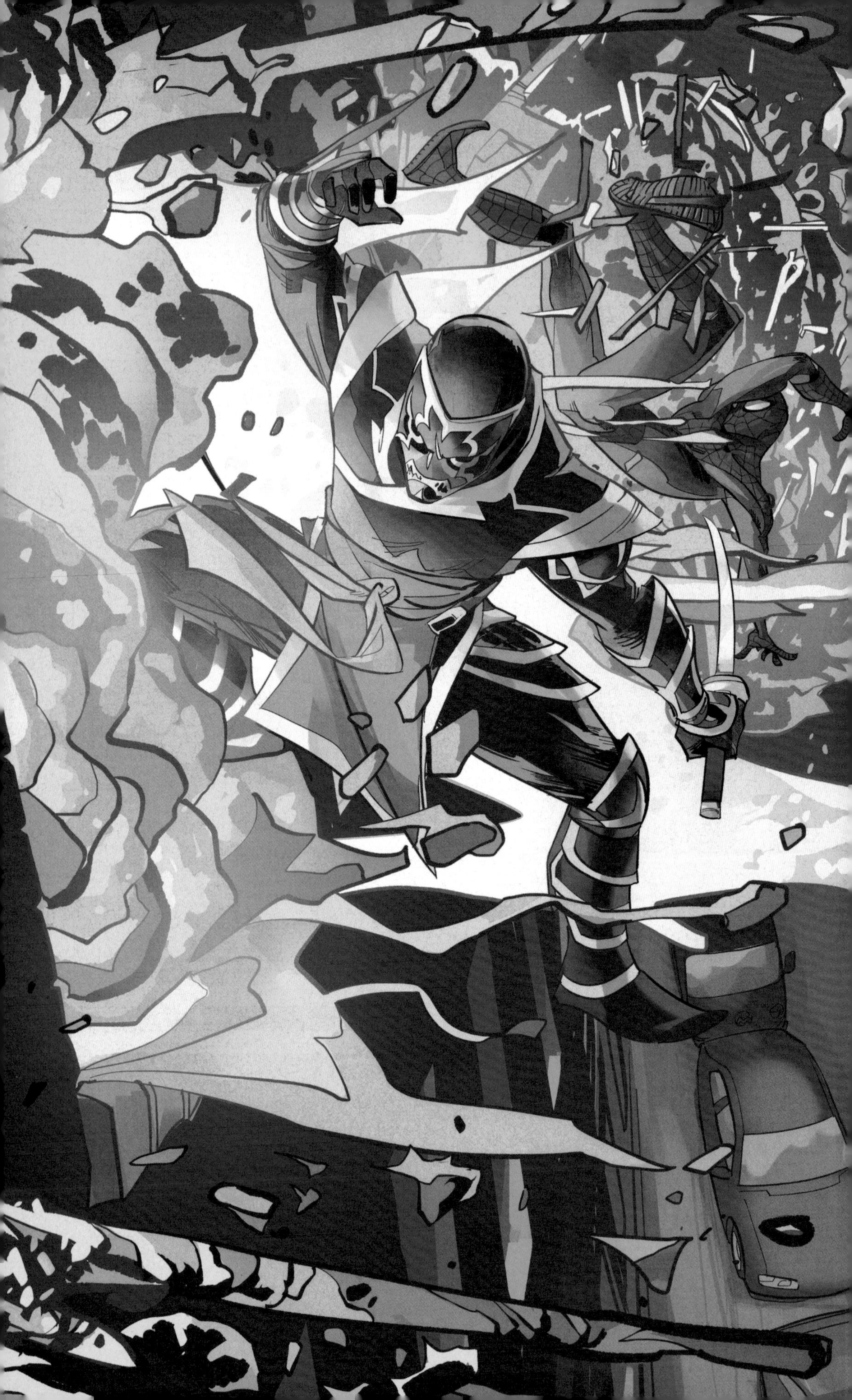

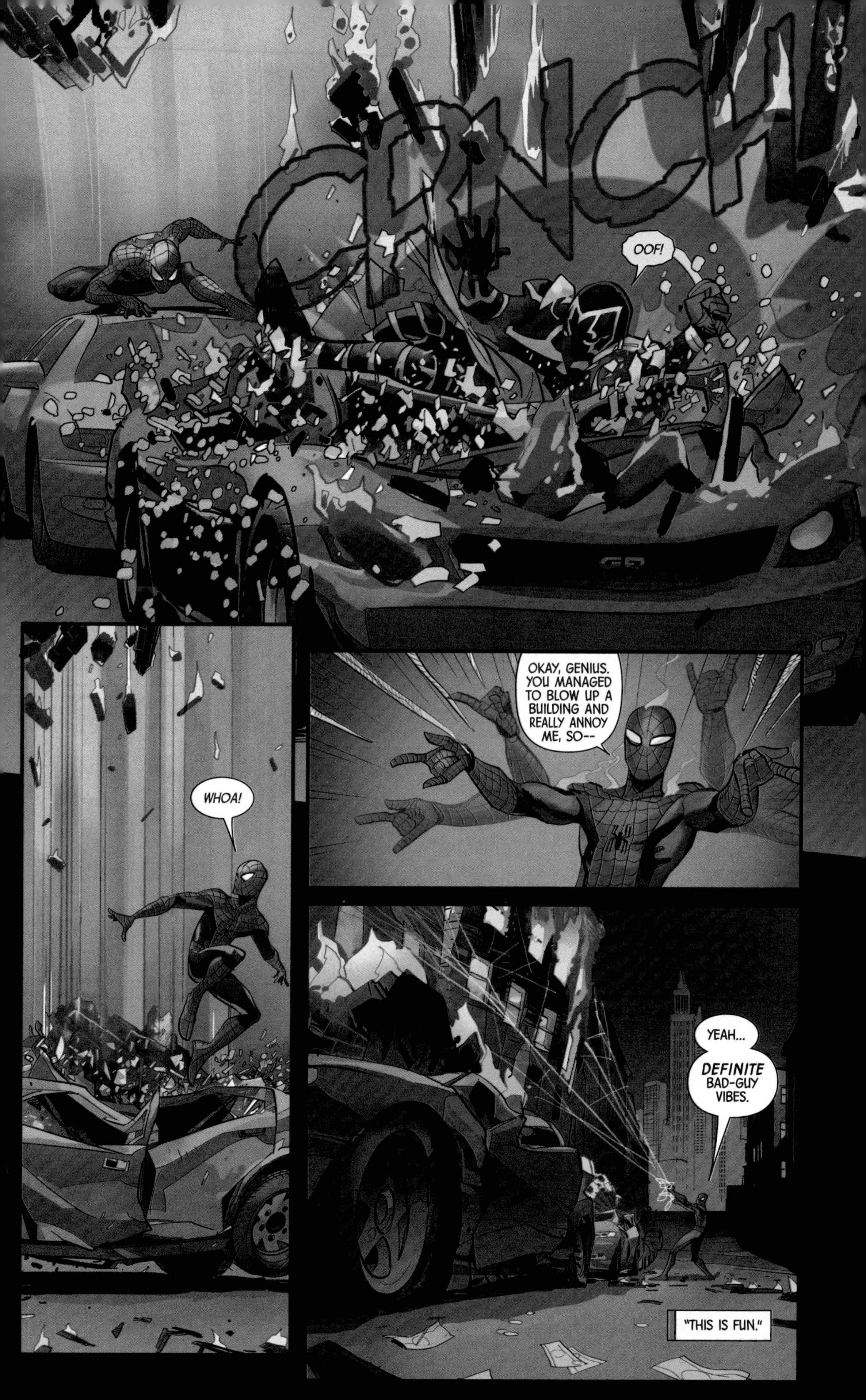
CRNCH!
OOF!
WHOA!
OKAY, GENIUS. YOU MANAGED TO BLOW UP A BUILDING AND REALLY ANNOY ME, SO--
YEAH...
DEFINITE BAD-GUY VIBES.
"THIS IS FUN."

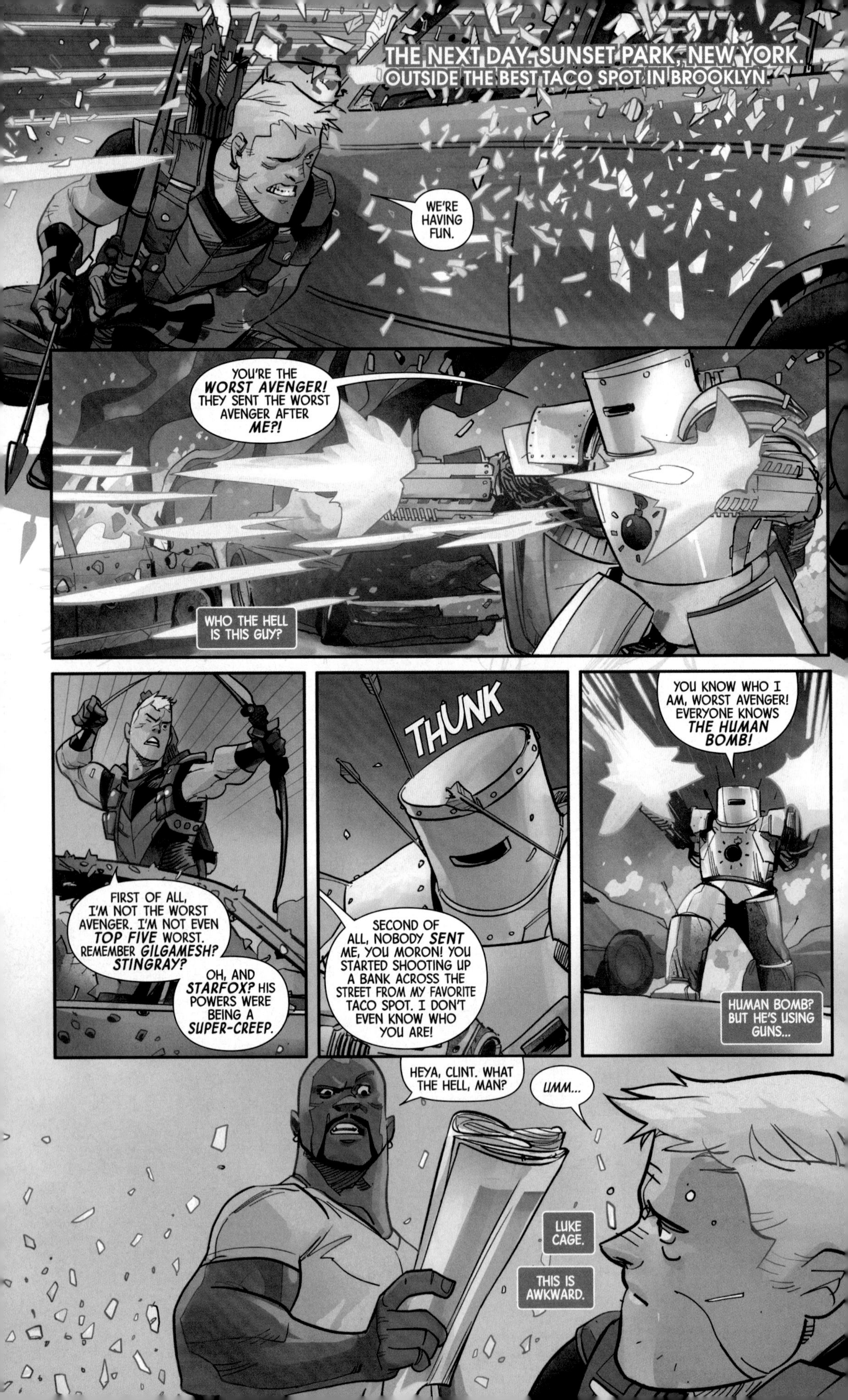
THE NEXT DAY. SUNSET PARK, NEW YORK.
OUTSIDE THE BEST TACO SPOT IN BROOKLYN.
WE'RE HAVING FUN.
YOU'RE THE WORST AVENGER! THEY SENT THE WORST AVENGER AFTER ME?!
WHO THE HELL IS THIS GUY?
FIRST OF ALL, I'M NOT THE WORST AVENGER. I'M NOT EVEN TOP FIVE WORST. REMEMBER GILGAMESH? STINGRAY?
OH, AND STARFOX? HIS POWERS WERE BEING A SUPER-CREEP.
THUNK
SECOND OF ALL, NOBODY SENT ME, YOU MORON! YOU STARTED SHOOTING UP A BANK ACROSS THE STREET FROM MY FAVORITE TACO SPOT. I DON'T EVEN KNOW WHO YOU ARE!
YOU KNOW WHO I AM, WORST AVENGER! EVERYONE KNOWS THE HUMAN BOMB!
HUMAN BOMB? BUT HE'S USING GUNS...
HEYA, CLINT. WHAT THE HELL, MAN?
UMM...
LUKE CAGE.
THIS IS AWKWARD.

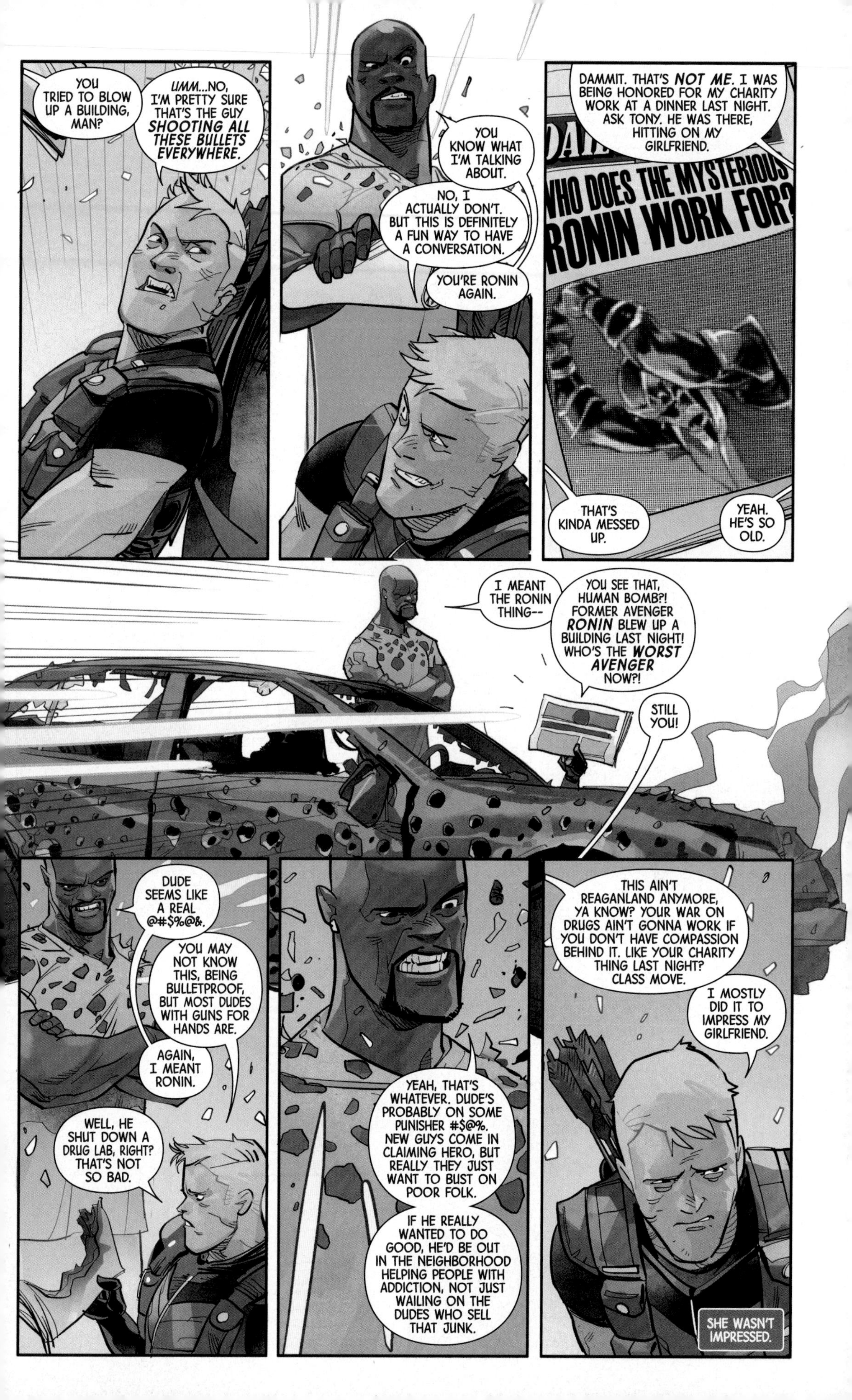
YOU TRIED TO BLOW UP A BUILDING, MAN?
UMM...NO, I'M PRETTY SURE THAT'S THE GUY SHOOTING ALL THESE BULLETS EVERYWHERE.
YOU KNOW WHAT I'M TALKING ABOUT.
NO, I ACTUALLY DON'T. BUT THIS IS DEFINITELY A FUN WAY TO HAVE A CONVERSATION.
YOU'RE RONIN AGAIN.
DAMMIT. THAT'S NOT ME. I WAS BEING HONORED FOR MY CHARITY WORK AT A DINNER LAST NIGHT. ASK TONY. HE WAS THERE, HITTING ON MY GIRLFRIEND.
WHO DOES THE MYSTERIOUS RONIN WORK FOR?
THAT'S KINDA MESSED UP.
YEAH. HE'S SO OLD.
I MEANT THE RONIN THING--
YOU SEE THAT, HUMAN BOMB?! FORMER AVENGER RONIN BLEW UP A BUILDING LAST NIGHT! WHO'S THE WORST AVENGER NOW?!
STILL YOU!
DUDE SEEMS LIKE A REAL @#$%@&.
YOU MAY NOT KNOW THIS, BEING BULLETPROOF, BUT MOST DUDES WITH GUNS FOR HANDS ARE.
AGAIN, I MEANT RONIN.
WELL, HE SHUT DOWN A DRUG LAB, RIGHT? THAT'S NOT SO BAD.
YEAH, THAT'S WHATEVER. DUDE'S PROBABLY ON SOME PUNISHER #$@%. NEW GUYS COME IN CLAIMING HERO, BUT REALLY THEY JUST WANT TO BUST ON POOR FOLK.
IF HE REALLY WANTED TO DO GOOD, HE'D BE OUT IN THE NEIGHBORHOOD HELPING PEOPLE WITH ADDICTION, NOT JUST WAILING ON THE DUDES WHO SELL THAT JUNK.
THIS AIN'T REAGANLAND ANYMORE, YA KNOW? YOUR WAR ON DRUGS AIN'T GONNA WORK IF YOU DON'T HAVE COMPASSION BEHIND IT. LIKE YOUR CHARITY THING LAST NIGHT? CLASS MOVE.
I MOSTLY DID IT TO IMPRESS MY GIRLFRIEND.
SHE WASN'T IMPRESSED.

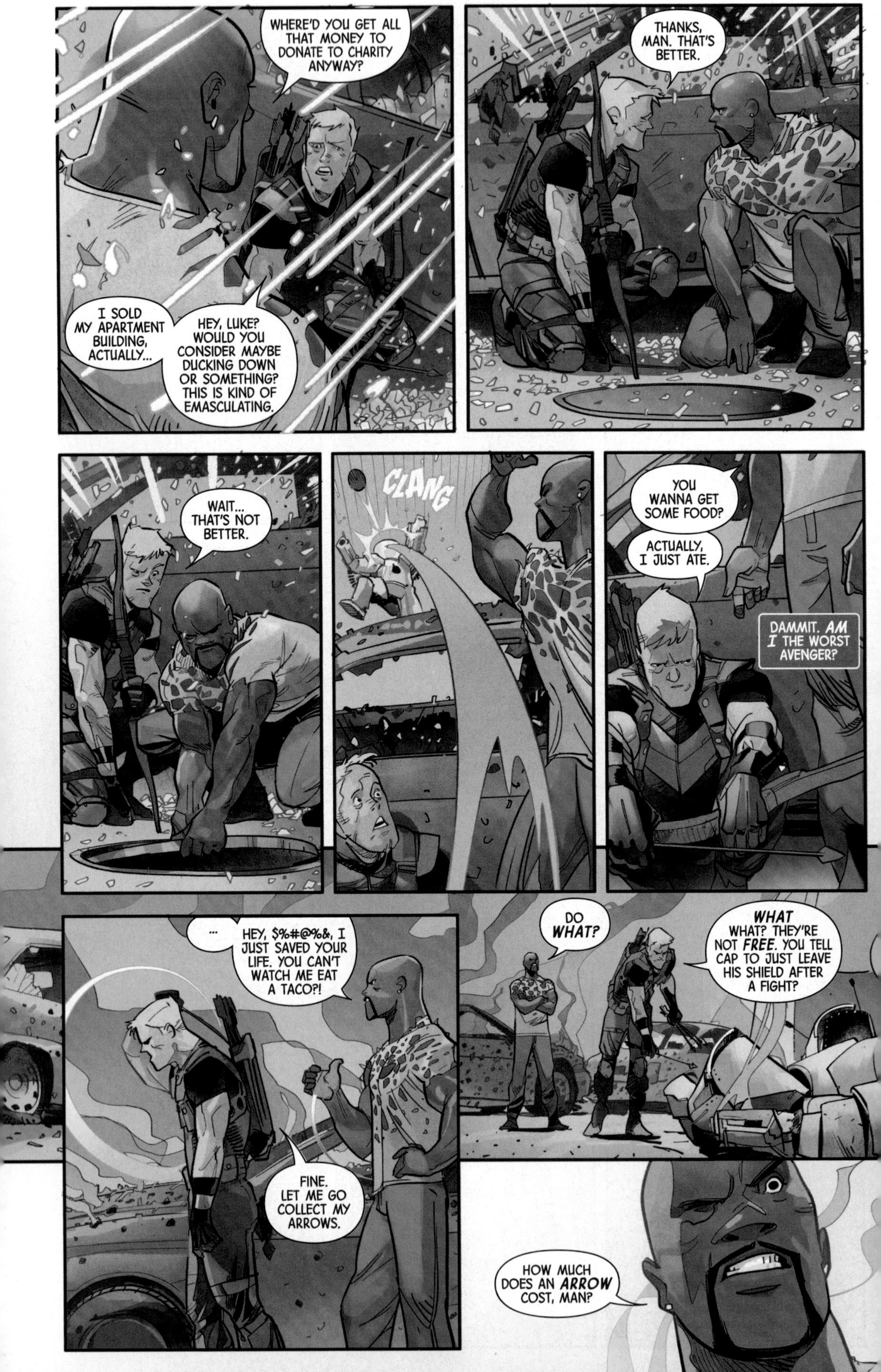
WHERE'D YOU GET ALL THAT MONEY TO DONATE TO CHARITY ANYWAY?
I SOLD MY APARTMENT BUILDING, ACTUALLY...
HEY, LUKE? WOULD YOU CONSIDER MAYBE DUCKING DOWN OR SOMETHING? THIS IS KIND OF EMASCULATING.
THANKS, MAN. THAT'S BETTER.
WAIT... THAT'S NOT BETTER.
CLANG
YOU WANNA GET SOME FOOD?
ACTUALLY, I JUST ATE.
DAMMIT. AM I THE WORST AVENGER?
...
HEY, $%#@%&, I JUST SAVED YOUR LIFE. YOU CAN'T WATCH ME EAT A TACO?!
FINE. LET ME GO COLLECT MY ARROWS.
DO WHAT?
WHAT WHAT? THEY'RE NOT FREE. YOU TELL CAP TO JUST LEAVE HIS SHIELD AFTER A FIGHT?
HOW MUCH DOES AN ARROW COST, MAN?

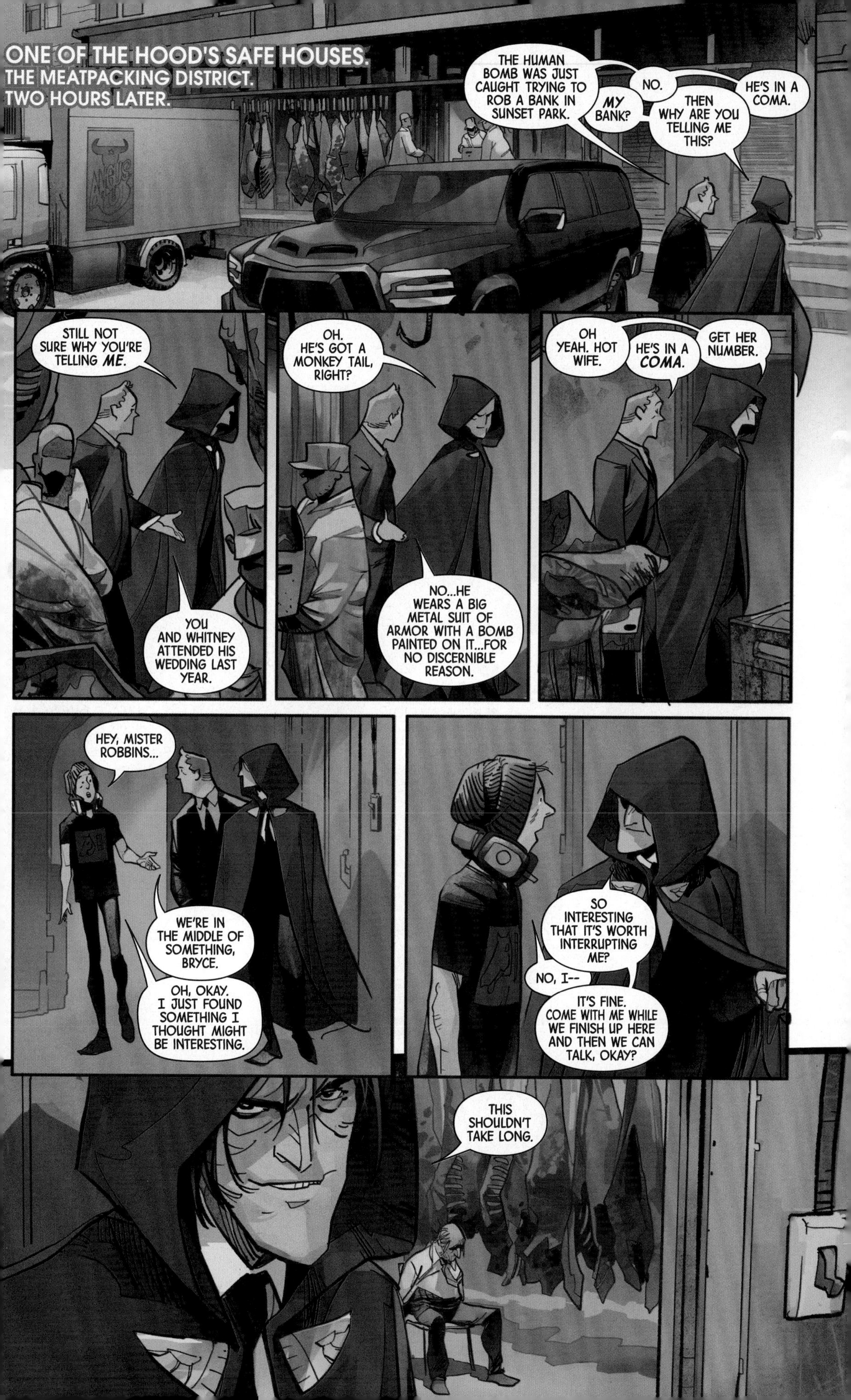
ONE OF THE HOOD'S SAFE HOUSES.
THE MEATPACKING DISTRICT.
TWO HOURS LATER.
THE HUMAN BOMB WAS JUST CAUGHT TRYING TO ROB A BANK IN SUNSET PARK.
MY BANK?
NO.
THEN WHY ARE YOU TELLING ME THIS?
HE'S IN A COMA.
STILL NOT SURE WHY YOU'RE TELLING ME.
YOU AND WHITNEY ATTENDED HIS WEDDING LAST YEAR.
OH. HE'S GOT A MONKEY TAIL, RIGHT?
NO...HE WEARS A BIG METAL SUIT OF ARMOR WITH A BOMB PAINTED ON IT...FOR NO DISCERNIBLE REASON.
OH YEAH. HOT WIFE.
HE'S IN A COMA.
GET HER NUMBER.
HEY, MISTER ROBBINS...
WE'RE IN THE MIDDLE OF SOMETHING, BRYCE.
OH, OKAY. I JUST FOUND SOMETHING I THOUGHT MIGHT BE INTERESTING.
SO INTERESTING THAT IT'S WORTH INTERRUPTING ME?
NO, I--
IT'S FINE. COME WITH ME WHILE WE FINISH UP HERE AND THEN WE CAN TALK, OKAY?
THIS SHOULDN'T TAKE LONG.

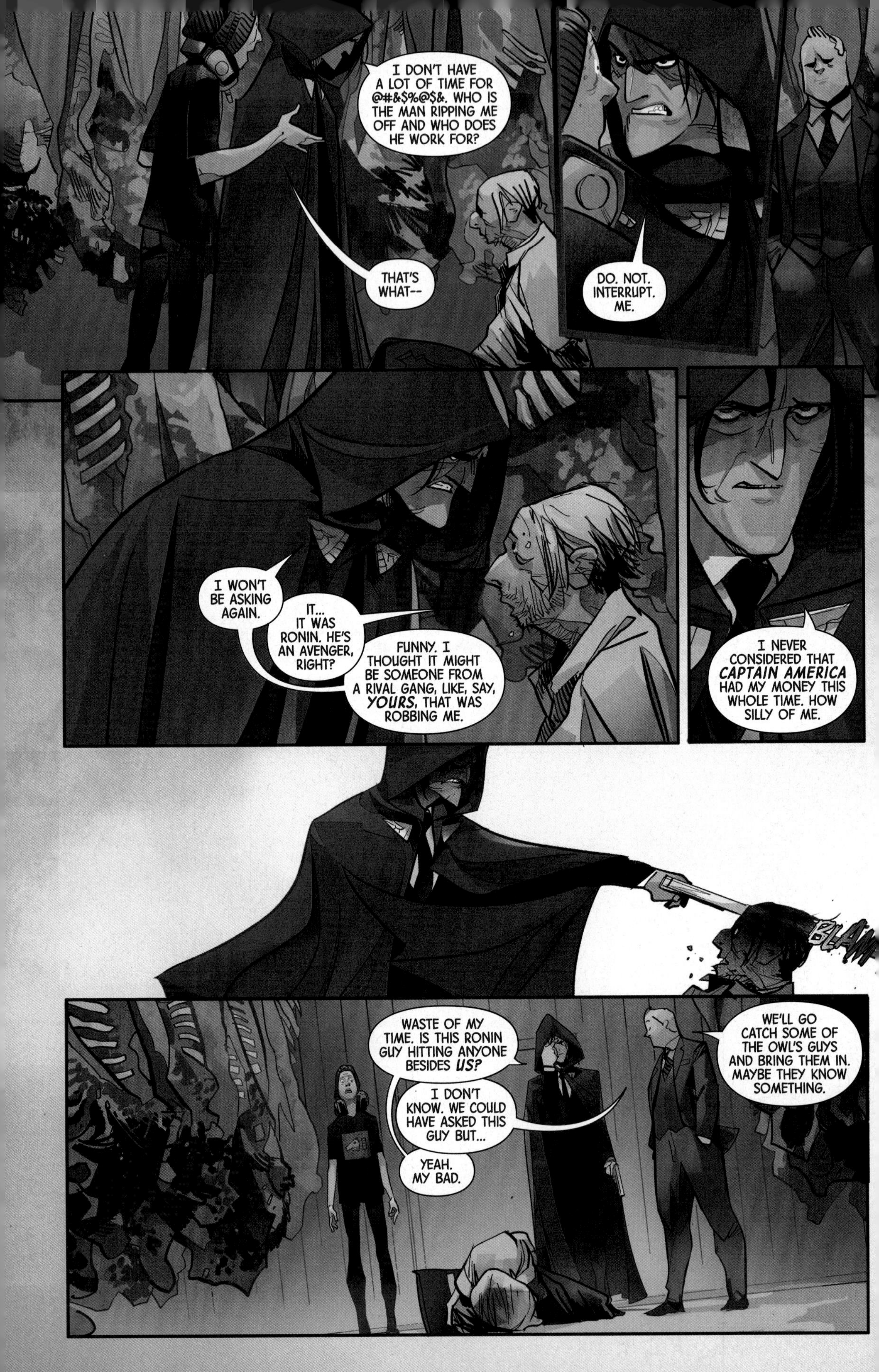
I DON'T HAVE A LOT OF TIME FOR @#&$%@$&. WHO IS THE MAN RIPPING ME OFF AND WHO DOES HE WORK FOR?
THAT'S WHAT--
DO. NOT. INTERRUPT. ME.
I WON'T BE ASKING AGAIN.
IT... IT WAS RONIN. HE'S AN AVENGER, RIGHT?
FUNNY. I THOUGHT IT MIGHT BE SOMEONE FROM A RIVAL GANG, LIKE, SAY, YOURS, THAT WAS ROBBING ME.
I NEVER CONSIDERED THAT CAPTAIN AMERICA HAD MY MONEY THIS WHOLE TIME. HOW SILLY OF ME.
BLAM
WASTE OF MY TIME. IS THIS RONIN GUY HITTING ANYONE BESIDES US?
I DON'T KNOW. WE COULD HAVE ASKED THIS GUY BUT...
YEAH. MY BAD.
WE'LL GO CATCH SOME OF THE OWL'S GUYS AND BRING THEM IN. MAYBE THEY KNOW SOMETHING.

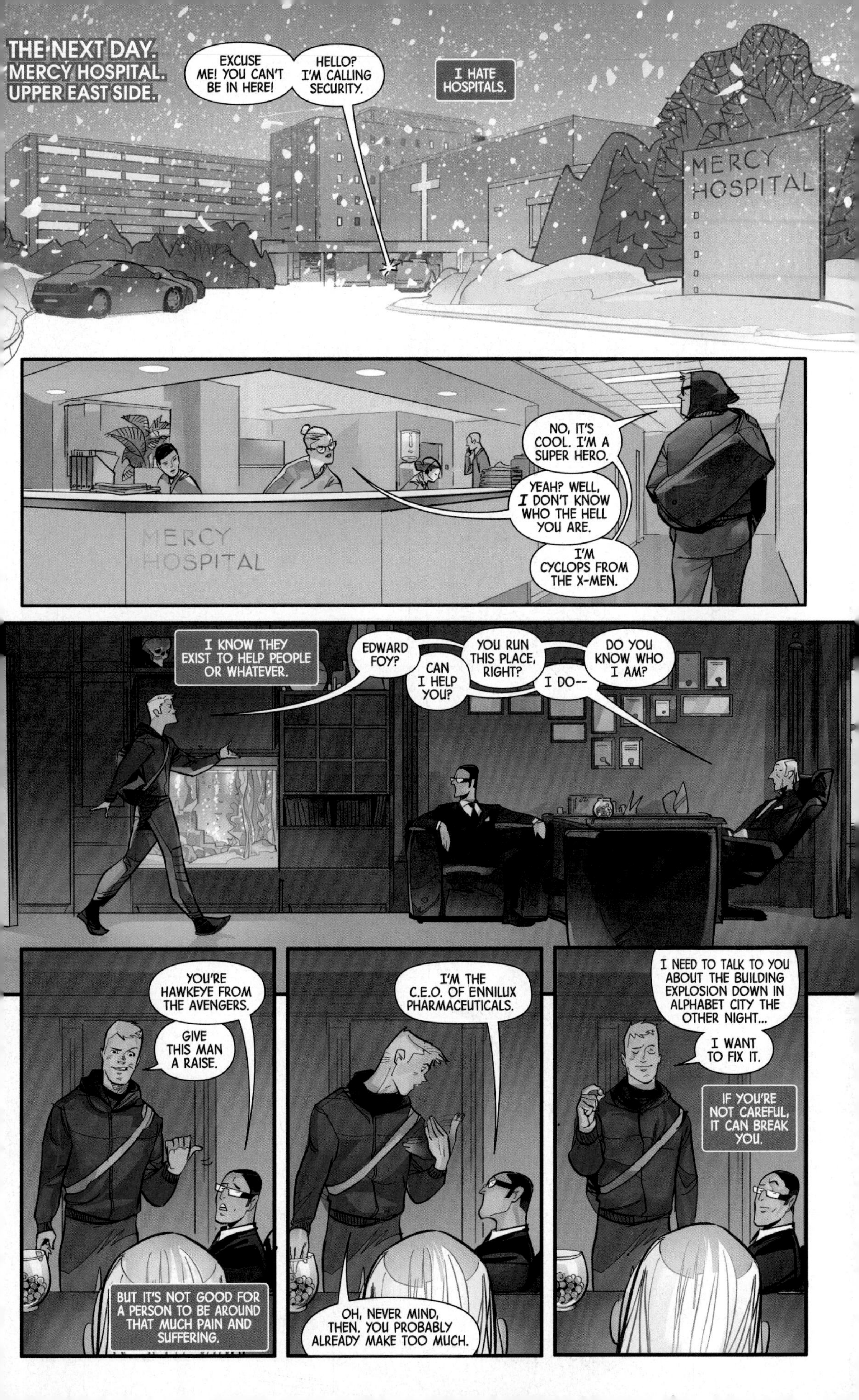
THE NEXT DAY. MERCY HOSPITAL. UPPER EAST SIDE.
EXCUSE ME! YOU CAN'T BE IN HERE!
HELLO? I'M CALLING SECURITY.
I HATE HOSPITALS.
MERCY HOSPITAL
NO, IT'S COOL. I'M A SUPER HERO.
YEAH? WELL, I DON'T KNOW WHO THE HELL YOU ARE.
I'M CYCLOPS FROM THE X-MEN.
MERCY HOSPITAL
I KNOW THEY EXIST TO HELP PEOPLE OR WHATEVER.
EDWARD FOY?
CAN I HELP YOU?
YOU RUN THIS PLACE, RIGHT?
I DO--
DO YOU KNOW WHO I AM?
YOU'RE HAWKEYE FROM THE AVENGERS.
GIVE THIS MAN A RAISE.
BUT IT'S NOT GOOD FOR A PERSON TO BE AROUND THAT MUCH PAIN AND SUFFERING.
I'M THE C.E.O. OF ENNILUX PHARMACEUTICALS.
OH, NEVER MIND, THEN. YOU PROBABLY ALREADY MAKE TOO MUCH.
I NEED TO TALK TO YOU ABOUT THE BUILDING EXPLOSION DOWN IN ALPHABET CITY THE OTHER NIGHT...
I WANT TO FIX IT.
IF YOU'RE NOT CAREFUL, IT CAN BREAK YOU.

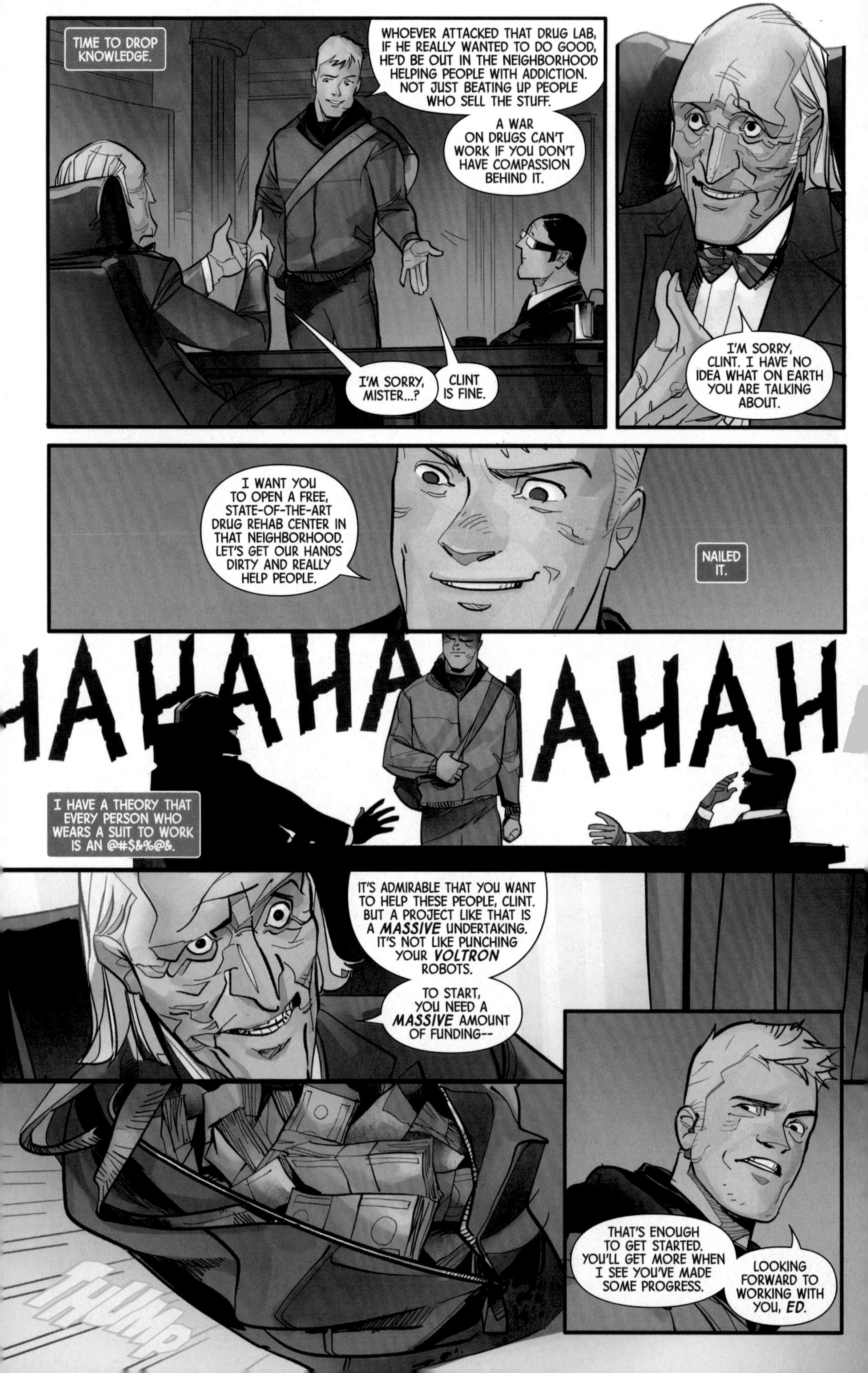

TIME TO DROP KNOWLEDGE.
WHOEVER ATTACKED THAT DRUG LAB, IF HE REALLY WANTED TO DO GOOD, HE'D BE OUT IN THE NEIGHBORHOOD HELPING PEOPLE WITH ADDICTION. NOT JUST BEATING UP PEOPLE WHO SELL THE STUFF.
A WAR ON DRUGS CAN'T WORK IF YOU DON'T HAVE COMPASSION BEHIND IT.
I'M SORRY, MISTER...?
CLINT IS FINE.
I'M SORRY, CLINT. I HAVE NO IDEA WHAT ON EARTH YOU ARE TALKING ABOUT.
I WANT YOU TO OPEN A FREE, STATE-OF-THE-ART DRUG REHAB CENTER IN THAT NEIGHBORHOOD. LET'S GET OUR HANDS DIRTY AND REALLY HELP PEOPLE.
NAILED IT.
HAHAHAHAHAHAH
I HAVE A THEORY THAT EVERY PERSON WHO WEARS A SUIT TO WORK IS AN @#$&%@&.
IT'S ADMIRABLE THAT YOU WANT TO HELP THESE PEOPLE, CLINT. BUT A PROJECT LIKE THAT IS A *MASSIVE* UNDERTAKING. IT'S NOT LIKE PUNCHING YOUR *VOLTRON* ROBOTS.
TO START, YOU NEED A *MASSIVE* AMOUNT OF FUNDING--
THUMP
THAT'S ENOUGH TO GET STARTED. YOU'LL GET MORE WHEN I SEE YOU'VE MADE SOME PROGRESS.
LOOKING FORWARD TO WORKING WITH YOU, *ED*.

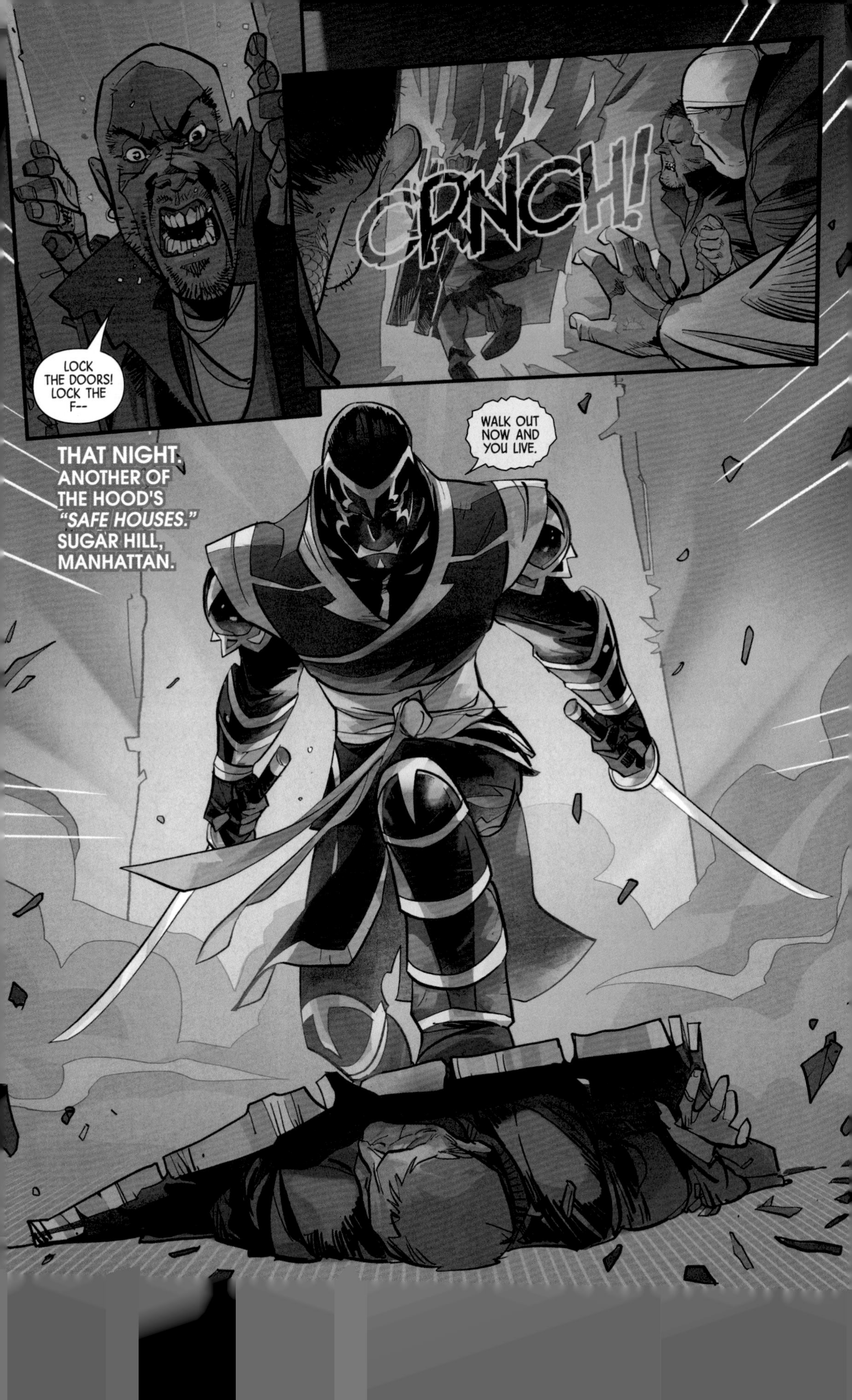
LOCK THE DOORS! LOCK THE F--
CRNCH!
THAT NIGHT. ANOTHER OF THE HOOD'S "SAFE HOUSES." SUGAR HILL, MANHATTAN.
WALK OUT NOW AND YOU LIVE.

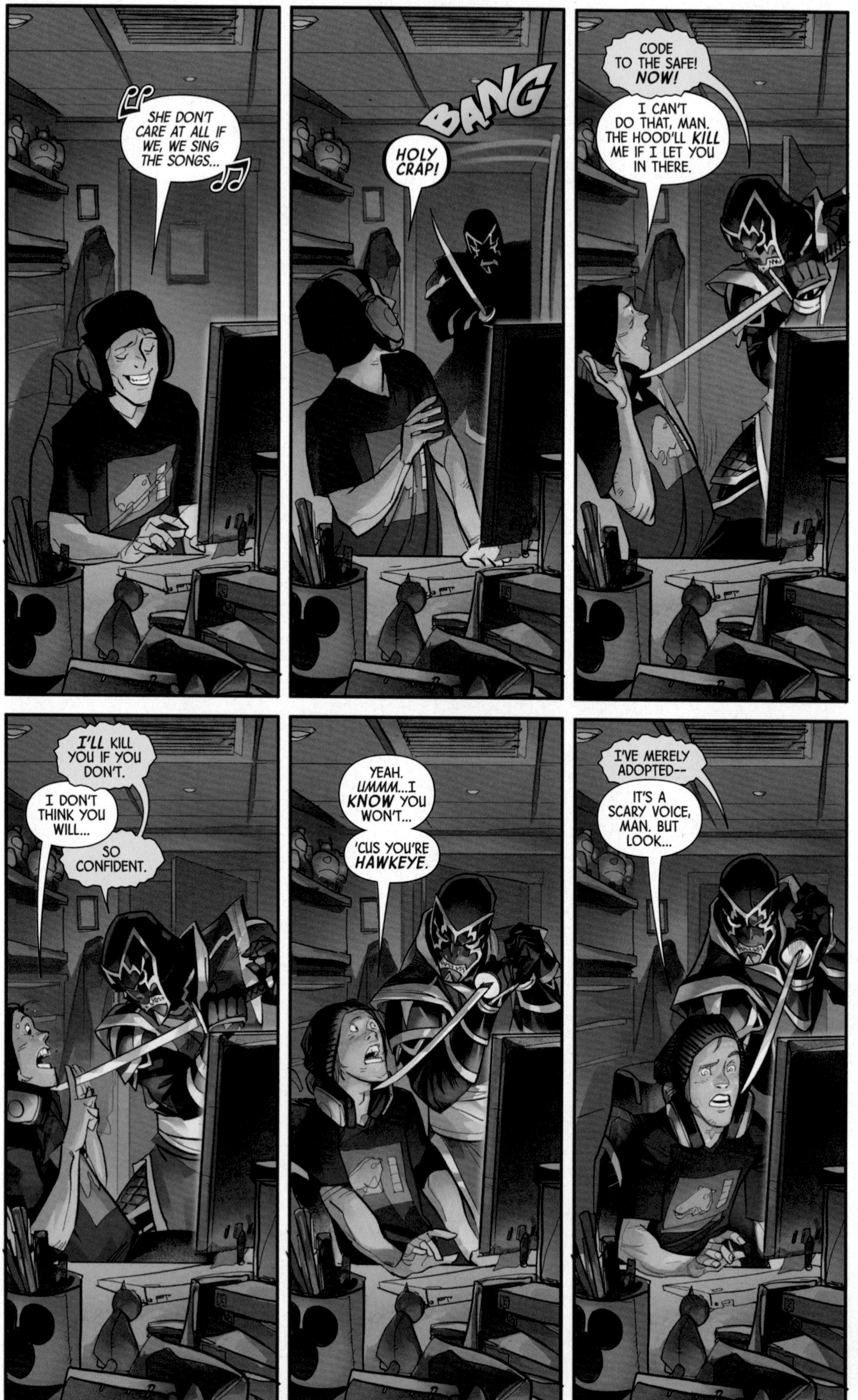

SHE DON'T CARE AT ALL IF WE, WE SING THE SONGS...
BANG
HOLY CRAP!
CODE TO THE SAFE! NOW!
I CAN'T DO THAT, MAN. THE HOOD'LL KILL ME IF I LET YOU IN THERE.
I'LL KILL YOU IF YOU DON'T.
I DON'T THINK YOU WILL...
SO CONFIDENT.
YEAH. UMMM...I KNOW YOU WON'T...
'CUS YOU'RE HAWKEYE.
I'VE MERELY ADOPTED--
IT'S A SCARY VOICE, MAN. BUT LOOK...

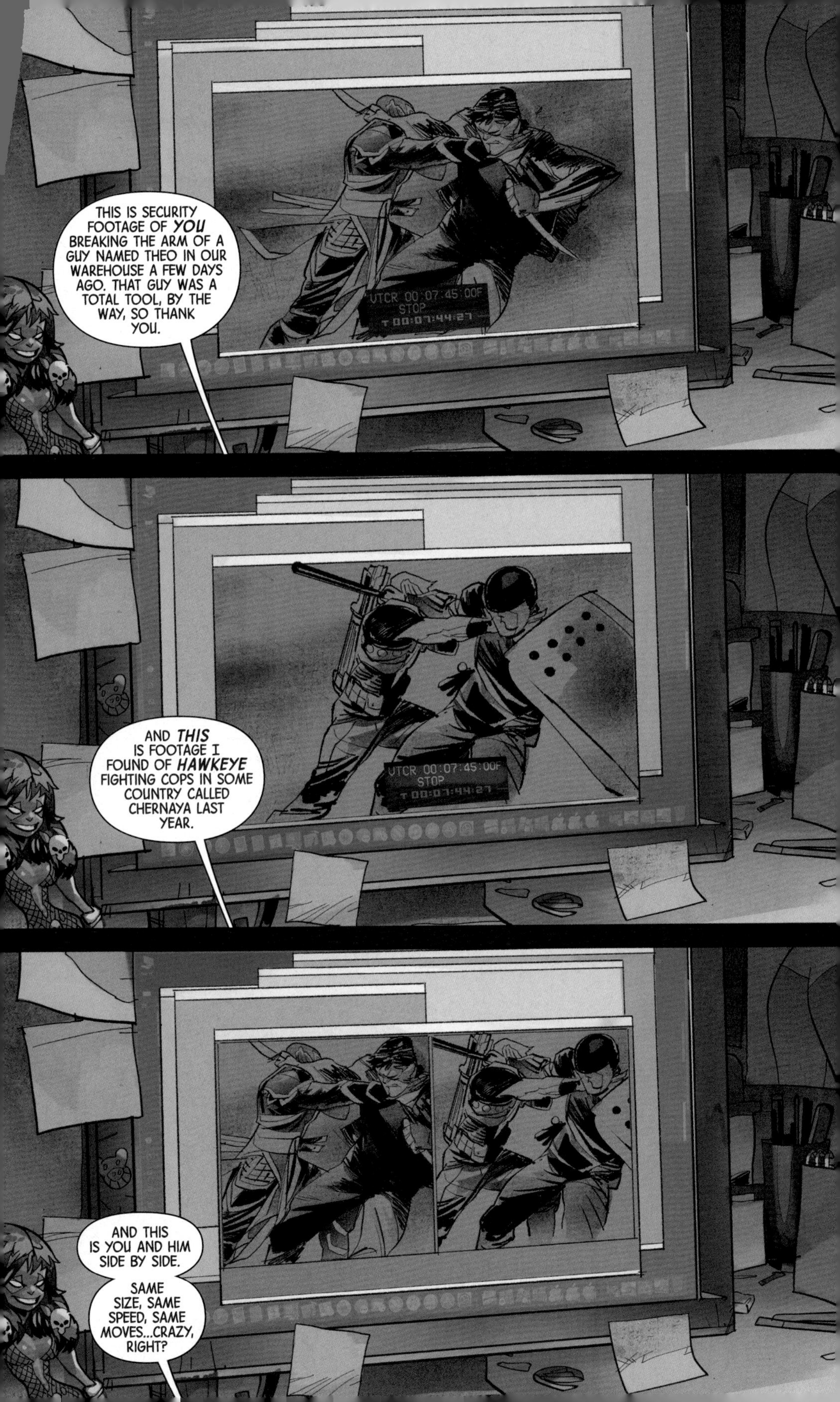

THIS IS SECURITY FOOTAGE OF YOU BREAKING THE ARM OF A GUY NAMED THEO IN OUR WAREHOUSE A FEW DAYS AGO. THAT GUY WAS A TOTAL TOOL, BY THE WAY, SO THANK YOU.
VTCR 00:07:45:00F
STOP
T 00:07:44:27
AND THIS IS FOOTAGE I FOUND OF HAWKEYE FIGHTING COPS IN SOME COUNTRY CALLED CHERNAYA LAST YEAR.
VTCR 00:07:45:00F
STOP
T 00:07:44:27
AND THIS IS YOU AND HIM SIDE BY SIDE.
SAME SIZE, SAME SPEED, SAME MOVES...CRAZY, RIGHT?

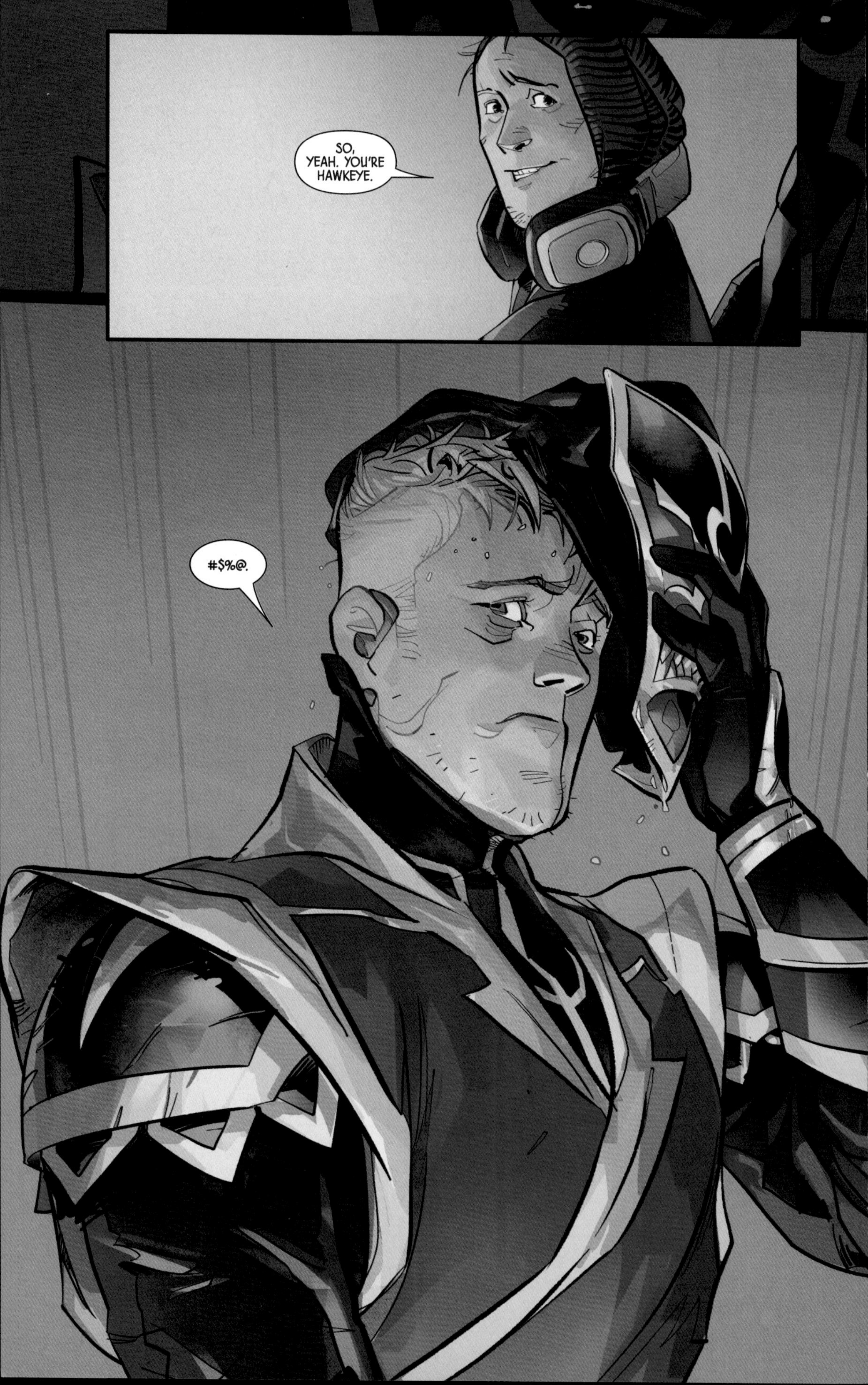
SO, YEAH. YOU'RE HAWKEYE.
#$%@.

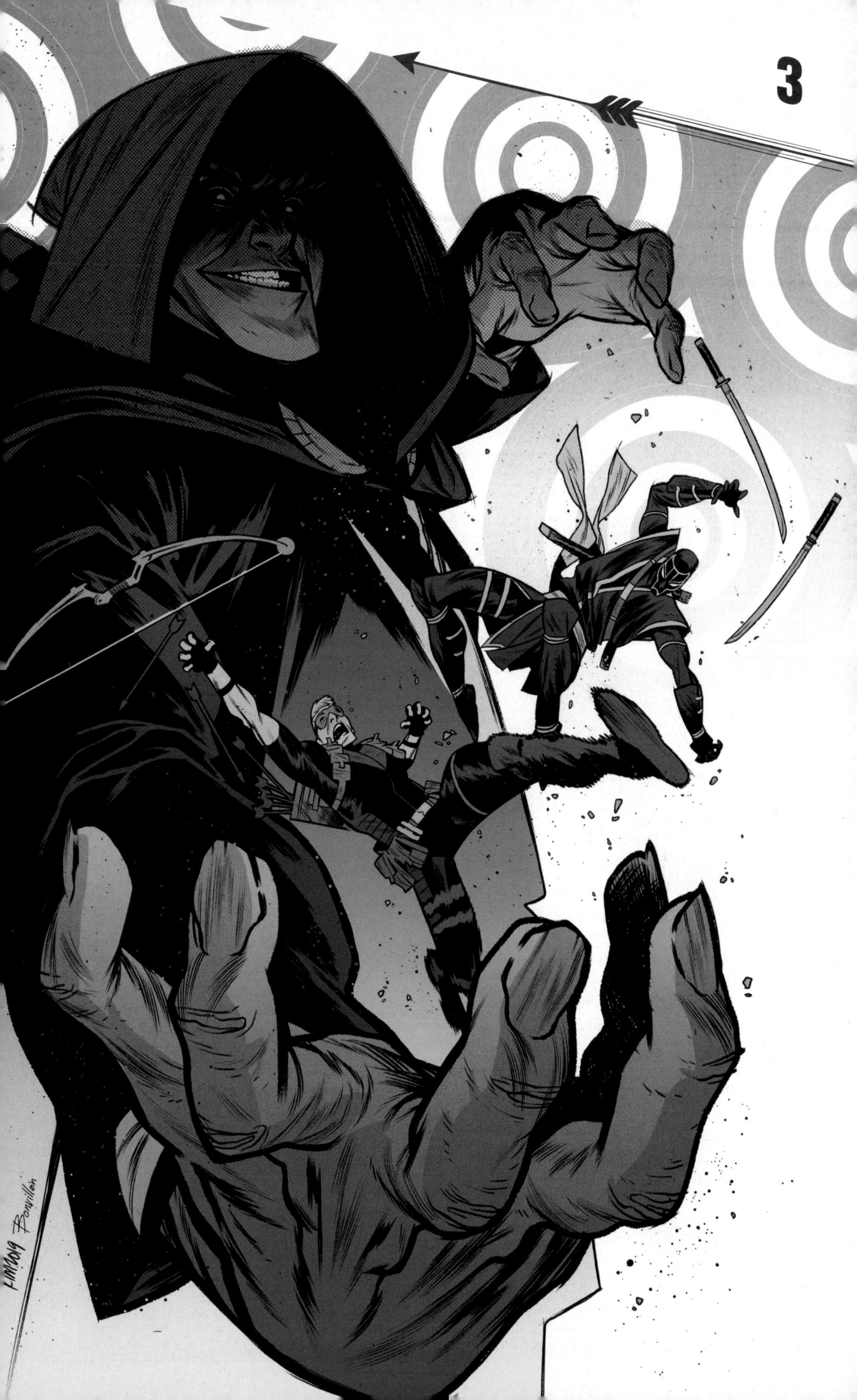
3

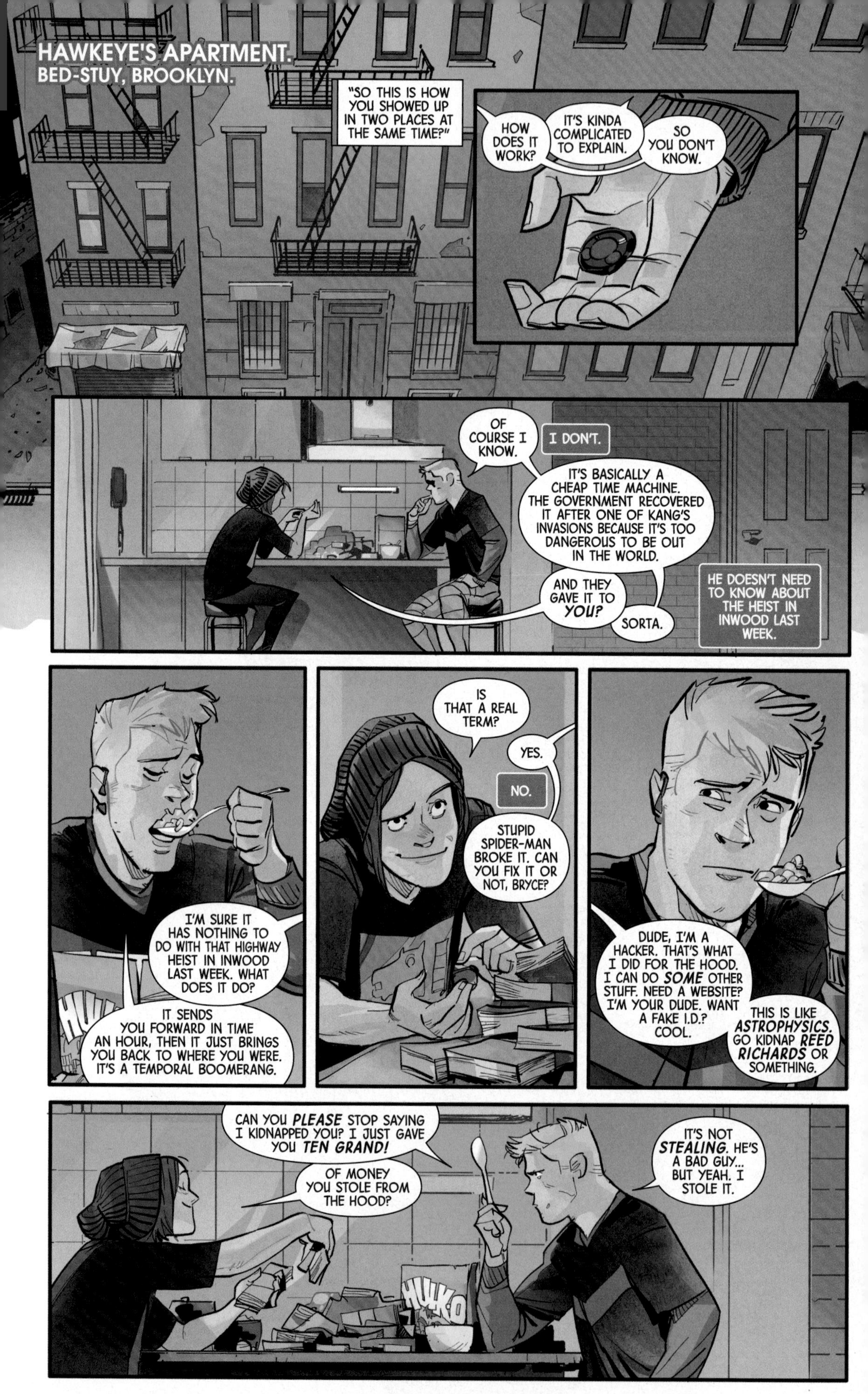
HAWKEYE'S APARTMENT.
BED-STUY, BROOKLYN.
"SO THIS IS HOW YOU SHOWED UP IN TWO PLACES AT THE SAME TIME?"
HOW DOES IT WORK?
IT'S KINDA COMPLICATED TO EXPLAIN.
SO YOU DON'T KNOW.
OF COURSE I KNOW.
I DON'T.
IT'S BASICALLY A CHEAP TIME MACHINE. THE GOVERNMENT RECOVERED IT AFTER ONE OF KANG'S INVASIONS BECAUSE IT'S TOO DANGEROUS TO BE OUT IN THE WORLD.
AND THEY GAVE IT TO YOU?
SORTA.
HE DOESN'T NEED TO KNOW ABOUT THE HEIST IN INWOOD LAST WEEK.
I'M SURE IT HAS NOTHING TO DO WITH THAT HIGHWAY HEIST IN INWOOD LAST WEEK. WHAT DOES IT DO?
IT SENDS YOU FORWARD IN TIME AN HOUR, THEN IT JUST BRINGS YOU BACK TO WHERE YOU WERE. IT'S A TEMPORAL BOOMERANG.
IS THAT A REAL TERM?
YES.
NO.
STUPID SPIDER-MAN BROKE IT. CAN YOU FIX IT OR NOT, BRYCE?
DUDE, I'M A HACKER. THAT'S WHAT I DID FOR THE HOOD. I CAN DO SOME OTHER STUFF. NEED A WEBSITE? I'M YOUR DUDE. WANT A FAKE I.D.? COOL.
THIS IS LIKE ASTROPHYSICS. GO KIDNAP REED RICHARDS OR SOMETHING.
CAN YOU PLEASE STOP SAYING I KIDNAPPED YOU? I JUST GAVE YOU TEN GRAND!
OF MONEY YOU STOLE FROM THE HOOD?
IT'S NOT STEALING. HE'S A BAD GUY... BUT YEAH. I STOLE IT.

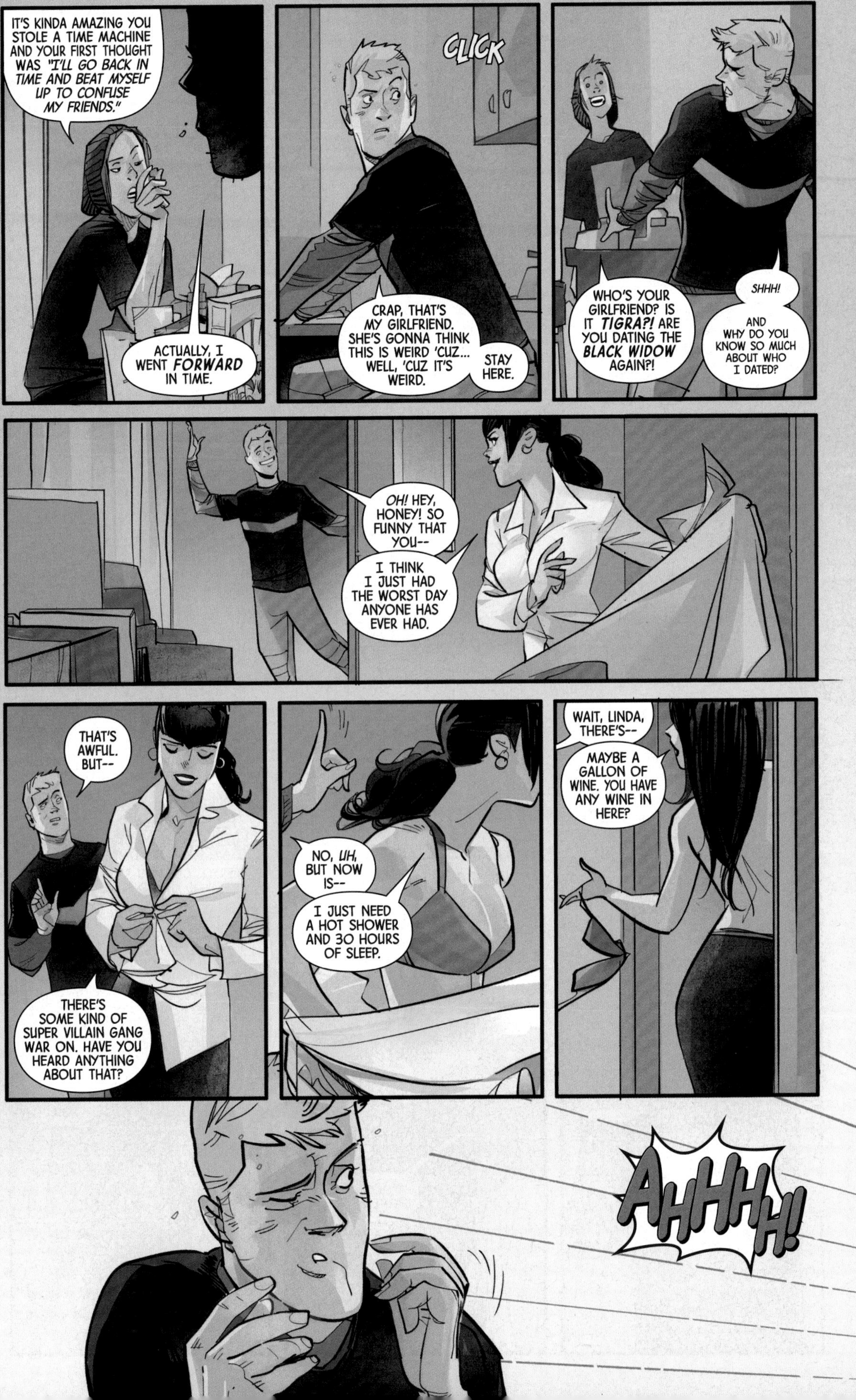
IT'S KINDA AMAZING YOU STOLE A TIME MACHINE AND YOUR FIRST THOUGHT WAS "I'LL GO BACK IN TIME AND BEAT MYSELF UP TO CONFUSE MY FRIENDS."
ACTUALLY, I WENT FORWARD IN TIME.
CLICK
CRAP, THAT'S MY GIRLFRIEND. SHE'S GONNA THINK THIS IS WEIRD 'CUZ... WELL, 'CUZ IT'S WEIRD.
STAY HERE.
WHO'S YOUR GIRLFRIEND? IS IT TIGRA?! ARE YOU DATING THE BLACK WIDOW AGAIN?!
SHHH!
AND WHY DO YOU KNOW SO MUCH ABOUT WHO I DATED?
OH! HEY, HONEY! SO FUNNY THAT YOU--
I THINK I JUST HAD THE WORST DAY ANYONE HAS EVER HAD.
THAT'S AWFUL. BUT--
THERE'S SOME KIND OF SUPER VILLAIN GANG WAR ON. HAVE YOU HEARD ANYTHING ABOUT THAT?
NO, UH, BUT NOW IS--
I JUST NEED A HOT SHOWER AND 30 HOURS OF SLEEP.
WAIT, LINDA, THERE'S--
MAYBE A GALLON OF WINE. YOU HAVE ANY WINE IN HERE?
AHHHH!

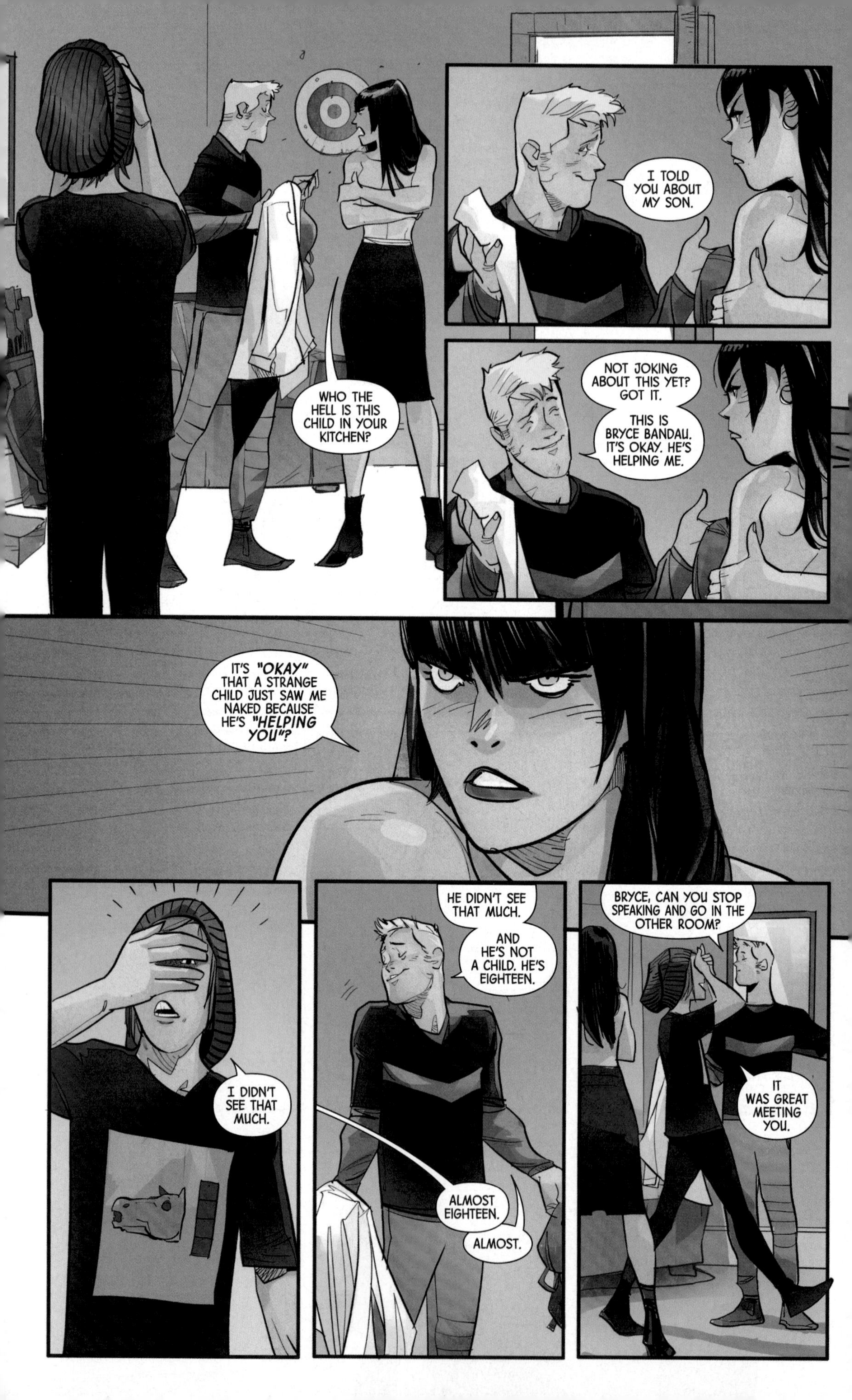
WHO THE HELL IS THIS CHILD IN YOUR KITCHEN?
I TOLD YOU ABOUT MY SON.
NOT JOKING ABOUT THIS YET? GOT IT.
THIS IS BRYCE BANDAU. IT'S OKAY. HE'S HELPING ME.
IT'S "OKAY" THAT A STRANGE CHILD JUST SAW ME NAKED BECAUSE HE'S "HELPING YOU"?
I DIDN'T SEE THAT MUCH.
HE DIDN'T SEE THAT MUCH.
AND HE'S NOT A CHILD. HE'S EIGHTEEN.
ALMOST EIGHTEEN.
ALMOST.
BRYCE, CAN YOU STOP SPEAKING AND GO IN THE OTHER ROOM?
IT WAS GREAT MEETING YOU.

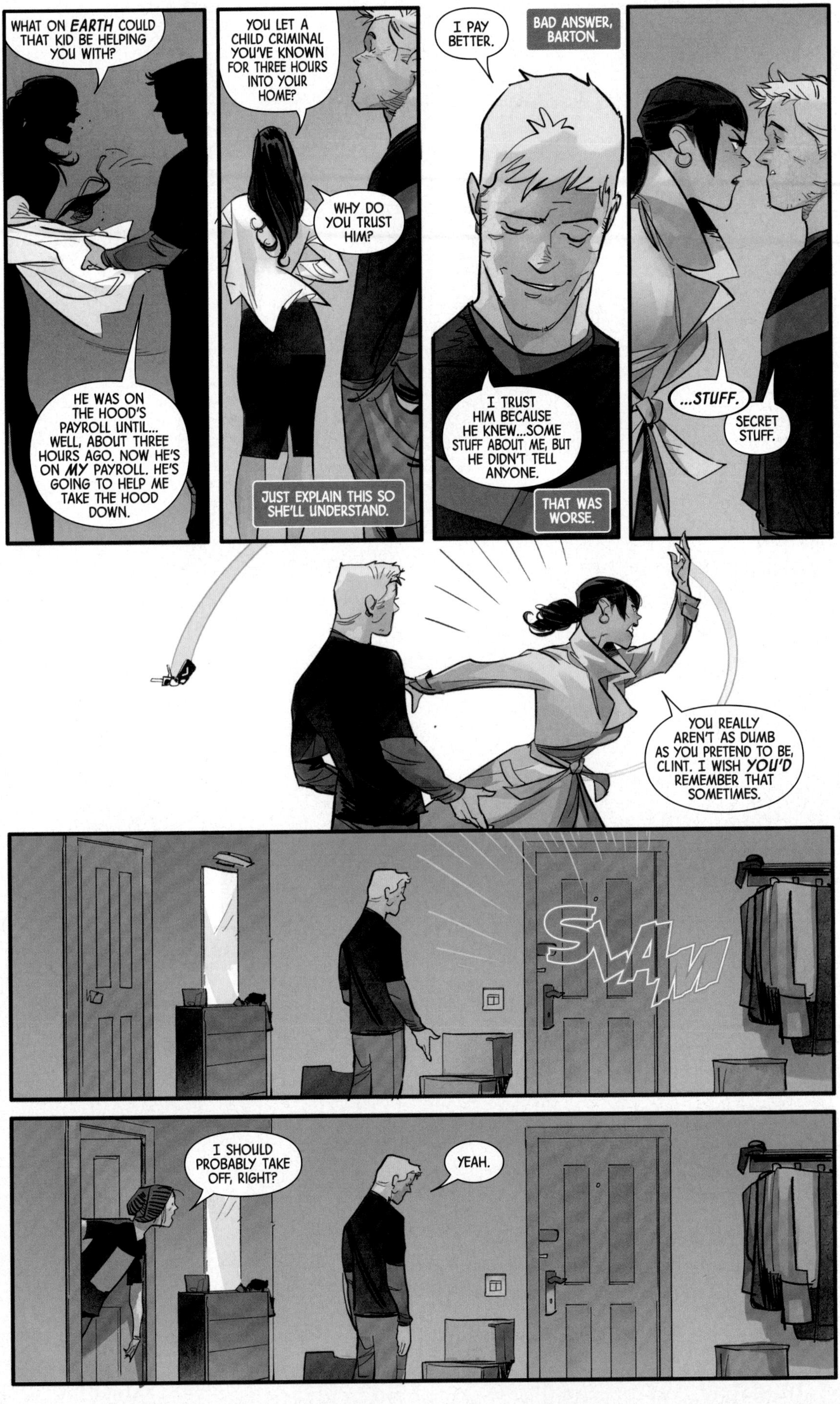
WHAT ON EARTH COULD THAT KID BE HELPING YOU WITH?
HE WAS ON THE HOOD'S PAYROLL UNTIL... WELL, ABOUT THREE HOURS AGO. NOW HE'S ON MY PAYROLL. HE'S GOING TO HELP ME TAKE THE HOOD DOWN.
YOU LET A CHILD CRIMINAL YOU'VE KNOWN FOR THREE HOURS INTO YOUR HOME?
WHY DO YOU TRUST HIM?
JUST EXPLAIN THIS SO SHE'LL UNDERSTAND.
I PAY BETTER.
BAD ANSWER, BARTON.
I TRUST HIM BECAUSE HE KNEW...SOME STUFF ABOUT ME, BUT HE DIDN'T TELL ANYONE.
THAT WAS WORSE.
...STUFF.
SECRET STUFF.
YOU REALLY AREN'T AS DUMB AS YOU PRETEND TO BE, CLINT. I WISH YOU'D REMEMBER THAT SOMETIMES.
SLAM
I SHOULD PROBABLY TAKE OFF, RIGHT?
YEAH.

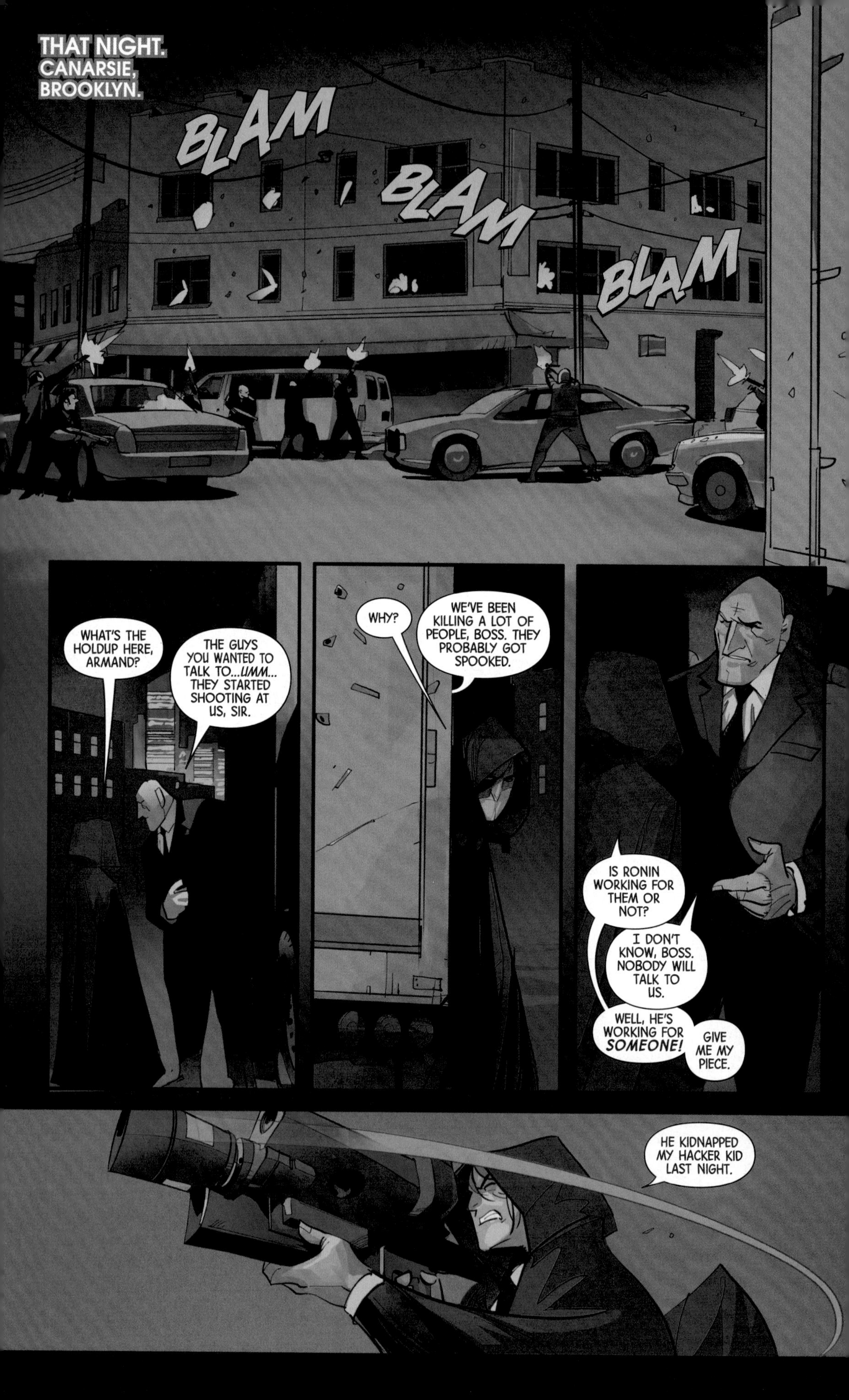
THAT NIGHT.
CANARSIE, BROOKLYN.
BLAM
BLAM
BLAM
WHAT'S THE HOLDUP HERE, ARMAND?
THE GUYS YOU WANTED TO TALK TO...UMM... THEY STARTED SHOOTING AT US, SIR.
WHY?
WE'VE BEEN KILLING A LOT OF PEOPLE, BOSS. THEY PROBABLY GOT SPOOKED.
IS RONIN WORKING FOR THEM OR NOT?
I DON'T KNOW, BOSS. NOBODY WILL TALK TO US.
WELL, HE'S WORKING FOR SOMEONE!
GIVE ME MY PIECE.
HE KIDNAPPED MY HACKER KID LAST NIGHT.

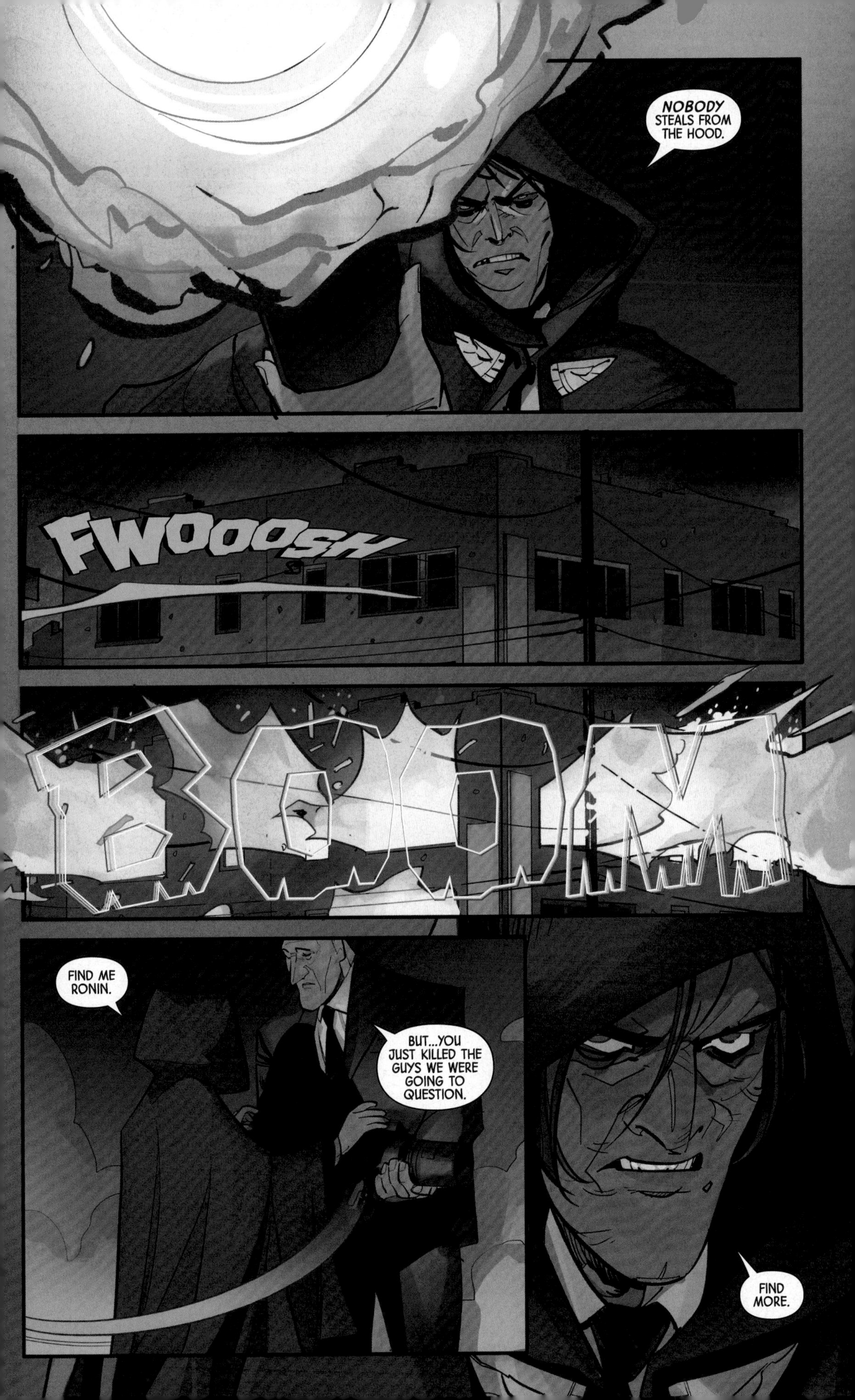
NOBODY STEALS FROM THE HOOD.
FWOOOSH
BOOM
FIND ME RONIN.
BUT...YOU JUST KILLED THE GUYS WE WERE GOING TO QUESTION.
FIND MORE.

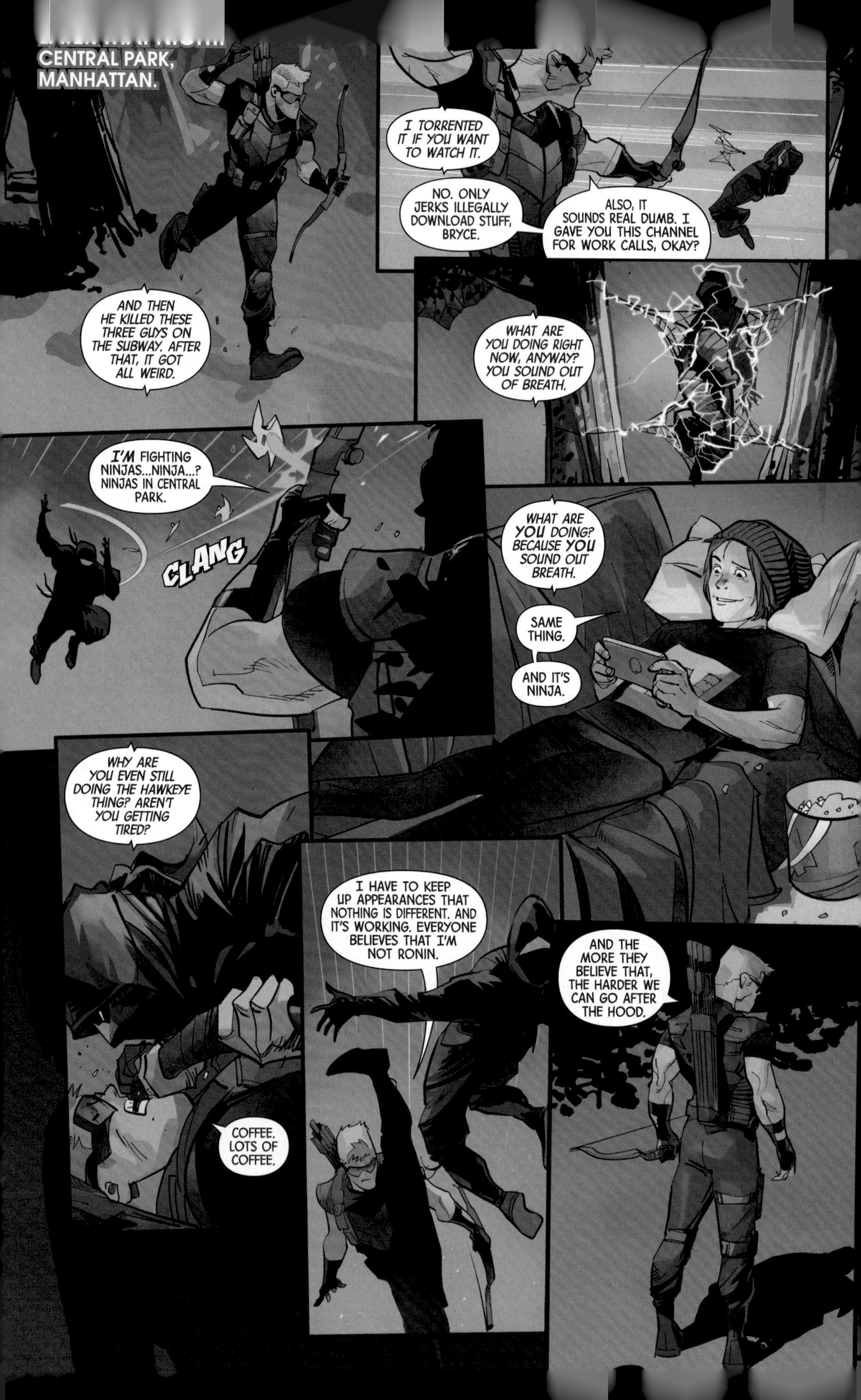
CENTRAL PARK, MANHATTAN.
AND THEN HE KILLED THESE THREE GUYS ON THE SUBWAY. AFTER THAT, IT GOT ALL WEIRD.
I TORRENTED IT IF YOU WANT TO WATCH IT.
NO. ONLY JERKS ILLEGALLY DOWNLOAD STUFF, BRYCE.
ALSO, IT SOUNDS REAL DUMB. I GAVE YOU THIS CHANNEL FOR WORK CALLS, OKAY?
WHAT ARE YOU DOING RIGHT NOW, ANYWAY? YOU SOUND OUT OF BREATH.
I'M FIGHTING NINJAS...NINJA...? NINJAS IN CENTRAL PARK.
CLANG
WHAT ARE YOU DOING? BECAUSE YOU SOUND OUT BREATH.
SAME THING.
AND IT'S NINJA.
WHY ARE YOU EVEN STILL DOING THE HAWKEYE THING? AREN'T YOU GETTING TIRED?
COFFEE. LOTS OF COFFEE.
I HAVE TO KEEP UP APPEARANCES THAT NOTHING IS DIFFERENT. AND IT'S WORKING. EVERYONE BELIEVES THAT I'M NOT RONIN.
AND THE MORE THEY BELIEVE THAT, THE HARDER WE CAN GO AFTER THE HOOD.

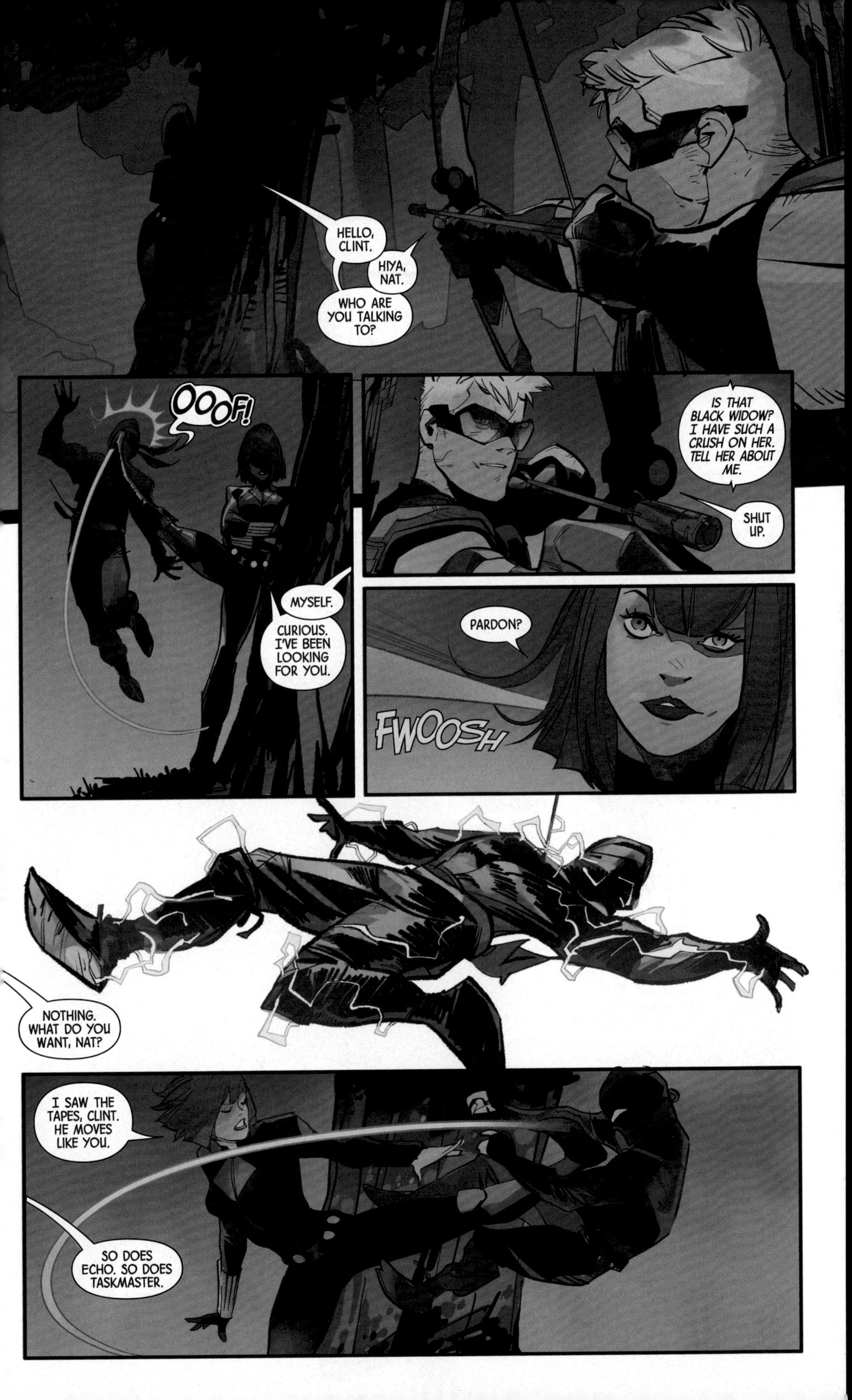
HELLO, CLINT.
HIYA, NAT.
WHO ARE YOU TALKING TO?
OOOF!
MYSELF.
CURIOUS. I'VE BEEN LOOKING FOR YOU.
IS THAT BLACK WIDOW? I HAVE SUCH A CRUSH ON HER. TELL HER ABOUT ME.
SHUT UP.
PARDON?
FWOOSH
NOTHING. WHAT DO YOU WANT, NAT?
I SAW THE TAPES, CLINT. HE MOVES LIKE YOU.
SO DOES ECHO. SO DOES TASKMASTER.

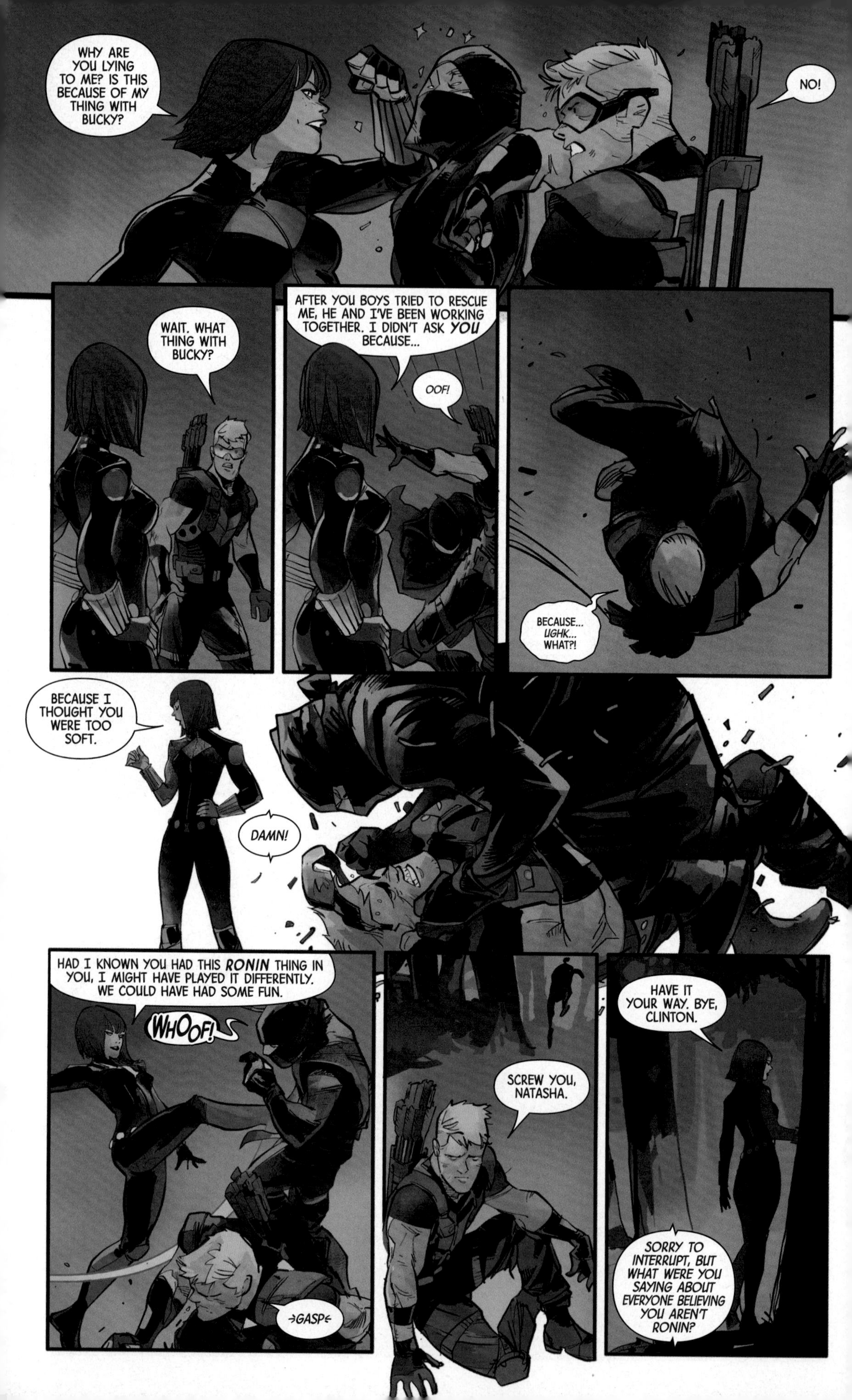
WHY ARE YOU LYING TO ME? IS THIS BECAUSE OF MY THING WITH BUCKY?
NO!
WAIT. WHAT THING WITH BUCKY?
AFTER YOU BOYS TRIED TO RESCUE ME, HE AND I'VE BEEN WORKING TOGETHER. I DIDN'T ASK YOU BECAUSE...
OOF!
BECAUSE... UGHK... WHAT?!
BECAUSE I THOUGHT YOU WERE TOO SOFT.
DAMN!
HAD I KNOWN YOU HAD THIS RONIN THING IN YOU, I MIGHT HAVE PLAYED IT DIFFERENTLY. WE COULD HAVE HAD SOME FUN.
WHOOF!
GASP
SCREW YOU, NATASHA.
HAVE IT YOUR WAY. BYE, CLINTON.
SORRY TO INTERRUPT, BUT WHAT WERE YOU SAYING ABOUT EVERYONE BELIEVING YOU AREN'T RONIN?

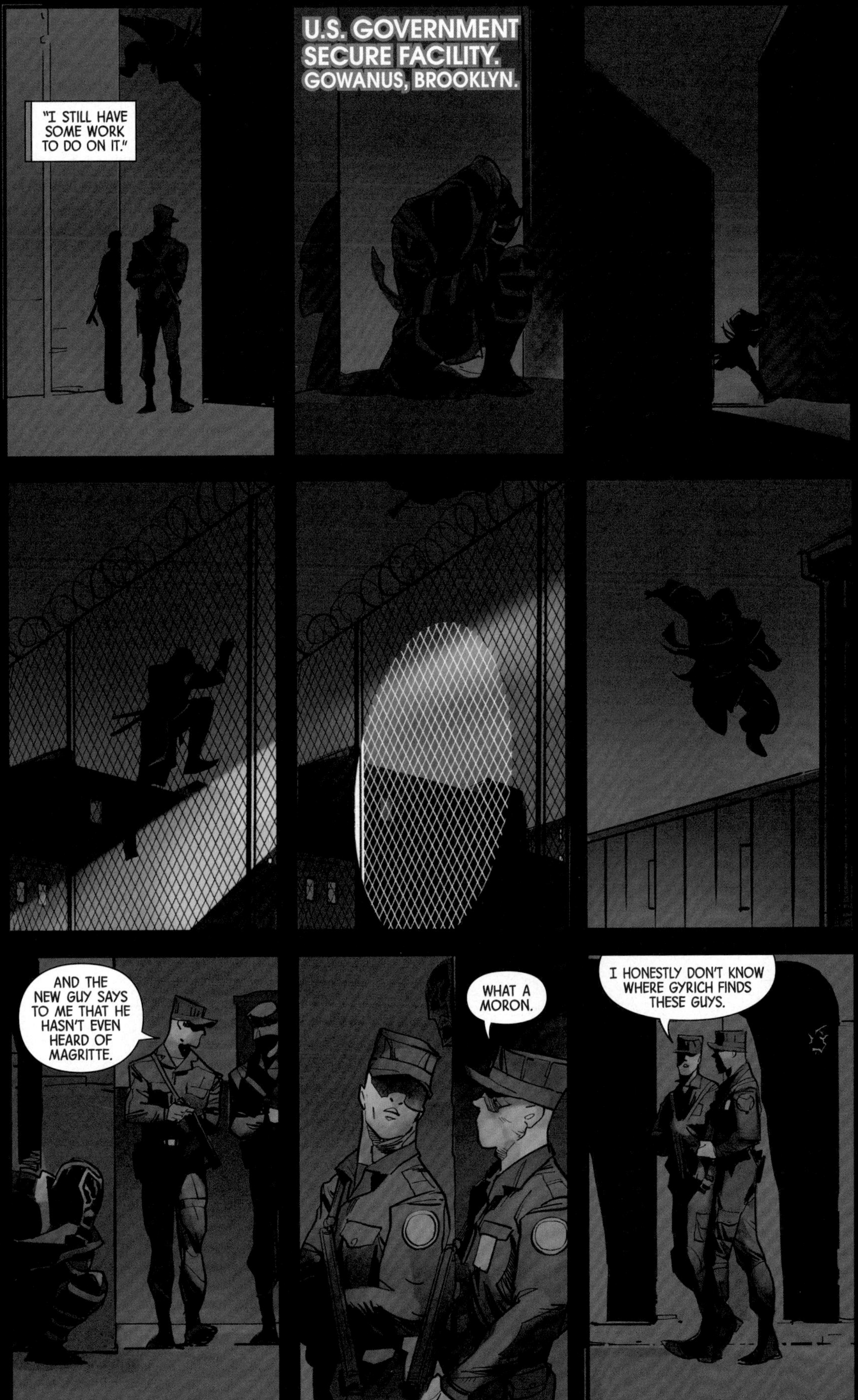
"I STILL HAVE SOME WORK TO DO ON IT."
U.S. GOVERNMENT SECURE FACILITY. GOWANUS, BROOKLYN.
AND THE NEW GUY SAYS TO ME THAT HE HASN'T EVEN HEARD OF MAGRITTE.
WHAT A MORON.
I HONESTLY DON'T KNOW WHERE GYRICH FINDS THESE GUYS.

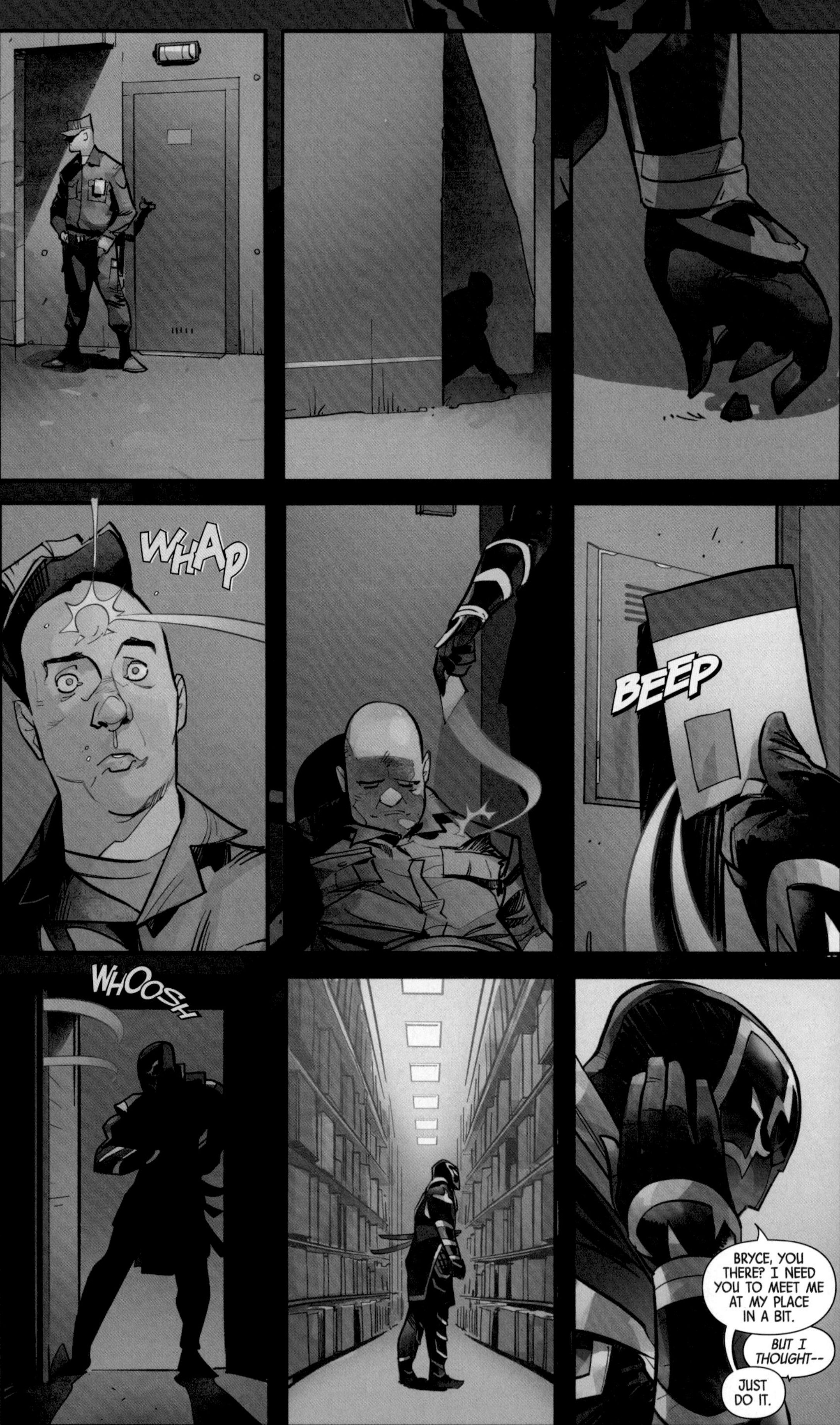
WHAP
BEEP
WHOOSH
BRYCE, YOU THERE? I NEED YOU TO MEET ME AT MY PLACE IN A BIT.
BUT I THOUGHT--
JUST DO IT.

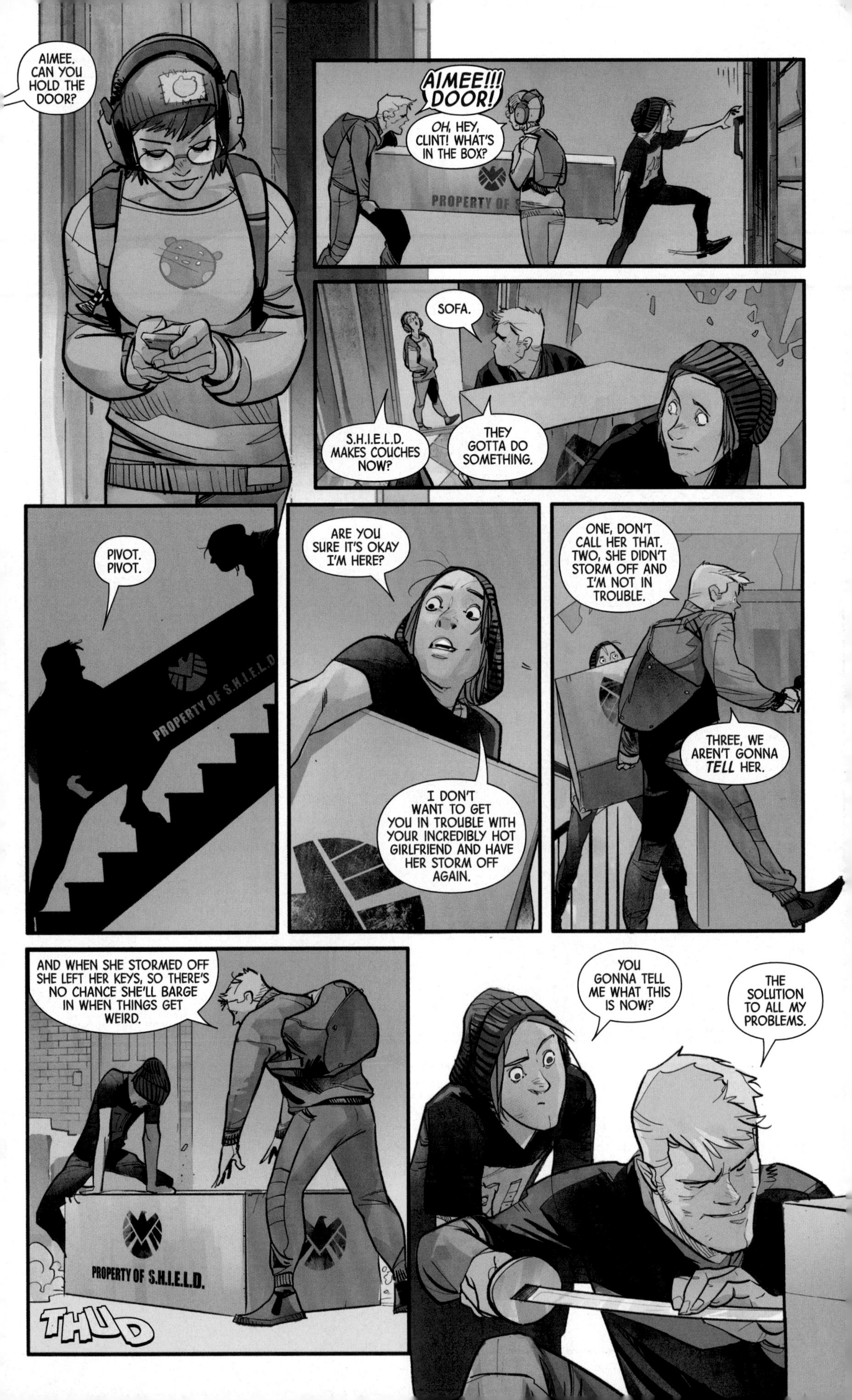

AIMEE. CAN YOU HOLD THE DOOR?
AIMEE!!! DOOR!
OH, HEY, CLINT! WHAT'S IN THE BOX?
PROPERTY OF S
SOFA.
S.H.I.E.L.D. MAKES COUCHES NOW?
THEY GOTTA DO SOMETHING.
PIVOT. PIVOT.
PROPERTY OF S.H.I.E.L.D
ARE YOU SURE IT'S OKAY I'M HERE?
I DON'T WANT TO GET YOU IN TROUBLE WITH YOUR INCREDIBLY HOT GIRLFRIEND AND HAVE HER STORM OFF AGAIN.
ONE, DON'T CALL HER THAT. TWO, SHE DIDN'T STORM OFF AND I'M NOT IN TROUBLE.
THREE, WE AREN'T GONNA TELL HER.
AND WHEN SHE STORMED OFF SHE LEFT HER KEYS, SO THERE'S NO CHANCE SHE'LL BARGE IN WHEN THINGS GET WEIRD.
PROPERTY OF S.H.I.E.L.D.
THUD
YOU GONNA TELL ME WHAT THIS IS NOW?
THE SOLUTION TO ALL MY PROBLEMS.

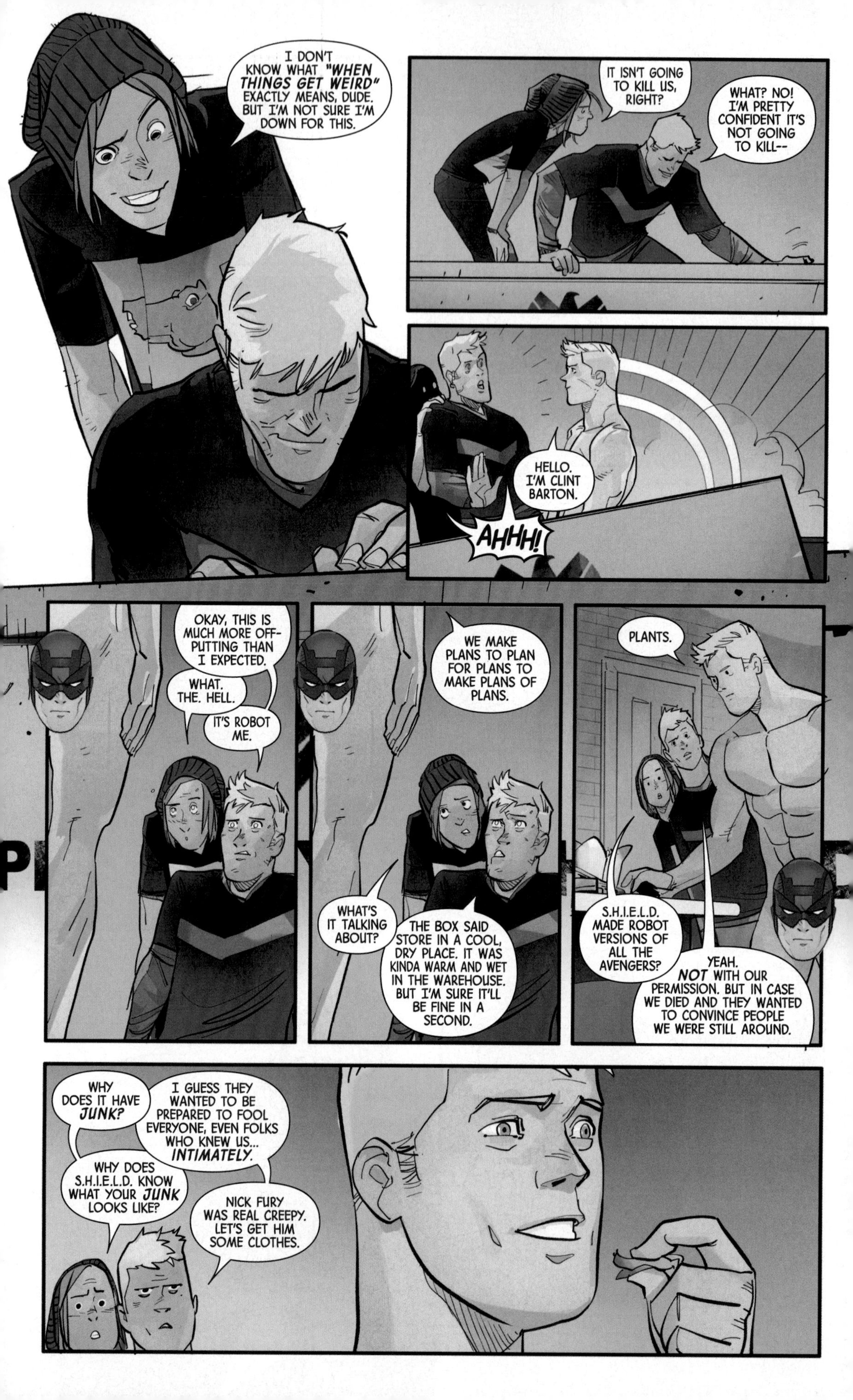
I DON'T KNOW WHAT "WHEN THINGS GET WEIRD" EXACTLY MEANS, DUDE. BUT I'M NOT SURE I'M DOWN FOR THIS.
IT ISN'T GOING TO KILL US, RIGHT?
WHAT? NO! I'M PRETTY CONFIDENT IT'S NOT GOING TO KILL--
HELLO. I'M CLINT BARTON.
AHHH!
OKAY, THIS IS MUCH MORE OFF-PUTTING THAN I EXPECTED.
WHAT. THE. HELL.
IT'S ROBOT ME.
WE MAKE PLANS TO PLAN FOR PLANS TO MAKE PLANS OF PLANS.
WHAT'S IT TALKING ABOUT?
THE BOX SAID STORE IN A COOL, DRY PLACE. IT WAS KINDA WARM AND WET IN THE WAREHOUSE. BUT I'M SURE IT'LL BE FINE IN A SECOND.
PLANTS.
S.H.I.E.L.D. MADE ROBOT VERSIONS OF ALL THE AVENGERS?
YEAH. NOT WITH OUR PERMISSION. BUT IN CASE WE DIED AND THEY WANTED TO CONVINCE PEOPLE WE WERE STILL AROUND.
WHY DOES IT HAVE JUNK?
I GUESS THEY WANTED TO BE PREPARED TO FOOL EVERYONE, EVEN FOLKS WHO KNEW US... INTIMATELY.
WHY DOES S.H.I.E.L.D. KNOW WHAT YOUR JUNK LOOKS LIKE?
NICK FURY WAS REAL CREEPY. LET'S GET HIM SOME CLOTHES.

YOU STAY. STAY.

YOU GOT A LOTTA PURPLE #$&%.

NO, IT'S PRINCE'S COLOR.

IT'S MY COLOR.

BZZZZZRR!

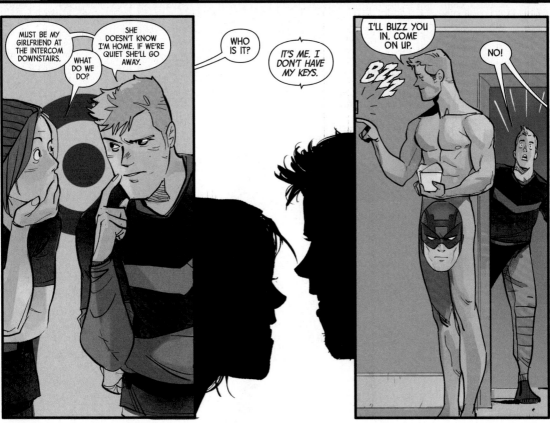

MUST BE MY GIRLFRIEND AT THE INTERCOM DOWNSTAIRS.

WHAT DO WE DO?

SHE DOESN'T KNOW I'M HOME. IF WE'RE QUIET SHE'LL GO AWAY.

WHO IS IT?

IT'S ME. I DON'T HAVE MY KEYS.

I'LL BUZZ YOU IN. COME ON UP.

BZZZ

NO!

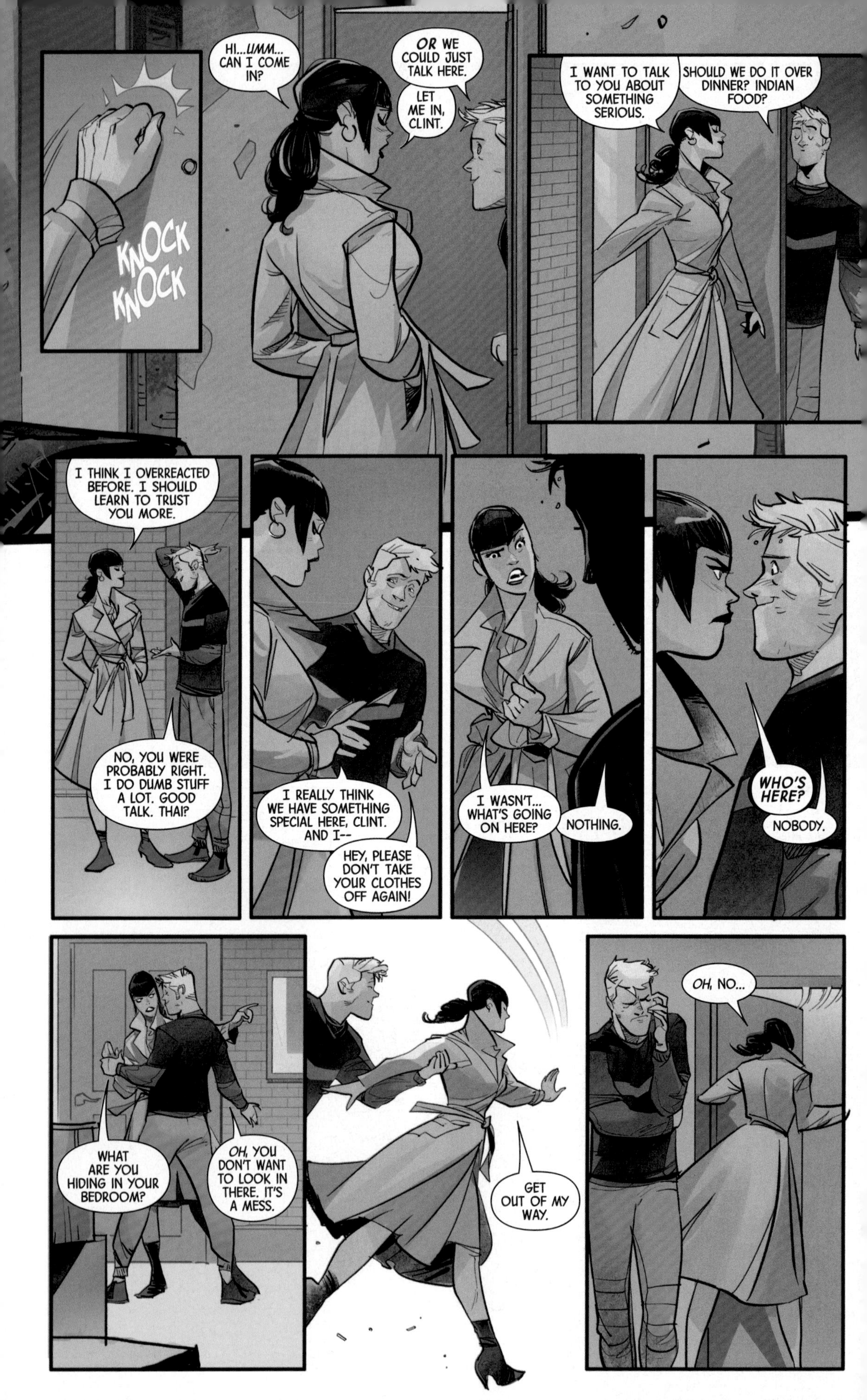
KNOCK KNOCK
HI...UMM... CAN I COME IN?
OR WE COULD JUST TALK HERE.
LET ME IN, CLINT.
I WANT TO TALK TO YOU ABOUT SOMETHING SERIOUS.
SHOULD WE DO IT OVER DINNER? INDIAN FOOD?
I THINK I OVERREACTED BEFORE. I SHOULD LEARN TO TRUST YOU MORE.
NO, YOU WERE PROBABLY RIGHT. I DO DUMB STUFF A LOT. GOOD TALK. THAI?
I REALLY THINK WE HAVE SOMETHING SPECIAL HERE, CLINT. AND I--
HEY, PLEASE DON'T TAKE YOUR CLOTHES OFF AGAIN!
I WASN'T... WHAT'S GOING ON HERE?
NOTHING.
WHO'S HERE?
NOBODY.
WHAT ARE YOU HIDING IN YOUR BEDROOM?
OH, YOU DON'T WANT TO LOOK IN THERE. IT'S A MESS.
GET OUT OF MY WAY.
OH, NO...

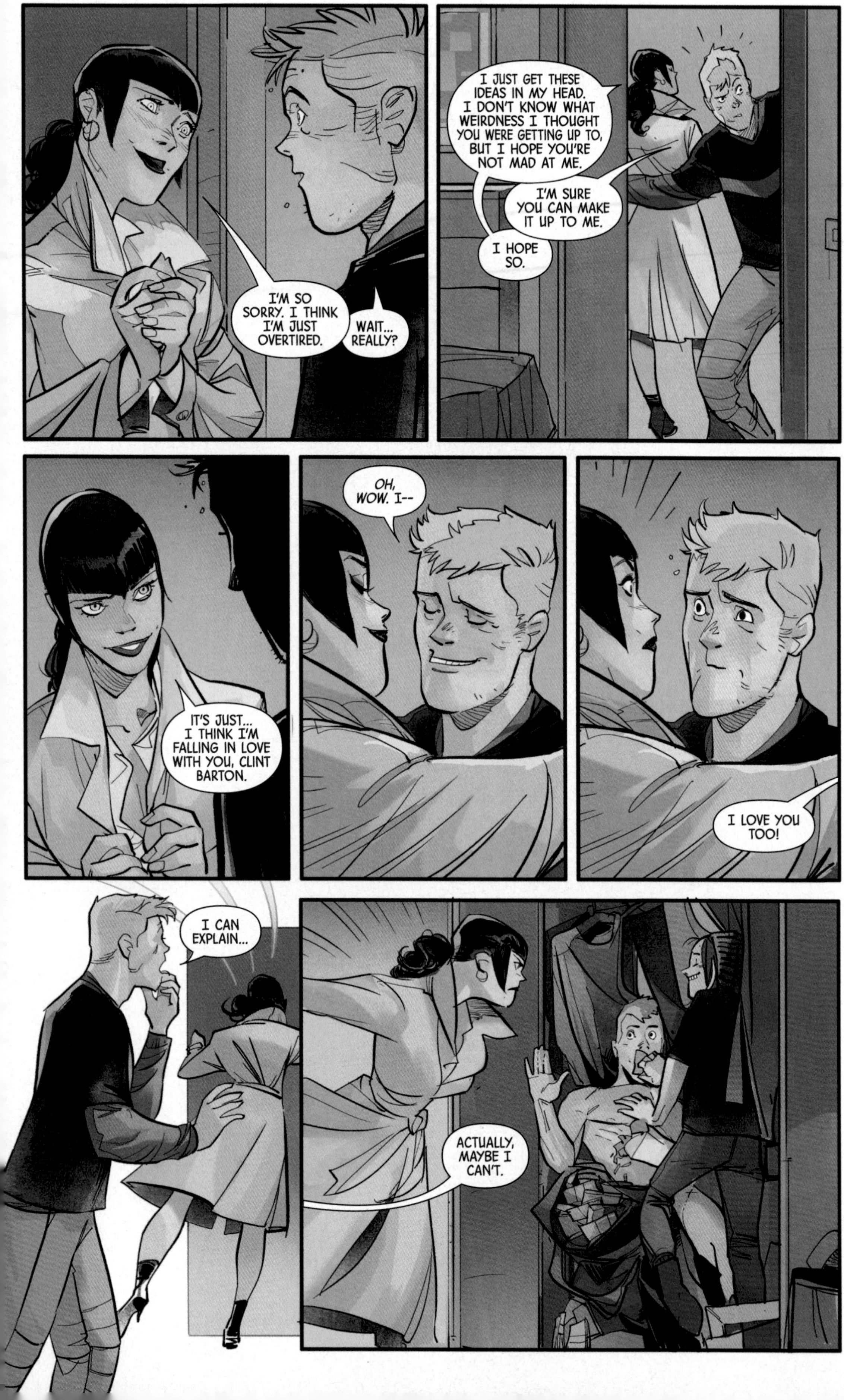
I'M SO SORRY. I THINK I'M JUST OVERTIRED.
WAIT... REALLY?
I JUST GET THESE IDEAS IN MY HEAD. I DON'T KNOW WHAT WEIRDNESS I THOUGHT YOU WERE GETTING UP TO, BUT I HOPE YOU'RE NOT MAD AT ME.
I'M SURE YOU CAN MAKE IT UP TO ME.
I HOPE SO.
IT'S JUST... I THINK I'M FALLING IN LOVE WITH YOU, CLINT BARTON.
OH, WOW. I--
I LOVE YOU TOO!
I CAN EXPLAIN...
ACTUALLY, MAYBE I CAN'T.

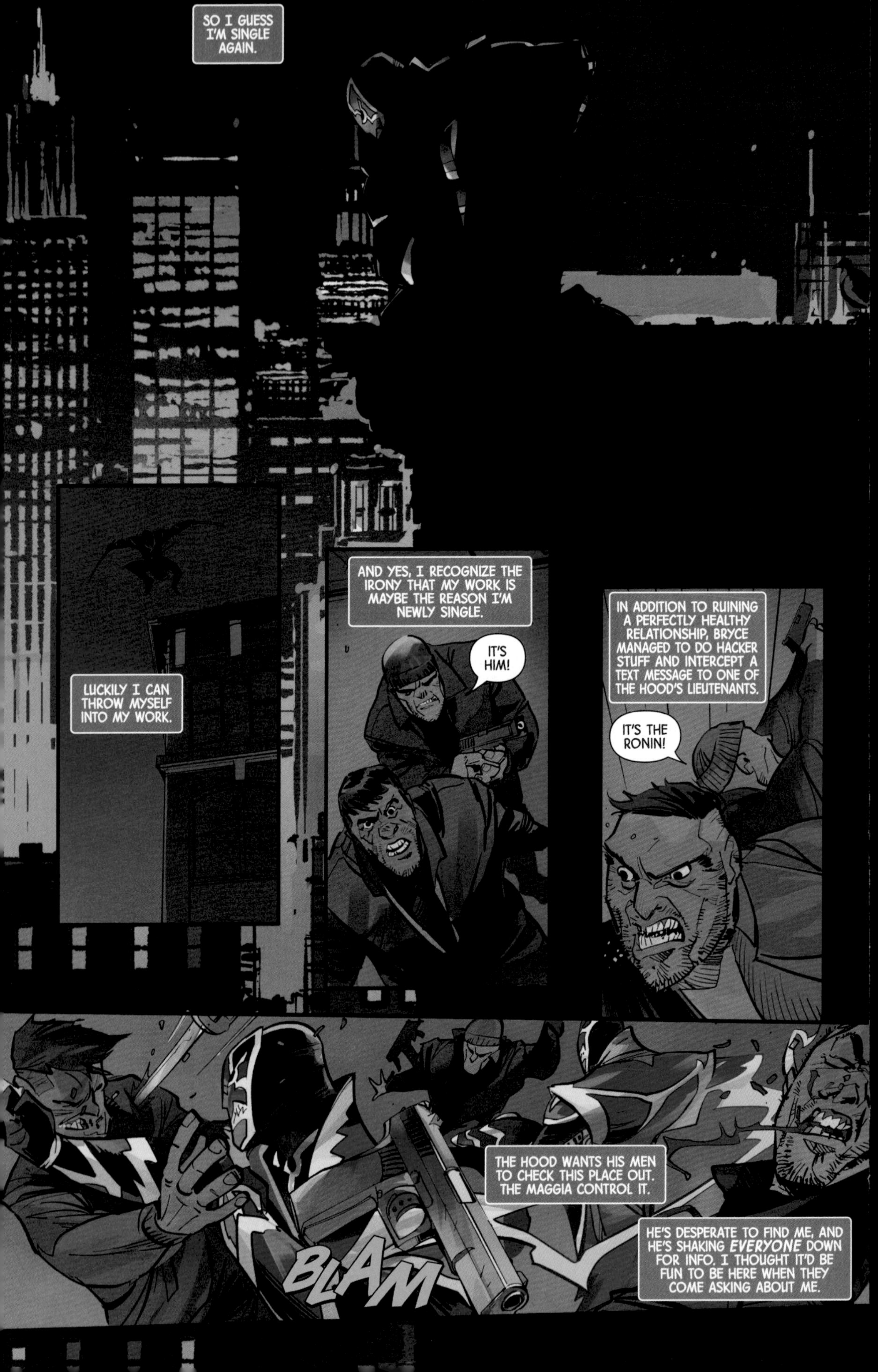
SO I GUESS I'M SINGLE AGAIN.
LUCKILY I CAN THROW MYSELF INTO MY WORK.
AND YES, I RECOGNIZE THE IRONY THAT MY WORK IS MAYBE THE REASON I'M NEWLY SINGLE.
IT'S HIM!
IN ADDITION TO RUINING A PERFECTLY HEALTHY RELATIONSHIP, BRYCE MANAGED TO DO HACKER STUFF AND INTERCEPT A TEXT MESSAGE TO ONE OF THE HOOD'S LIEUTENANTS.
IT'S THE RONIN!
THE HOOD WANTS HIS MEN TO CHECK THIS PLACE OUT. THE MAGGIA CONTROL IT.
HE'S DESPERATE TO FIND ME, AND HE'S SHAKING *EVERYONE* DOWN FOR INFO. I THOUGHT IT'D BE FUN TO BE HERE WHEN THEY COME ASKING ABOUT ME.
BLAM

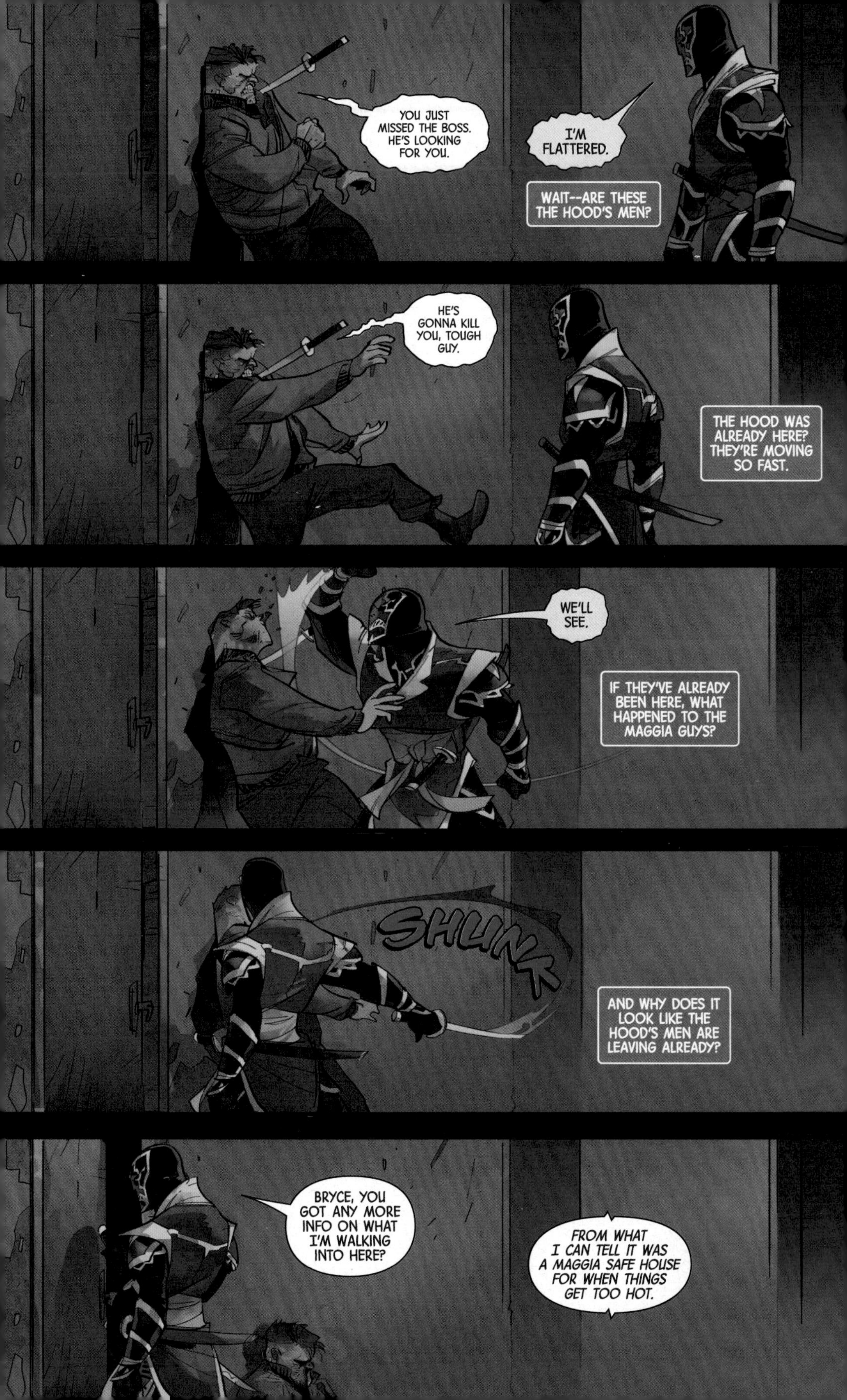
YOU JUST MISSED THE BOSS. HE'S LOOKING FOR YOU.
I'M FLATTERED.
WAIT--ARE THESE THE HOOD'S MEN?
HE'S GONNA KILL YOU, TOUGH GUY.
THE HOOD WAS ALREADY HERE? THEY'RE MOVING SO FAST.
WE'LL SEE.
IF THEY'VE ALREADY BEEN HERE, WHAT HAPPENED TO THE MAGGIA GUYS?
SHLINK
AND WHY DOES IT LOOK LIKE THE HOOD'S MEN ARE LEAVING ALREADY?
BRYCE, YOU GOT ANY MORE INFO ON WHAT I'M WALKING INTO HERE?
FROM WHAT I CAN TELL IT WAS A MAGGIA SAFE HOUSE FOR WHEN THINGS GET TOO HOT.

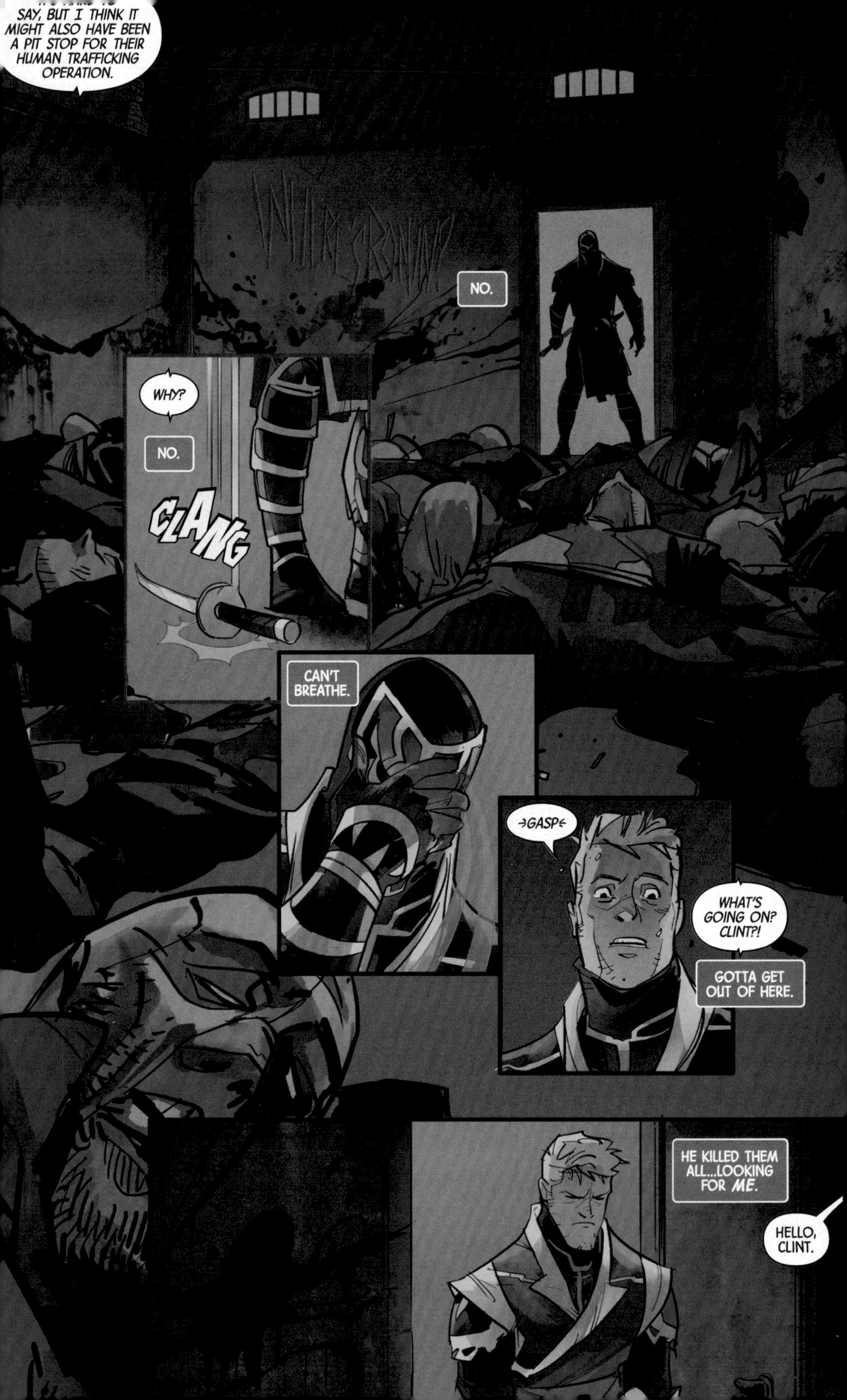
SAY, BUT I THINK IT MIGHT ALSO HAVE BEEN A PIT STOP FOR THEIR HUMAN TRAFFICKING OPERATION.
NO.
WHY?
NO.
CLANG
CAN'T BREATHE.
→GASP←
WHAT'S GOING ON? CLINT?!
GOTTA GET OUT OF HERE.
HE KILLED THEM ALL...LOOKING FOR *ME*.
HELLO, CLINT.

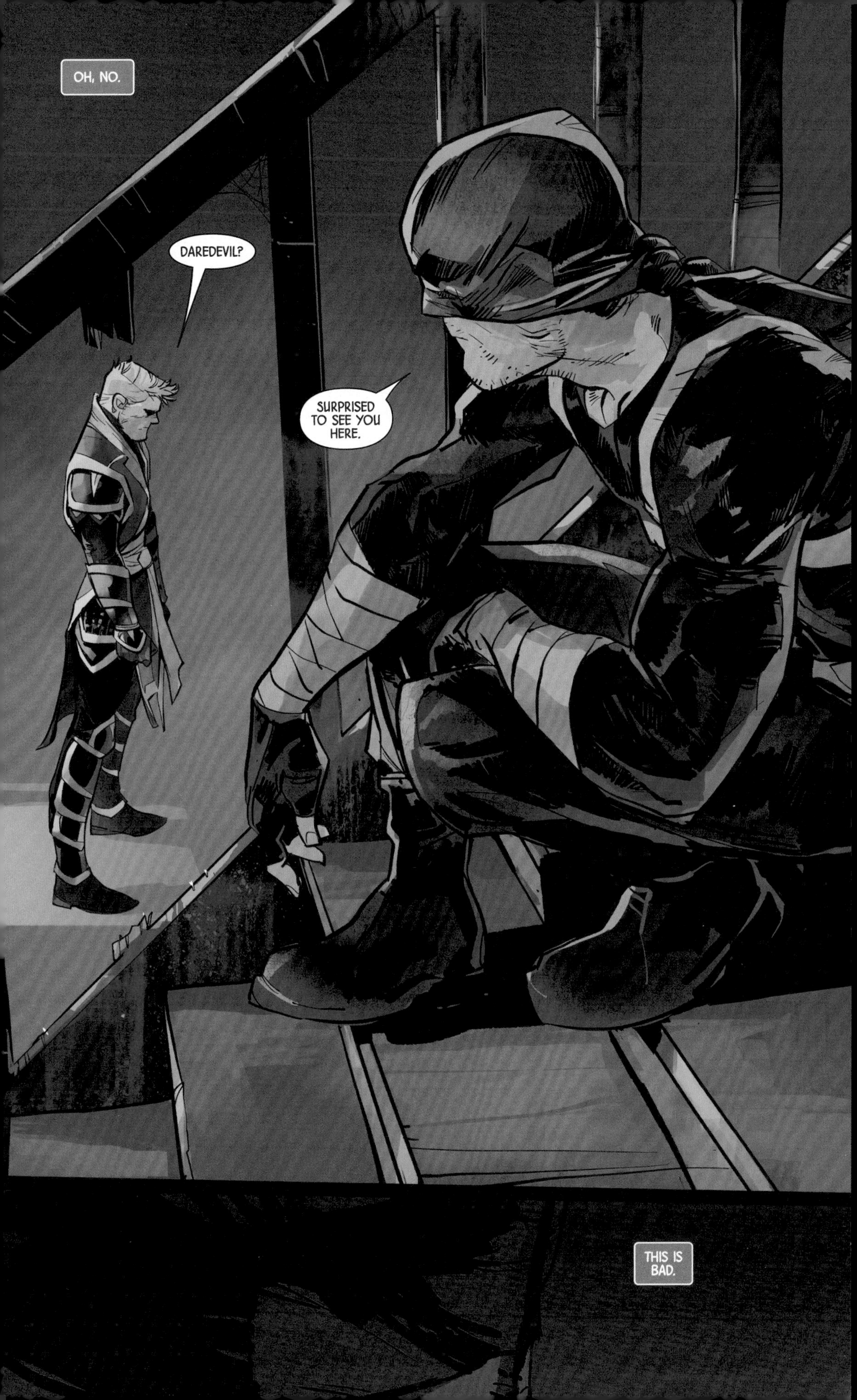

OH, NO.
DAREDEVIL?
SURPRISED TO SEE YOU HERE.
THIS IS BAD.

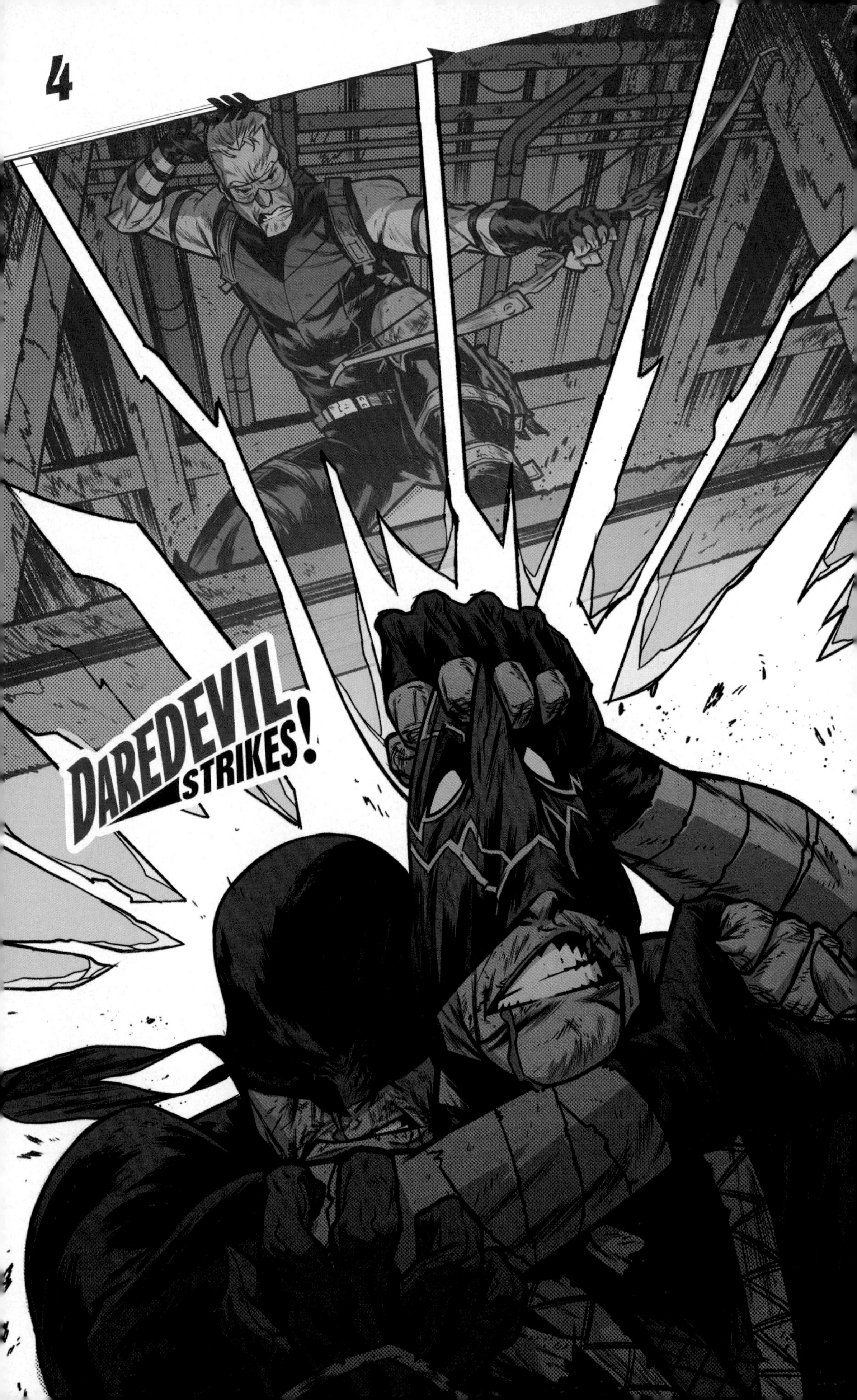
4
DAREDEVIL STRIKES!

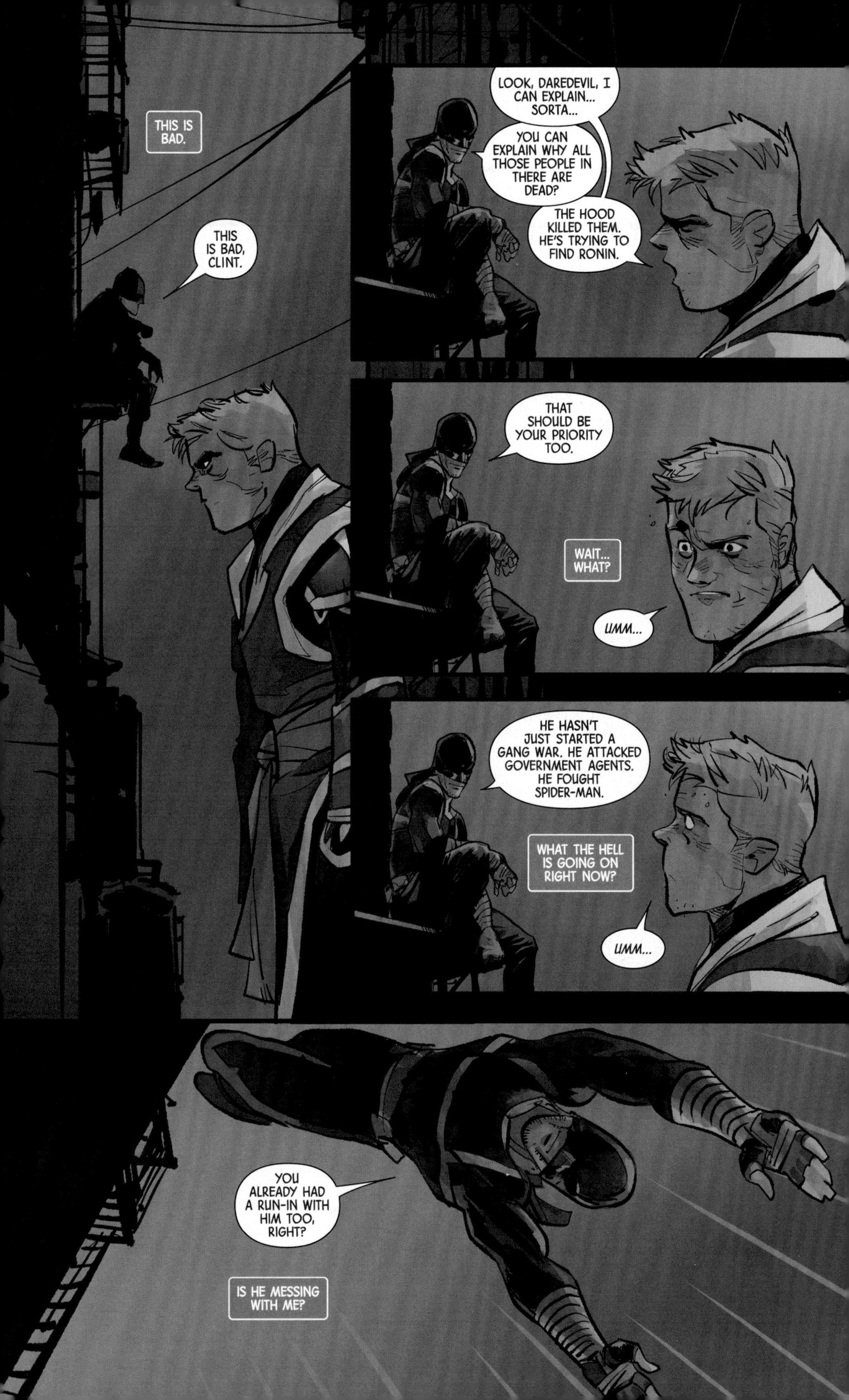
THIS IS BAD.
THIS IS BAD, CLINT.
LOOK, DAREDEVIL, I CAN EXPLAIN... SORTA...
YOU CAN EXPLAIN WHY ALL THOSE PEOPLE IN THERE ARE DEAD?
THE HOOD KILLED THEM. HE'S TRYING TO FIND RONIN.
THAT SHOULD BE YOUR PRIORITY TOO.
WAIT... WHAT?
UMM...
HE HASN'T JUST STARTED A GANG WAR. HE ATTACKED GOVERNMENT AGENTS. HE FOUGHT SPIDER-MAN.
WHAT THE HELL IS GOING ON RIGHT NOW?
UMM...
YOU ALREADY HAD A RUN-IN WITH HIM TOO, RIGHT?
IS HE MESSING WITH ME?

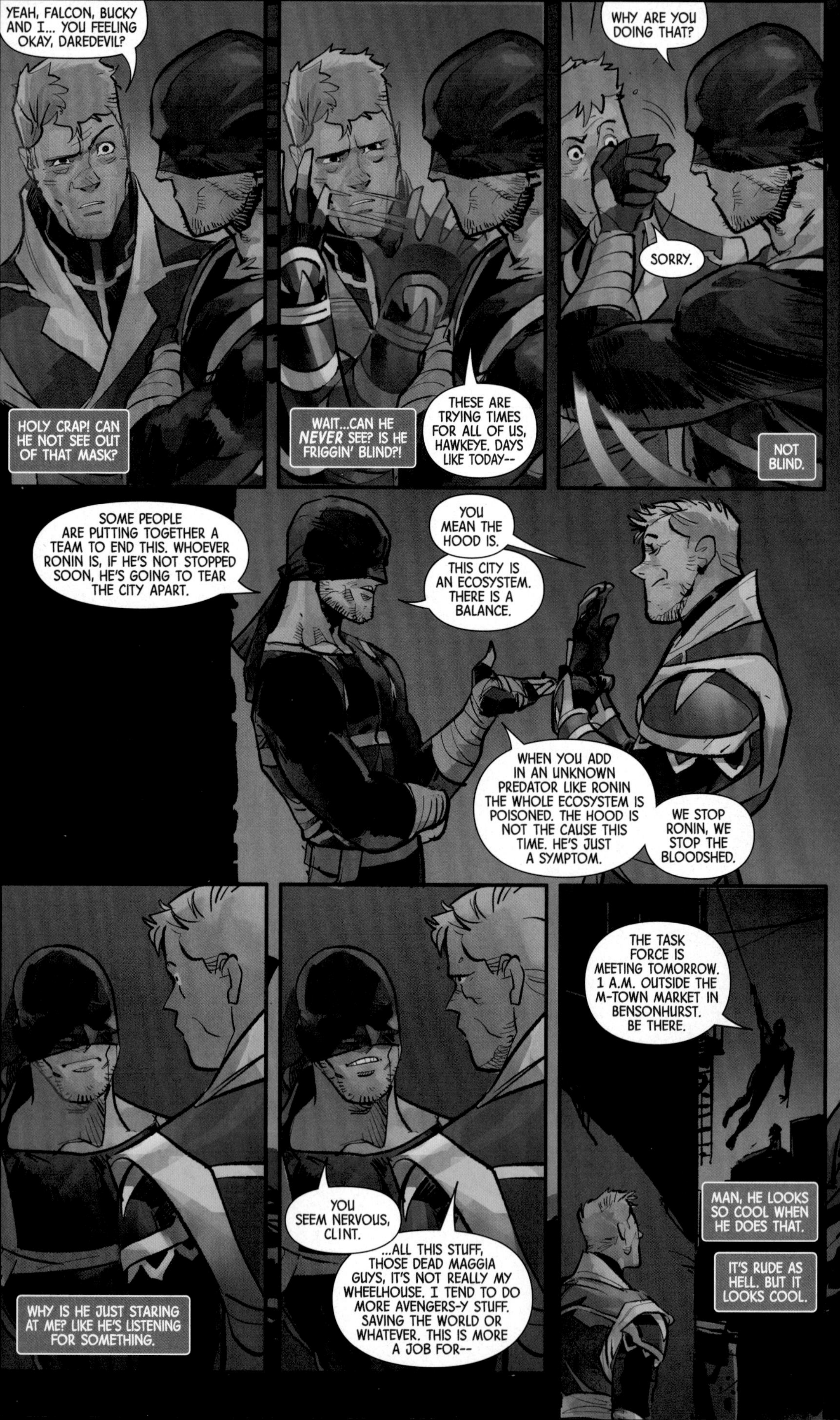
YEAH, FALCON, BUCKY AND I... YOU FEELING OKAY, DAREDEVIL?
HOLY CRAP! CAN HE NOT SEE OUT OF THAT MASK?
WAIT...CAN HE NEVER SEE? IS HE FRIGGIN' BLIND?!
THESE ARE TRYING TIMES FOR ALL OF US, HAWKEYE. DAYS LIKE TODAY--
WHY ARE YOU DOING THAT?
SORRY.
NOT BLIND.
SOME PEOPLE ARE PUTTING TOGETHER A TEAM TO END THIS. WHOEVER RONIN IS, IF HE'S NOT STOPPED SOON, HE'S GOING TO TEAR THE CITY APART.
YOU MEAN THE HOOD IS.
THIS CITY IS AN ECOSYSTEM. THERE IS A BALANCE.
WHEN YOU ADD IN AN UNKNOWN PREDATOR LIKE RONIN THE WHOLE ECOSYSTEM IS POISONED. THE HOOD IS NOT THE CAUSE THIS TIME. HE'S JUST A SYMPTOM.
WE STOP RONIN, WE STOP THE BLOODSHED.
WHY IS HE JUST STARING AT ME? LIKE HE'S LISTENING FOR SOMETHING.
YOU SEEM NERVOUS, CLINT.
...ALL THIS STUFF, THOSE DEAD MAGGIA GUYS, IT'S NOT REALLY MY WHEELHOUSE. I TEND TO DO MORE AVENGERS-Y STUFF. SAVING THE WORLD OR WHATEVER. THIS IS MORE A JOB FOR--
THE TASK FORCE IS MEETING TOMORROW. 1 A.M. OUTSIDE THE M-TOWN MARKET IN BENSONHURST. BE THERE.
MAN, HE LOOKS SO COOL WHEN HE DOES THAT.
IT'S RUDE AS HELL. BUT IT LOOKS COOL.

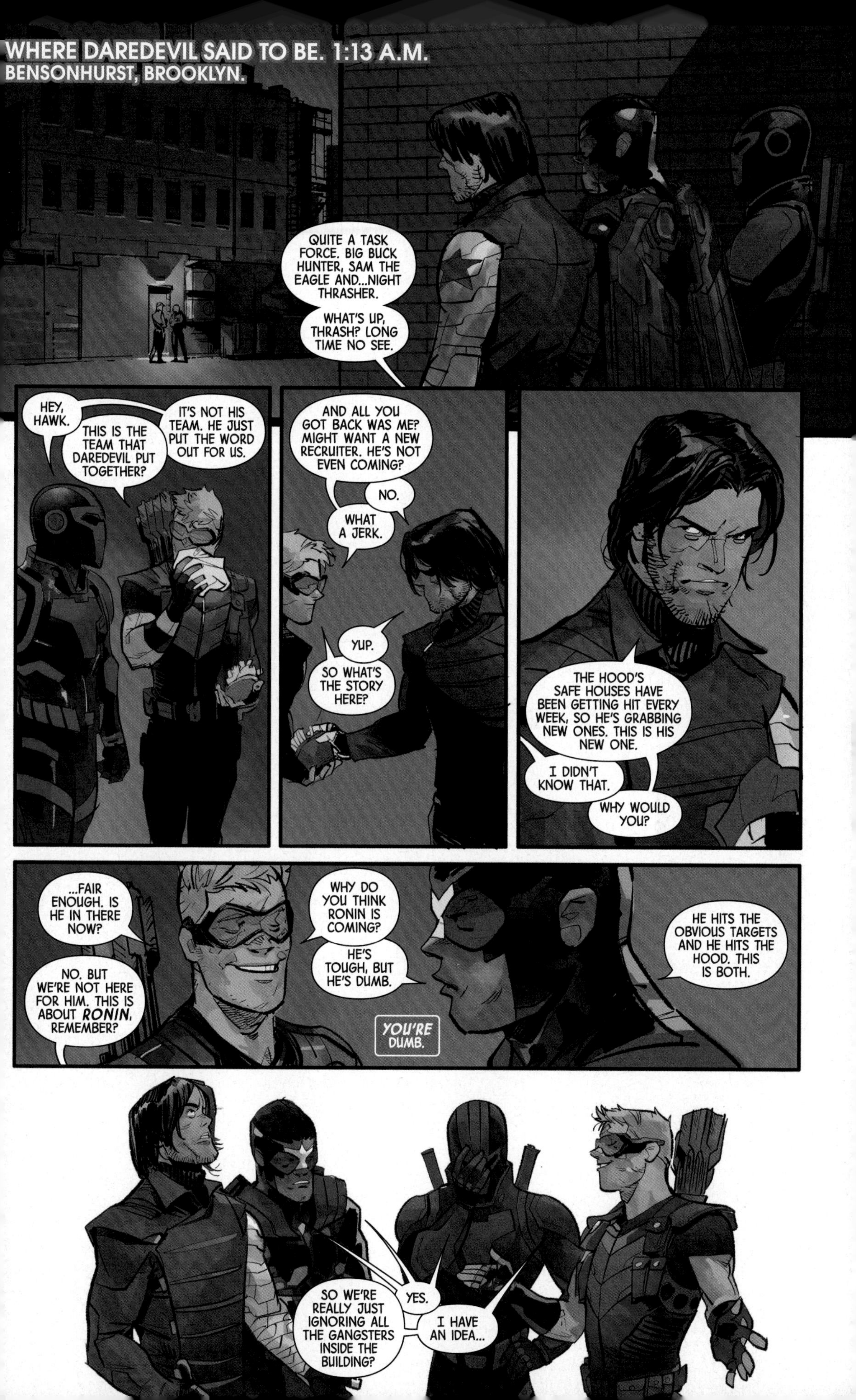
WHERE DAREDEVIL SAID TO BE. 1:13 A.M.
BENSONHURST, BROOKLYN.
QUITE A TASK FORCE. BIG BUCK HUNTER, SAM THE EAGLE AND...NIGHT THRASHER.
WHAT'S UP, THRASH? LONG TIME NO SEE.
HEY, HAWK.
THIS IS THE TEAM THAT DAREDEVIL PUT TOGETHER?
IT'S NOT HIS TEAM. HE JUST PUT THE WORD OUT FOR US.
AND ALL YOU GOT BACK WAS ME? MIGHT WANT A NEW RECRUITER. HE'S NOT EVEN COMING?
NO.
WHAT A JERK.
YUP.
SO WHAT'S THE STORY HERE?
THE HOOD'S SAFE HOUSES HAVE BEEN GETTING HIT EVERY WEEK, SO HE'S GRABBING NEW ONES. THIS IS HIS NEW ONE.
I DIDN'T KNOW THAT.
WHY WOULD YOU?
...FAIR ENOUGH. IS HE IN THERE NOW?
NO. BUT WE'RE NOT HERE FOR HIM. THIS IS ABOUT RONIN, REMEMBER?
WHY DO YOU THINK RONIN IS COMING?
HE'S TOUGH, BUT HE'S DUMB.
YOU'RE DUMB.
HE HITS THE OBVIOUS TARGETS AND HE HITS THE HOOD. THIS IS BOTH.
SO WE'RE REALLY JUST IGNORING ALL THE GANGSTERS INSIDE THE BUILDING?
YES.
I HAVE AN IDEA...

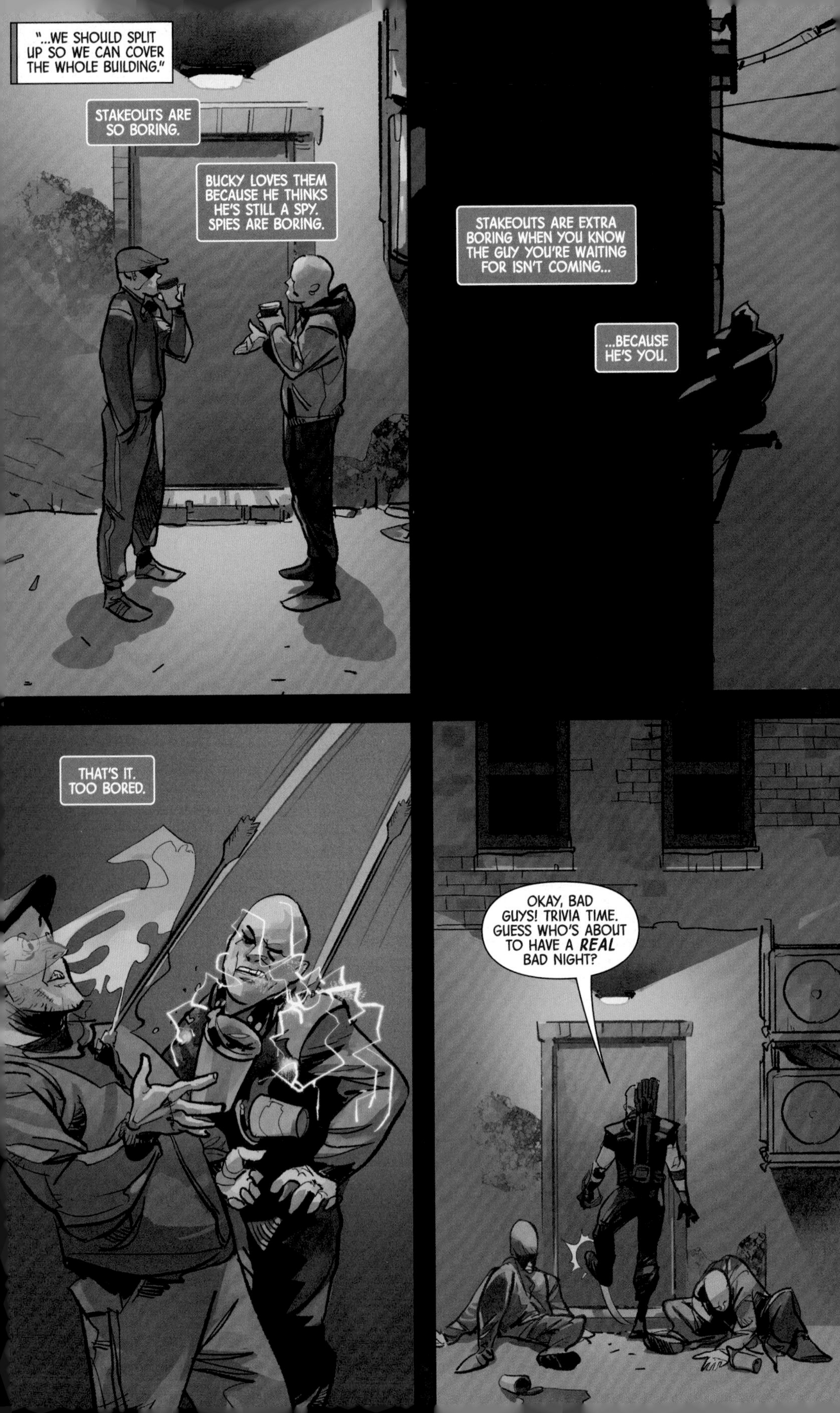
"...WE SHOULD SPLIT UP SO WE CAN COVER THE WHOLE BUILDING."
STAKEOUTS ARE SO BORING.
BUCKY LOVES THEM BECAUSE HE THINKS HE'S STILL A SPY. SPIES ARE BORING.
STAKEOUTS ARE EXTRA BORING WHEN YOU KNOW THE GUY YOU'RE WAITING FOR ISN'T COMING...
...BECAUSE HE'S YOU.
THAT'S IT. TOO BORED.
OKAY, BAD GUYS! TRIVIA TIME. GUESS WHO'S ABOUT TO HAVE A *REAL* BAD NIGHT?

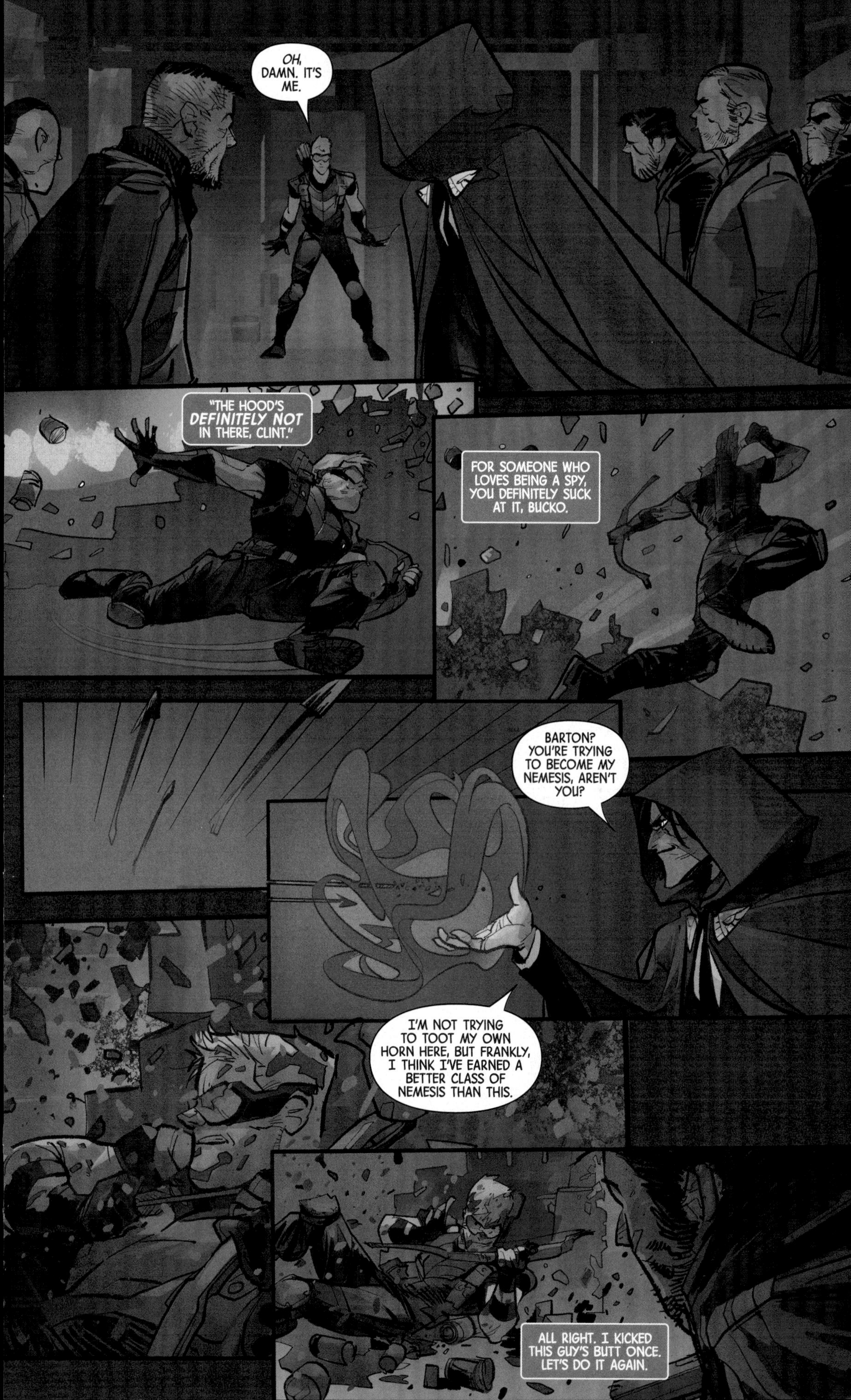
OH, DAMN. IT'S ME.
"THE HOOD'S DEFINITELY NOT IN THERE, CLINT."
FOR SOMEONE WHO LOVES BEING A SPY, YOU DEFINITELY SUCK AT IT, BUCKO.
BARTON? YOU'RE TRYING TO BECOME MY NEMESIS, AREN'T YOU?
I'M NOT TRYING TO TOOT MY OWN HORN HERE, BUT FRANKLY, I THINK I'VE EARNED A BETTER CLASS OF NEMESIS THAN THIS.
ALL RIGHT. I KICKED THIS GUY'S BUTT ONCE. LET'S DO IT AGAIN.

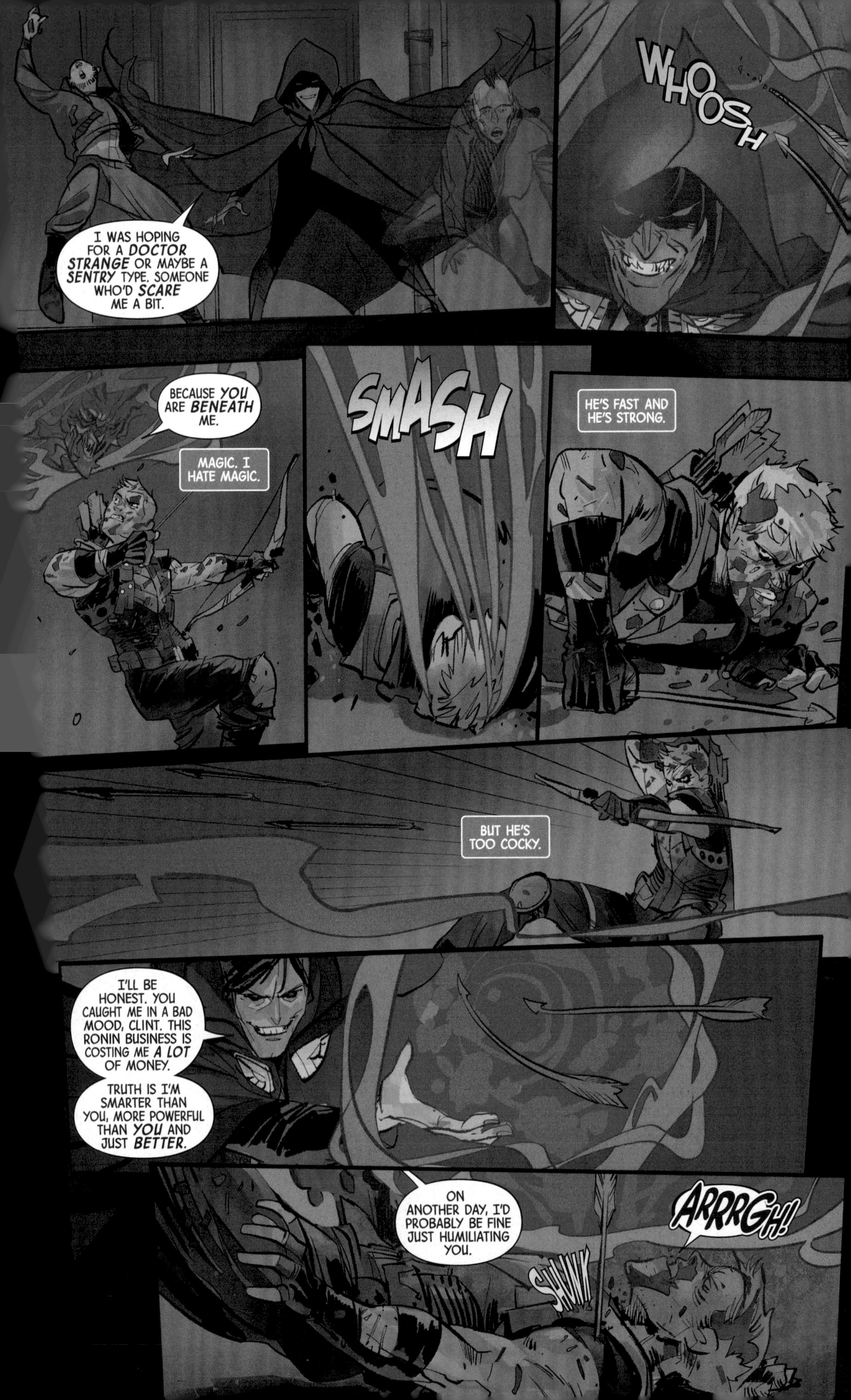
I WAS HOPING FOR A DOCTOR STRANGE OR MAYBE A SENTRY TYPE. SOMEONE WHO'D SCARE ME A BIT.
WHOOSH
BECAUSE YOU ARE BENEATH ME.
MAGIC. I HATE MAGIC.
SMASH
HE'S FAST AND HE'S STRONG.
BUT HE'S TOO COCKY.
I'LL BE HONEST. YOU CAUGHT ME IN A BAD MOOD, CLINT. THIS RONIN BUSINESS IS COSTING ME A LOT OF MONEY.
TRUTH IS I'M SMARTER THAN YOU, MORE POWERFUL THAN YOU AND JUST BETTER.
ON ANOTHER DAY, I'D PROBABLY BE FINE JUST HUMILIATING YOU.
ARRRGH!
SHUNK

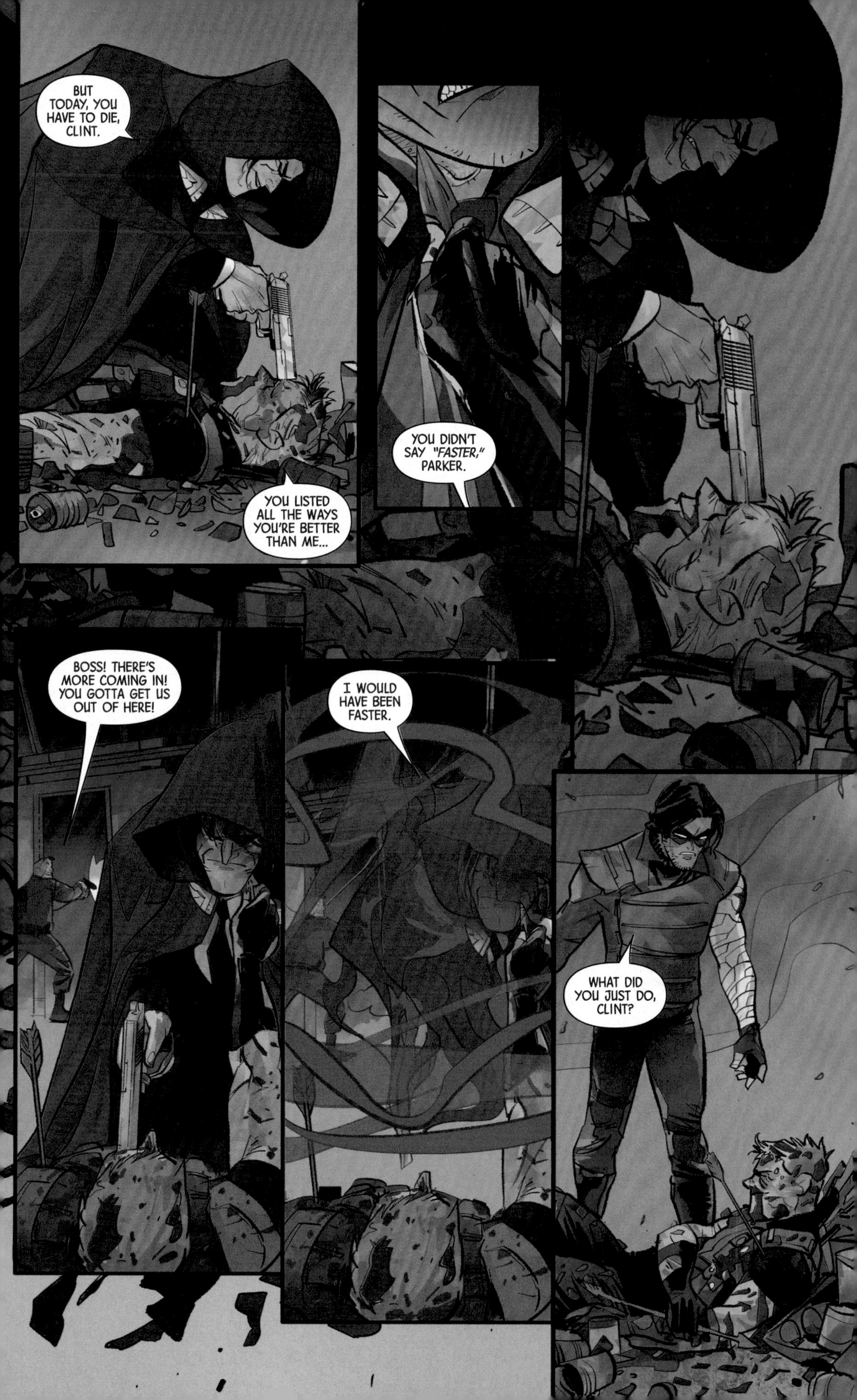
BUT TODAY, YOU HAVE TO DIE, CLINT.
YOU LISTED ALL THE WAYS YOU'RE BETTER THAN ME...
YOU DIDN'T SAY "FASTER," PARKER.
BOSS! THERE'S MORE COMING IN! YOU GOTTA GET US OUT OF HERE!
I WOULD HAVE BEEN FASTER.
WHAT DID YOU JUST DO, CLINT?

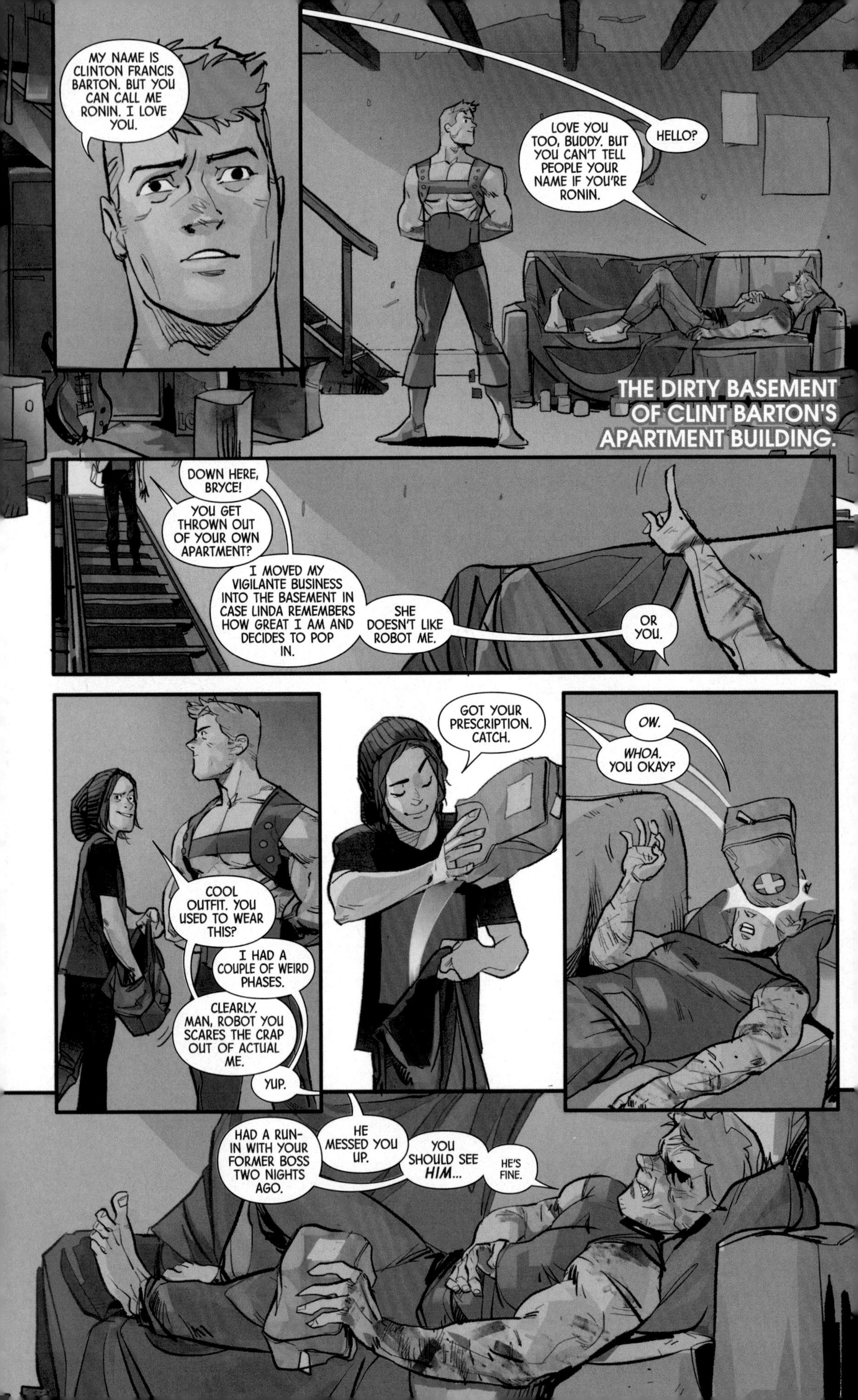
MY NAME IS CLINTON FRANCIS BARTON. BUT YOU CAN CALL ME RONIN. I LOVE YOU.
HELLO?
LOVE YOU TOO, BUDDY. BUT YOU CAN'T TELL PEOPLE YOUR NAME IF YOU'RE RONIN.
THE DIRTY BASEMENT OF CLINT BARTON'S APARTMENT BUILDING.
DOWN HERE, BRYCE!
YOU GET THROWN OUT OF YOUR OWN APARTMENT?
I MOVED MY VIGILANTE BUSINESS INTO THE BASEMENT IN CASE LINDA REMEMBERS HOW GREAT I AM AND DECIDES TO POP IN.
SHE DOESN'T LIKE ROBOT ME.
OR YOU.
COOL OUTFIT. YOU USED TO WEAR THIS?
I HAD A COUPLE OF WEIRD PHASES.
CLEARLY. MAN, ROBOT YOU SCARES THE CRAP OUT OF ACTUAL ME.
YUP.
GOT YOUR PRESCRIPTION. CATCH.
OW.
WHOA. YOU OKAY?
HAD A RUN-IN WITH YOUR FORMER BOSS TWO NIGHTS AGO.
HE MESSED YOU UP.
YOU SHOULD SEE HIM...
HE'S FINE.

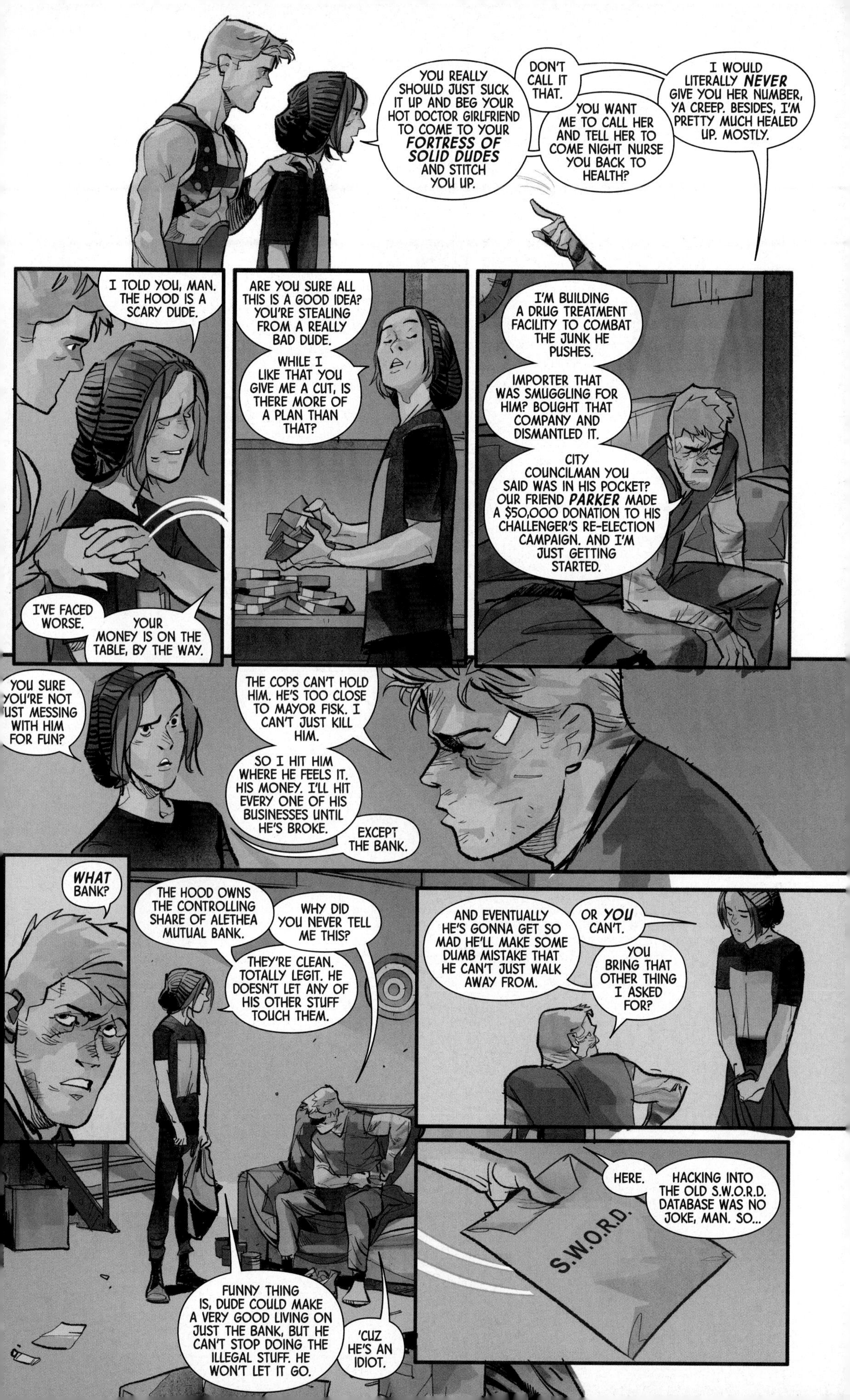

YOU REALLY SHOULD JUST SUCK IT UP AND BEG YOUR HOT DOCTOR GIRLFRIEND TO COME TO YOUR FORTRESS OF SOLID DUDES AND STITCH YOU UP.
DON'T CALL IT THAT.
YOU WANT ME TO CALL HER AND TELL HER TO COME NIGHT NURSE YOU BACK TO HEALTH?
I WOULD LITERALLY NEVER GIVE YOU HER NUMBER, YA CREEP. BESIDES, I'M PRETTY MUCH HEALED UP. MOSTLY.
I TOLD YOU, MAN. THE HOOD IS A SCARY DUDE.
I'VE FACED WORSE.
YOUR MONEY IS ON THE TABLE, BY THE WAY.
ARE YOU SURE ALL THIS IS A GOOD IDEA? YOU'RE STEALING FROM A REALLY BAD DUDE.
WHILE I LIKE THAT YOU GIVE ME A CUT, IS THERE MORE OF A PLAN THAN THAT?
I'M BUILDING A DRUG TREATMENT FACILITY TO COMBAT THE JUNK HE PUSHES.
IMPORTER THAT WAS SMUGGLING FOR HIM? BOUGHT THAT COMPANY AND DISMANTLED IT.
CITY COUNCILMAN YOU SAID WAS IN HIS POCKET? OUR FRIEND PARKER MADE A $50,000 DONATION TO HIS CHALLENGER'S RE-ELECTION CAMPAIGN. AND I'M JUST GETTING STARTED.
YOU SURE YOU'RE NOT JUST MESSING WITH HIM FOR FUN?
THE COPS CAN'T HOLD HIM. HE'S TOO CLOSE TO MAYOR FISK. I CAN'T JUST KILL HIM.
SO I HIT HIM WHERE HE FEELS IT. HIS MONEY. I'LL HIT EVERY ONE OF HIS BUSINESSES UNTIL HE'S BROKE.
EXCEPT THE BANK.
WHAT BANK?
THE HOOD OWNS THE CONTROLLING SHARE OF ALETHEA MUTUAL BANK.
WHY DID YOU NEVER TELL ME THIS?
THEY'RE CLEAN. TOTALLY LEGIT. HE DOESN'T LET ANY OF HIS OTHER STUFF TOUCH THEM.
FUNNY THING IS, DUDE COULD MAKE A VERY GOOD LIVING ON JUST THE BANK, BUT HE CAN'T STOP DOING THE ILLEGAL STUFF. HE WON'T LET IT GO.
'CUZ HE'S AN IDIOT.
AND EVENTUALLY HE'S GONNA GET SO MAD HE'LL MAKE SOME DUMB MISTAKE THAT HE CAN'T JUST WALK AWAY FROM.
OR YOU CAN'T.
YOU BRING THAT OTHER THING I ASKED FOR?
HERE.
HACKING INTO THE OLD S.W.O.R.D. DATABASE WAS NO JOKE, MAN. SO...
S.W.O.R.D.

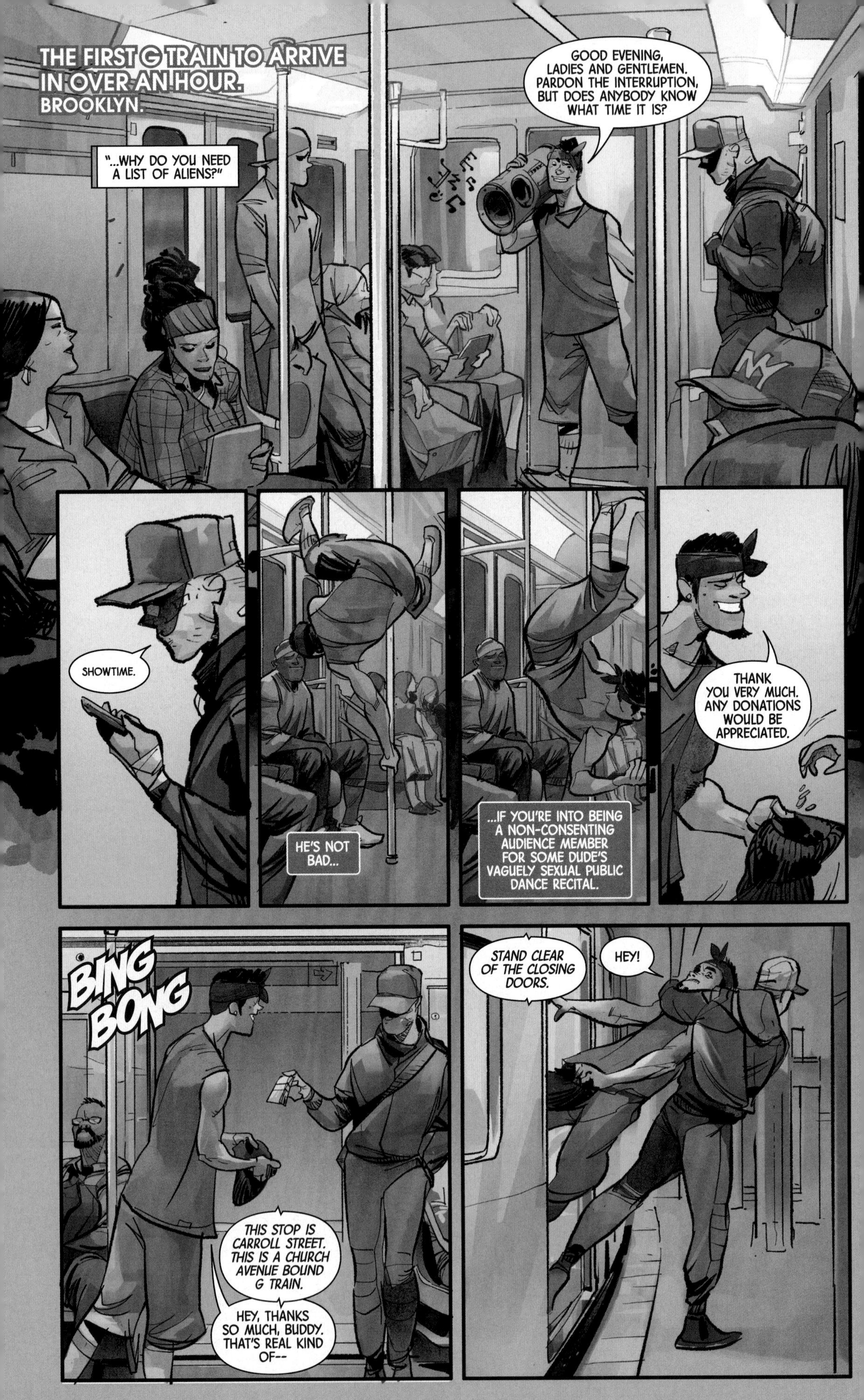
THE FIRST G TRAIN TO ARRIVE IN OVER AN HOUR.
BROOKLYN.
GOOD EVENING, LADIES AND GENTLEMEN. PARDON THE INTERRUPTION, BUT DOES ANYBODY KNOW WHAT TIME IT IS?
"...WHY DO YOU NEED A LIST OF ALIENS?"
SHOWTIME.
HE'S NOT BAD...
...IF YOU'RE INTO BEING A NON-CONSENTING AUDIENCE MEMBER FOR SOME DUDE'S VAGUELY SEXUAL PUBLIC DANCE RECITAL.
THANK YOU VERY MUCH. ANY DONATIONS WOULD BE APPRECIATED.
BING BONG
THIS STOP IS CARROLL STREET. THIS IS A CHURCH AVENUE BOUND G TRAIN.
HEY, THANKS SO MUCH, BUDDY. THAT'S REAL KIND OF--
STAND CLEAR OF THE CLOSING DOORS.
HEY!

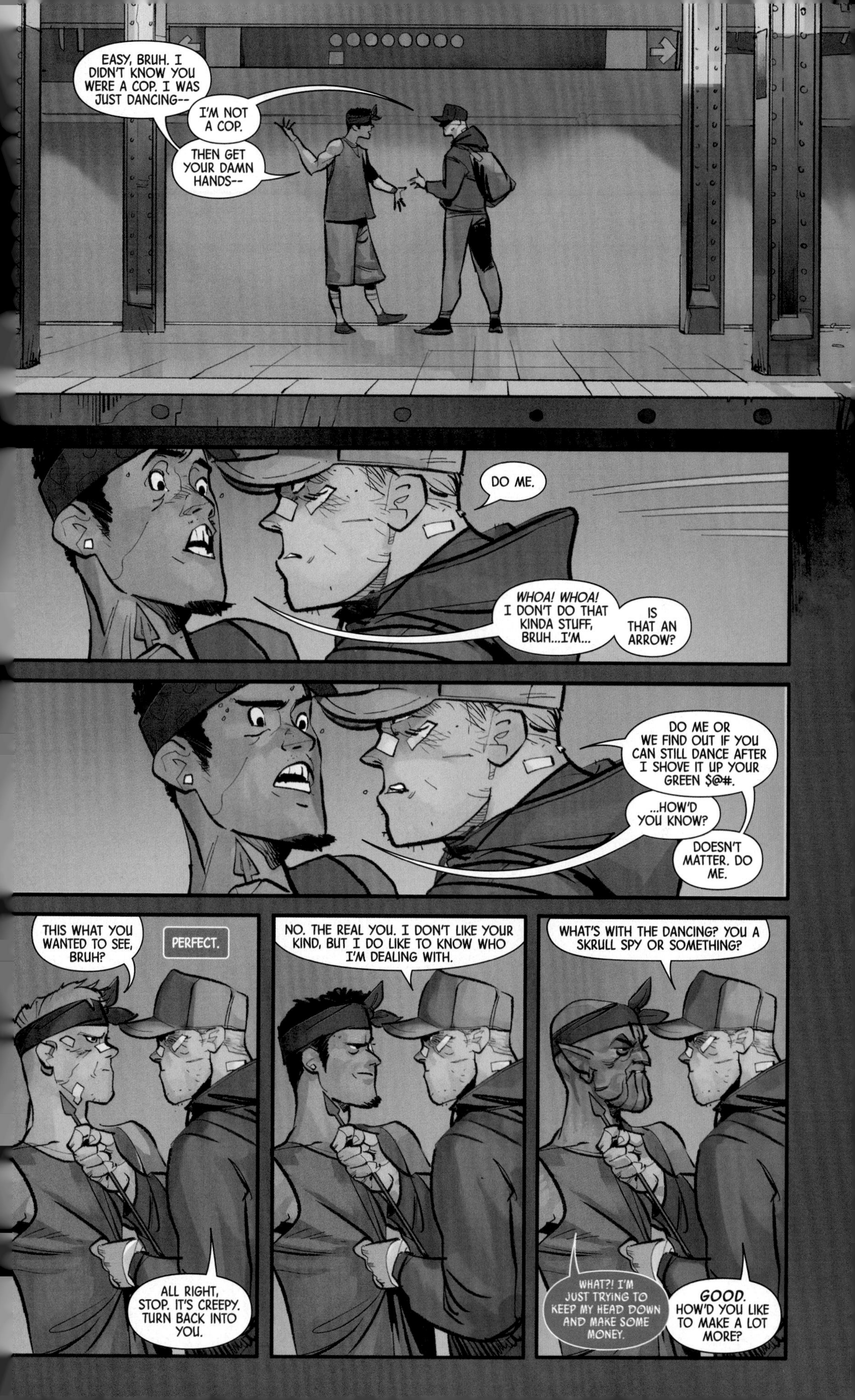
EASY, BRUH. I DIDN'T KNOW YOU WERE A COP. I WAS JUST DANCING--
I'M NOT A COP.
THEN GET YOUR DAMN HANDS--
DO ME.
WHOA! WHOA! I DON'T DO THAT KINDA STUFF, BRUH...I'M...
IS THAT AN ARROW?
DO ME OR WE FIND OUT IF YOU CAN STILL DANCE AFTER I SHOVE IT UP YOUR GREEN $@#.
...HOW'D YOU KNOW?
DOESN'T MATTER. DO ME.
THIS WHAT YOU WANTED TO SEE, BRUH?
PERFECT.
ALL RIGHT, STOP. IT'S CREEPY. TURN BACK INTO YOU.
NO. THE REAL YOU. I DON'T LIKE YOUR KIND, BUT I DO LIKE TO KNOW WHO I'M DEALING WITH.
WHAT'S WITH THE DANCING? YOU A SKRULL SPY OR SOMETHING?
WHAT?! I'M JUST TRYING TO KEEP MY HEAD DOWN AND MAKE SOME MONEY.
GOOD. HOW'D YOU LIKE TO MAKE A LOT MORE?

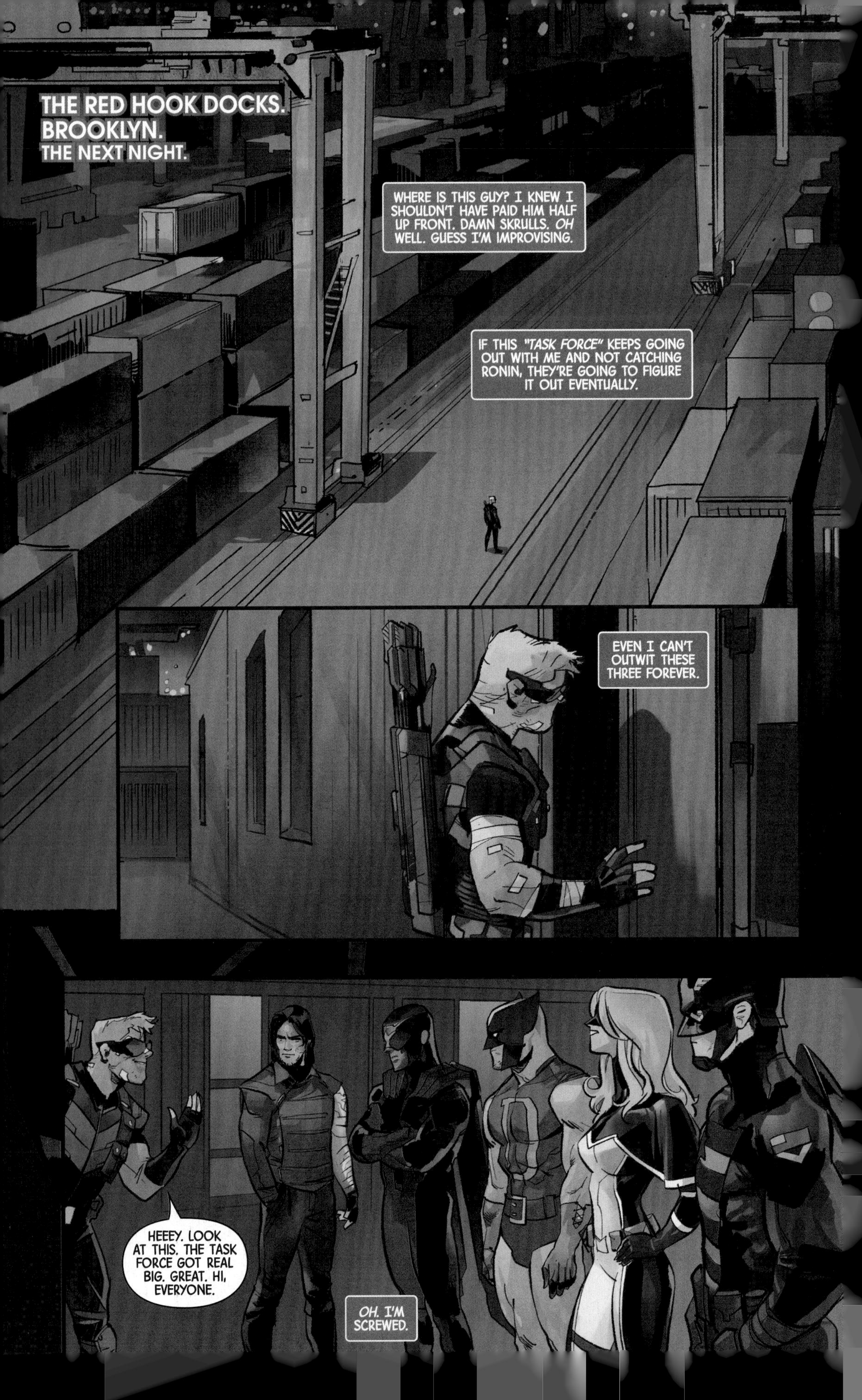
THE RED HOOK DOCKS.
BROOKLYN.
THE NEXT NIGHT.
WHERE IS THIS GUY? I KNEW I SHOULDN'T HAVE PAID HIM HALF UP FRONT. DAMN SKRULLS. *OH* WELL. GUESS I'M IMPROVISING.
IF THIS *"TASK FORCE"* KEEPS GOING OUT WITH ME AND NOT CATCHING RONIN, THEY'RE GOING TO FIGURE IT OUT EVENTUALLY.
EVEN I CAN'T OUTWIT THESE THREE FOREVER.
HEEEY. LOOK AT THIS. THE TASK FORCE GOT REAL BIG. GREAT. HI, EVERYONE.
OH. I'M SCREWED.

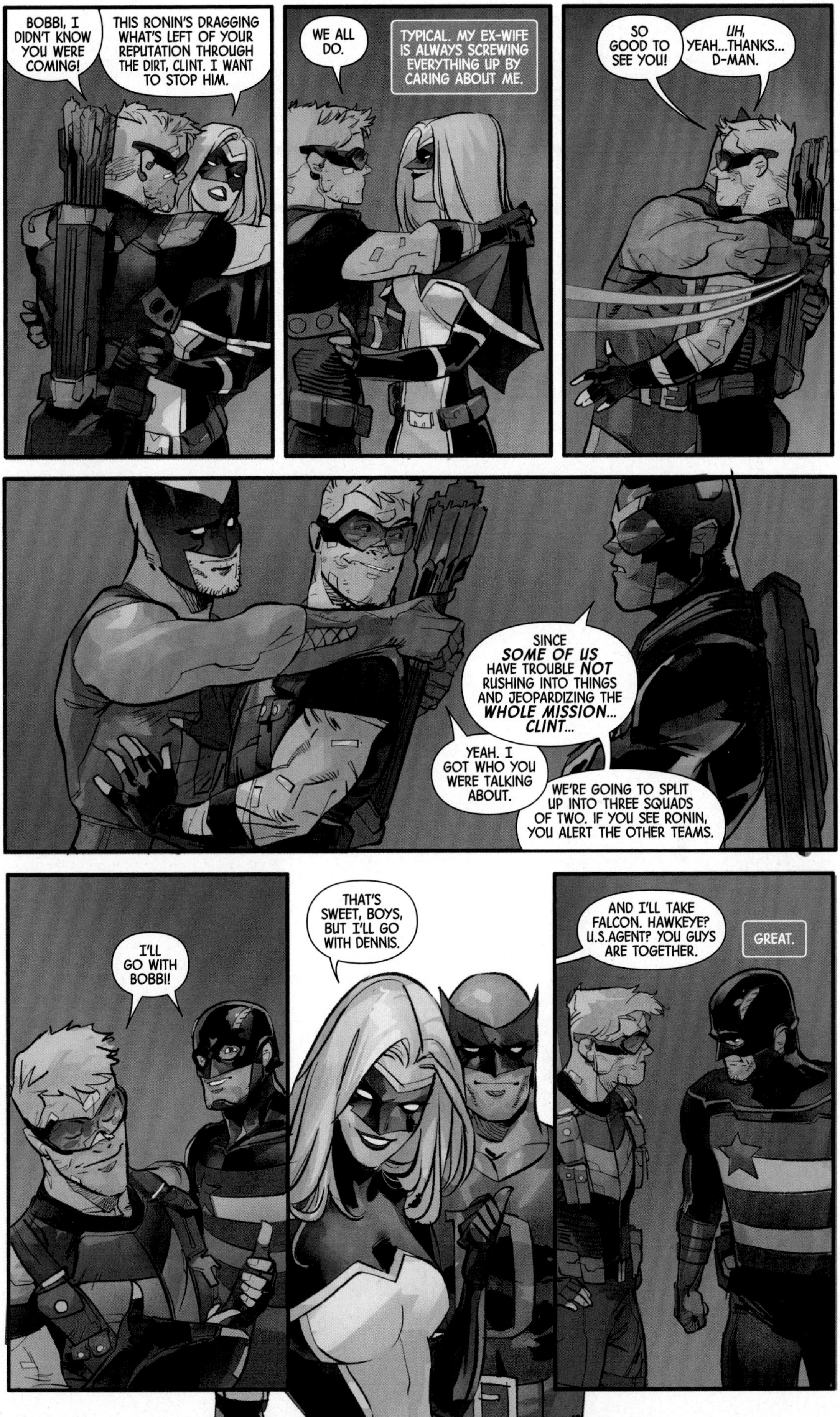
BOBBI, I DIDN'T KNOW YOU WERE COMING!
THIS RONIN'S DRAGGING WHAT'S LEFT OF YOUR REPUTATION THROUGH THE DIRT, CLINT. I WANT TO STOP HIM.
WE ALL DO.
TYPICAL. MY EX-WIFE IS ALWAYS SCREWING EVERYTHING UP BY CARING ABOUT ME.
SO GOOD TO SEE YOU!
UH, YEAH...THANKS... D-MAN.
SINCE SOME OF US HAVE TROUBLE NOT RUSHING INTO THINGS AND JEOPARDIZING THE WHOLE MISSION... CLINT...
YEAH. I GOT WHO YOU WERE TALKING ABOUT.
WE'RE GOING TO SPLIT UP INTO THREE SQUADS OF TWO. IF YOU SEE RONIN, YOU ALERT THE OTHER TEAMS.
I'LL GO WITH BOBBI!
THAT'S SWEET, BOYS, BUT I'LL GO WITH DENNIS.
AND I'LL TAKE FALCON. HAWKEYE? U.S.AGENT? YOU GUYS ARE TOGETHER.
GREAT.

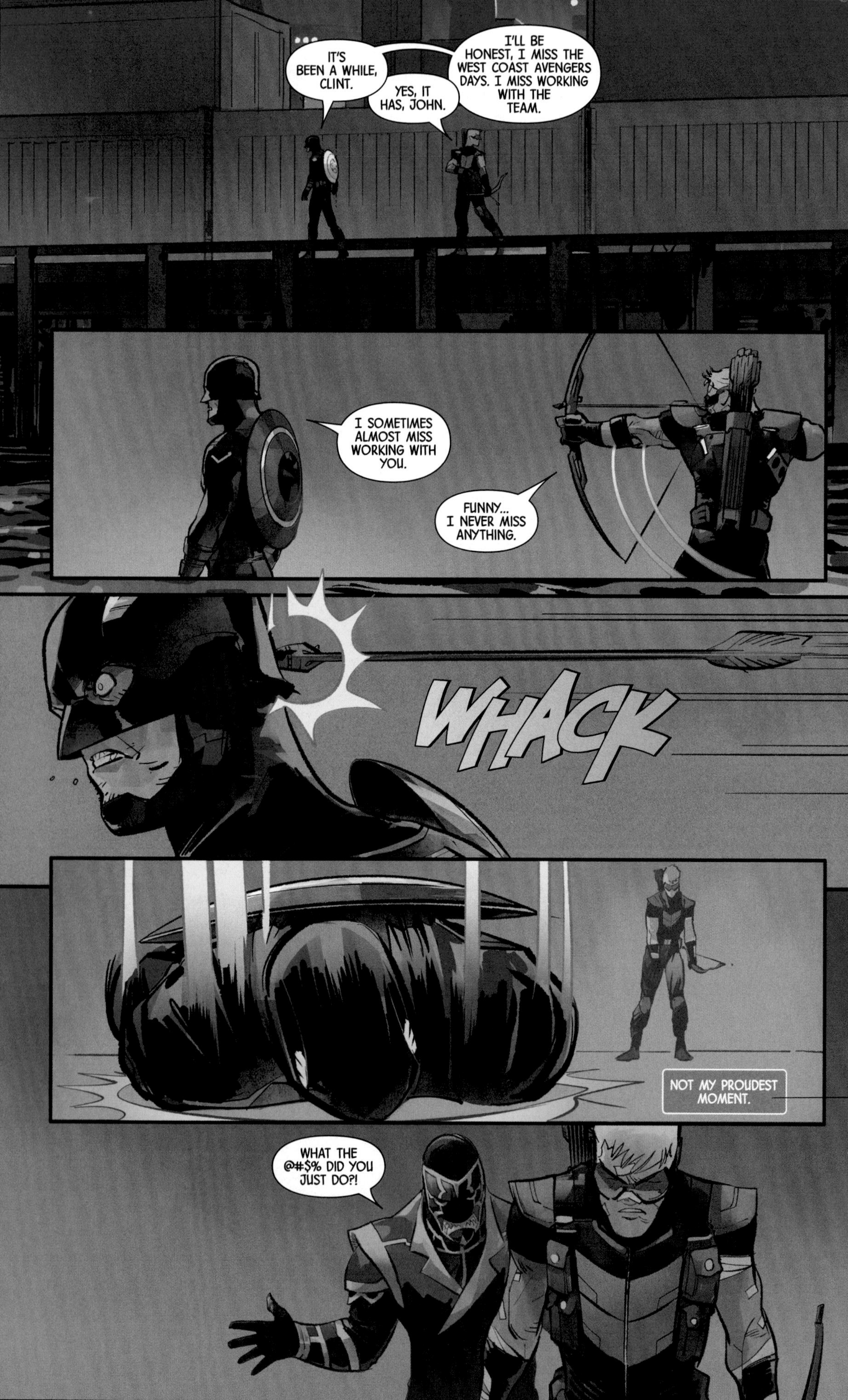
IT'S BEEN A WHILE, CLINT.
YES, IT HAS, JOHN.
I'LL BE HONEST, I MISS THE WEST COAST AVENGERS DAYS. I MISS WORKING WITH THE TEAM.
I SOMETIMES ALMOST MISS WORKING WITH YOU.
FUNNY... I NEVER MISS ANYTHING.
WHACK
NOT MY PROUDEST MOMENT.
WHAT THE @#$% DID YOU JUST DO?!

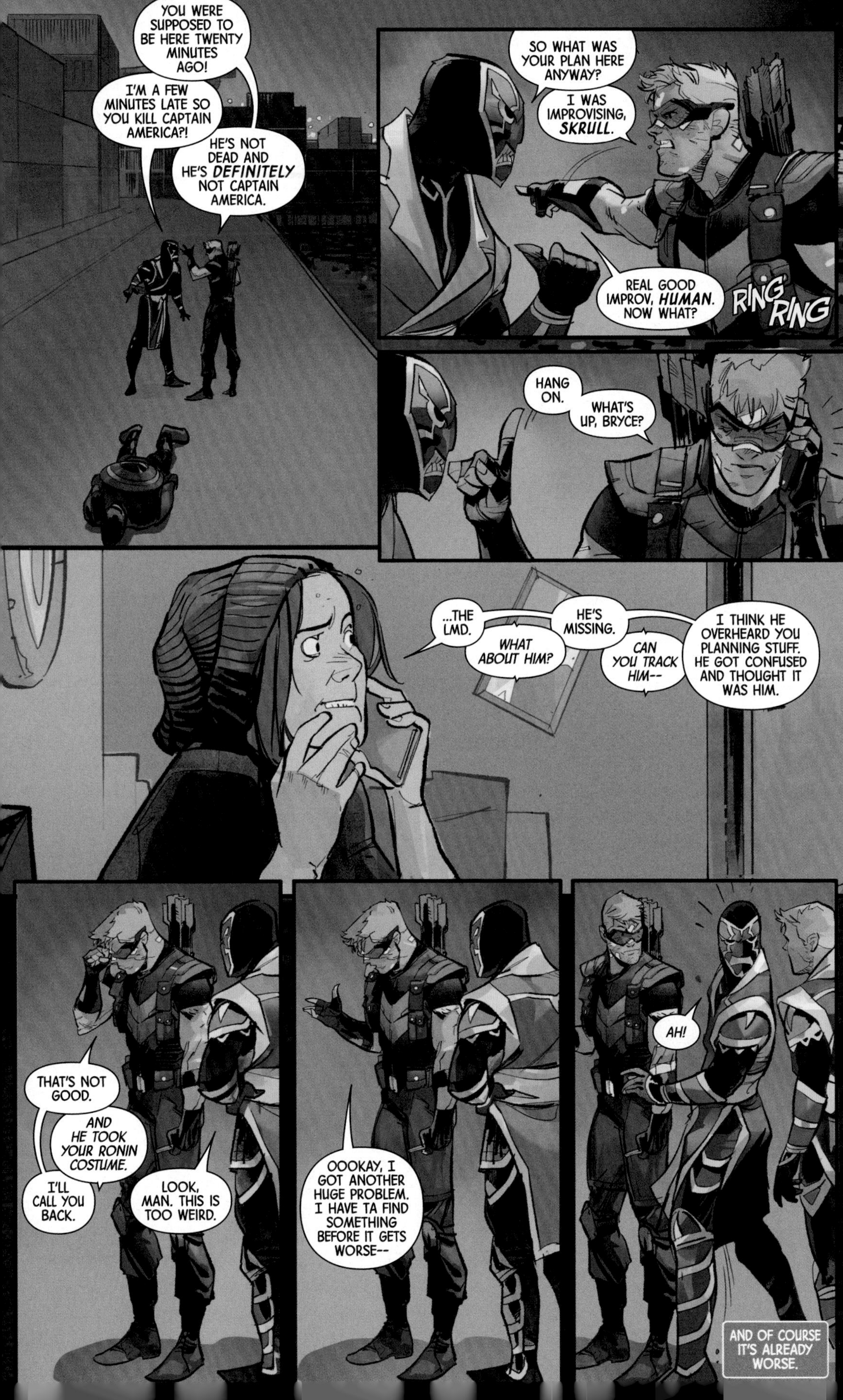
YOU WERE SUPPOSED TO BE HERE TWENTY MINUTES AGO!
I'M A FEW MINUTES LATE SO YOU KILL CAPTAIN AMERICA?!
HE'S NOT DEAD AND HE'S DEFINITELY NOT CAPTAIN AMERICA.
SO WHAT WAS YOUR PLAN HERE ANYWAY?
I WAS IMPROVISING, SKRULL.
REAL GOOD IMPROV, HUMAN. NOW WHAT?
RING RING
HANG ON.
WHAT'S UP, BRYCE?
...THE LMD.
WHAT ABOUT HIM?
HE'S MISSING.
CAN YOU TRACK HIM--
I THINK HE OVERHEARD YOU PLANNING STUFF. HE GOT CONFUSED AND THOUGHT IT WAS HIM.
THAT'S NOT GOOD.
AND HE TOOK YOUR RONIN COSTUME.
I'LL CALL YOU BACK.
LOOK, MAN. THIS IS TOO WEIRD.
OOOKAY, I GOT ANOTHER HUGE PROBLEM. I HAVE TA FIND SOMETHING BEFORE IT GETS WORSE--
AH!
AND OF COURSE IT'S ALREADY WORSE.

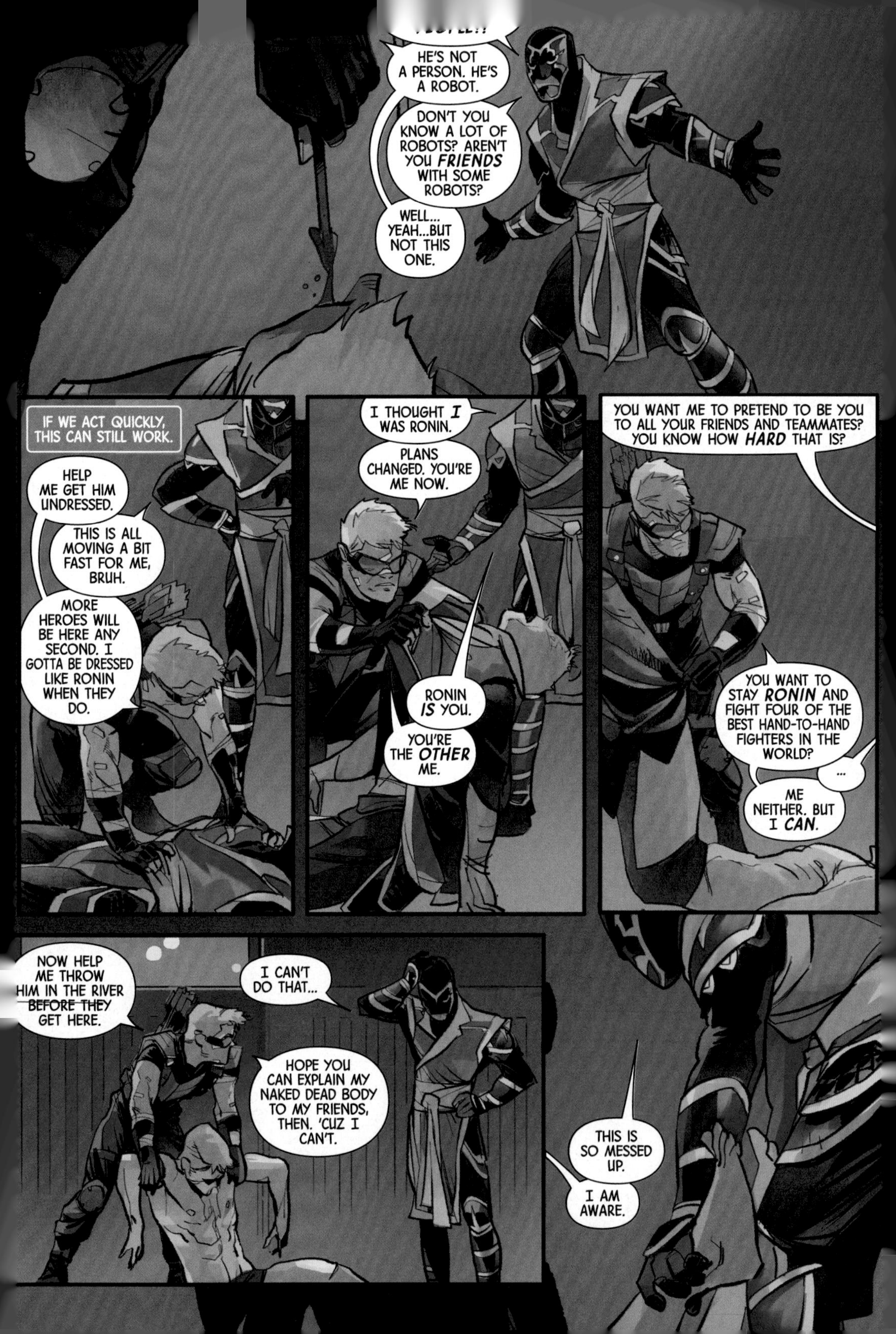

HE'S NOT A PERSON. HE'S A ROBOT.
DON'T YOU KNOW A LOT OF ROBOTS? AREN'T YOU FRIENDS WITH SOME ROBOTS?
WELL... YEAH...BUT NOT THIS ONE.
IF WE ACT QUICKLY, THIS CAN STILL WORK.
HELP ME GET HIM UNDRESSED.
THIS IS ALL MOVING A BIT FAST FOR ME, BRUH.
MORE HEROES WILL BE HERE ANY SECOND. I GOTTA BE DRESSED LIKE RONIN WHEN THEY DO.
I THOUGHT I WAS RONIN.
PLANS CHANGED. YOU'RE ME NOW.
RONIN IS YOU.
YOU'RE THE OTHER ME.
YOU WANT ME TO PRETEND TO BE YOU TO ALL YOUR FRIENDS AND TEAMMATES? YOU KNOW HOW HARD THAT IS?
YOU WANT TO STAY RONIN AND FIGHT FOUR OF THE BEST HAND-TO-HAND FIGHTERS IN THE WORLD?
...
ME NEITHER. BUT I CAN.
NOW HELP ME THROW HIM IN THE RIVER BEFORE THEY GET HERE.
I CAN'T DO THAT...
HOPE YOU CAN EXPLAIN MY NAKED DEAD BODY TO MY FRIENDS, THEN. 'CUZ I CAN'T.
THIS IS SO MESSED UP.
I AM AWARE.

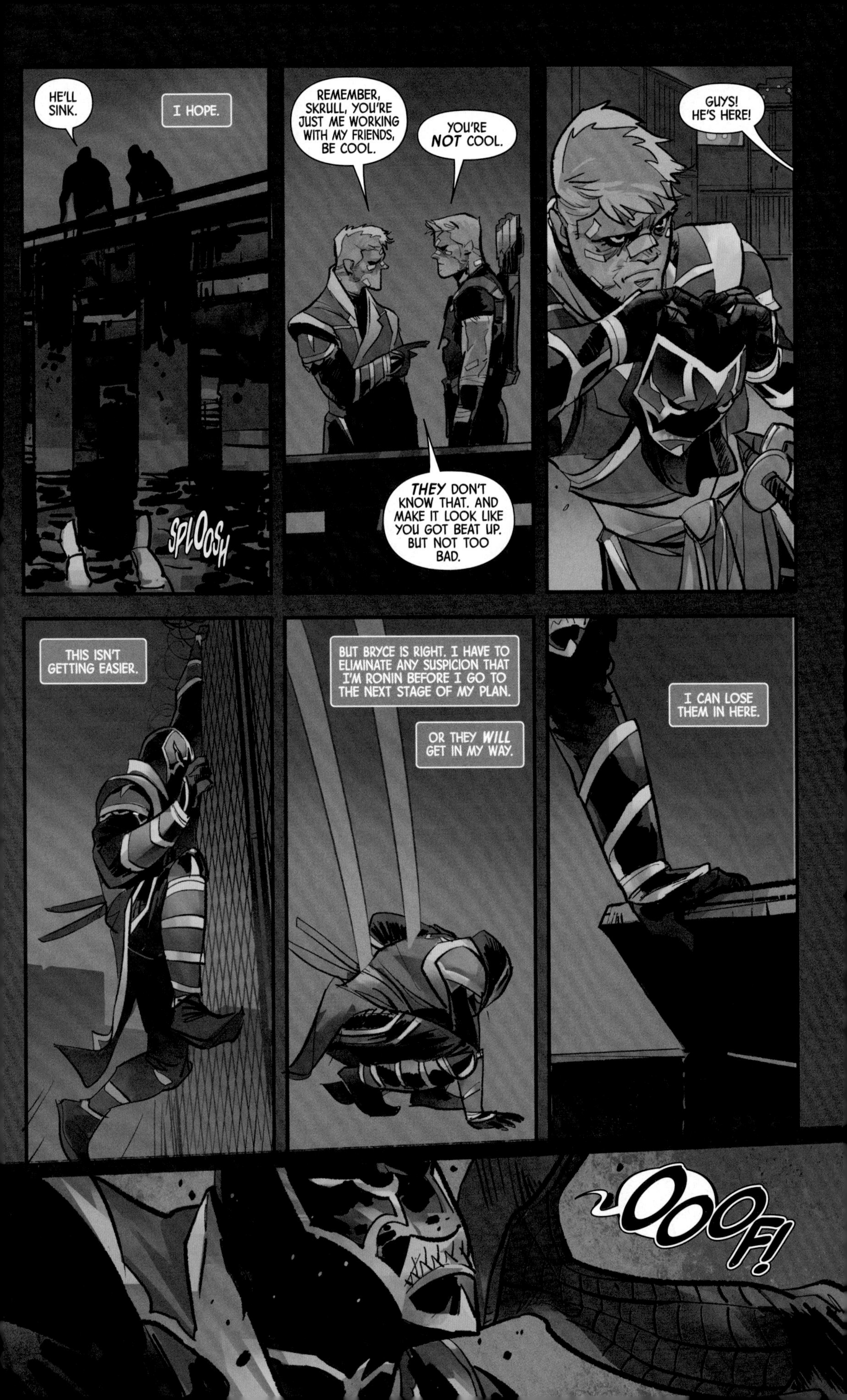
HE'LL SINK.
I HOPE.
SPLOOSH
REMEMBER, SKRULL, YOU'RE JUST ME WORKING WITH MY FRIENDS, BE COOL.
YOU'RE NOT COOL.
THEY DON'T KNOW THAT. AND MAKE IT LOOK LIKE YOU GOT BEAT UP. BUT NOT TOO BAD.
GUYS! HE'S HERE!
THIS ISN'T GETTING EASIER.
BUT BRYCE IS RIGHT. I HAVE TO ELIMINATE ANY SUSPICION THAT I'M RONIN BEFORE I GO TO THE NEXT STAGE OF MY PLAN.
OR THEY WILL GET IN MY WAY.
I CAN LOSE THEM IN HERE.
OOOF!

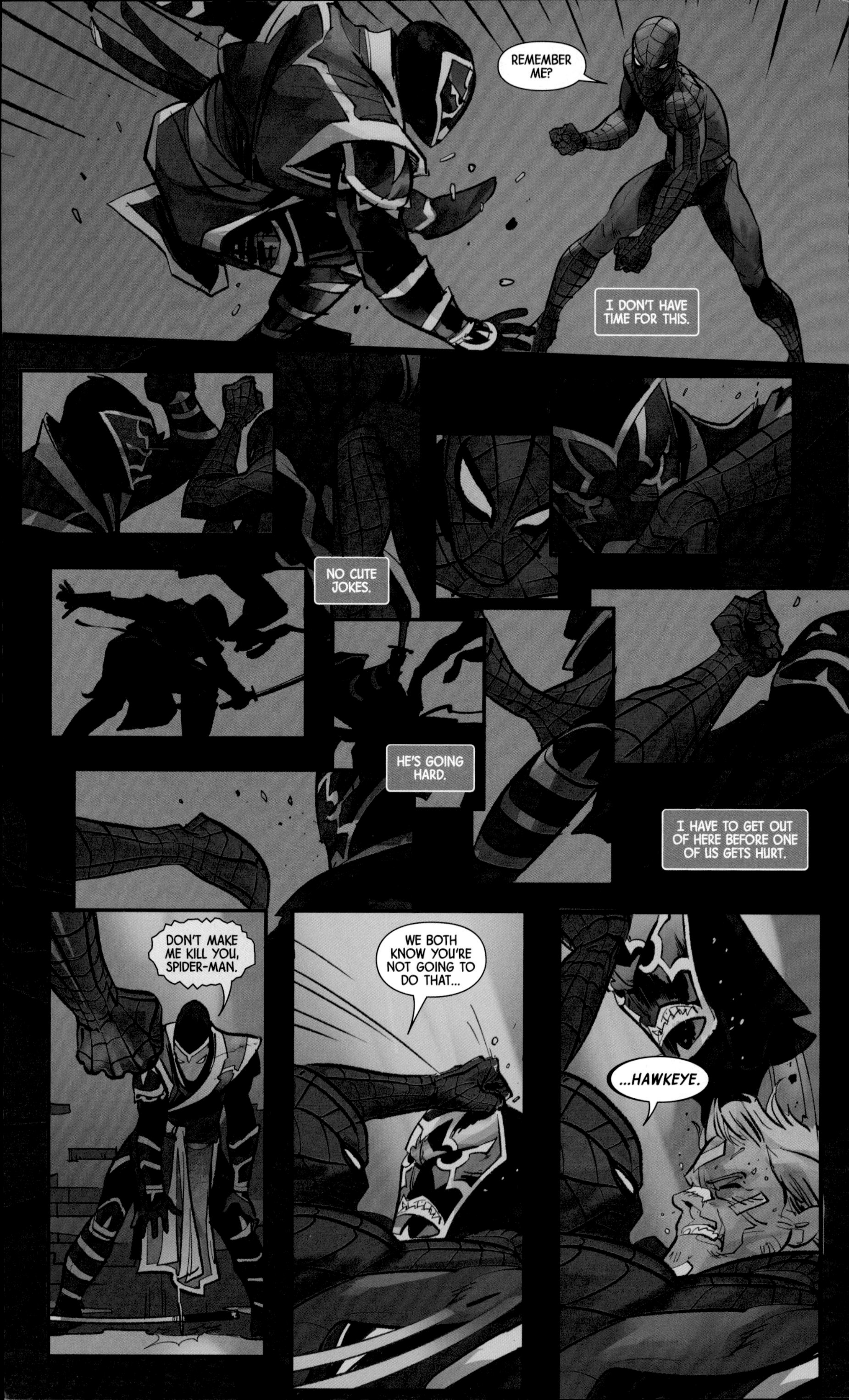
REMEMBER ME?
I DON'T HAVE TIME FOR THIS.
NO CUTE JOKES.
HE'S GOING HARD.
I HAVE TO GET OUT OF HERE BEFORE ONE OF US GETS HURT.
DON'T MAKE ME KILL YOU, SPIDER-MAN.
WE BOTH KNOW YOU'RE NOT GOING TO DO THAT...
...HAWKEYE.

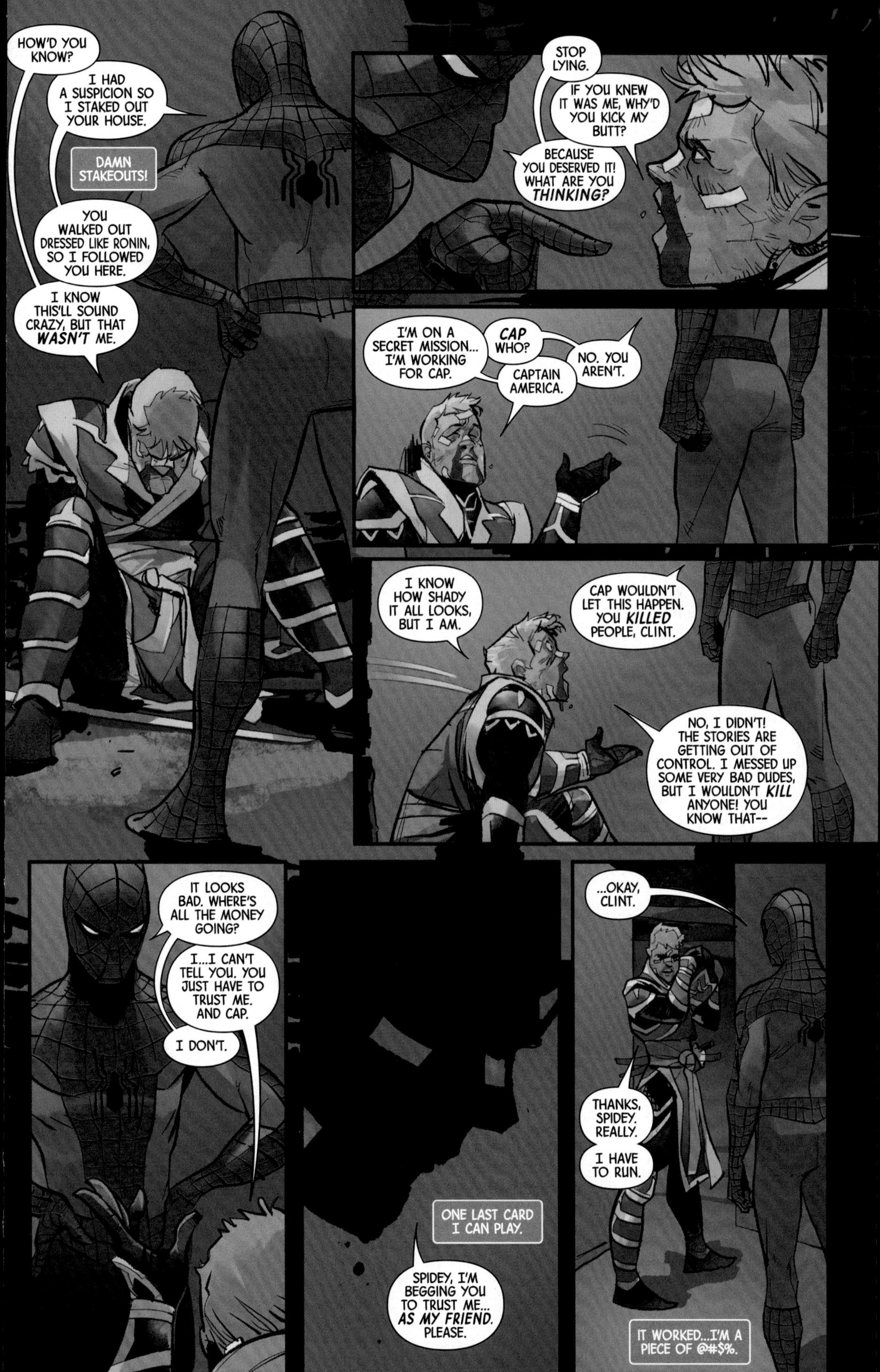
HOW'D YOU KNOW?
I HAD A SUSPICION SO I STAKED OUT YOUR HOUSE.
DAMN STAKEOUTS!
YOU WALKED OUT DRESSED LIKE RONIN, SO I FOLLOWED YOU HERE.
I KNOW THIS'LL SOUND CRAZY, BUT THAT WASN'T ME.
STOP LYING.
IF YOU KNEW IT WAS ME, WHY'D YOU KICK MY BUTT?
BECAUSE YOU DESERVED IT! WHAT ARE YOU THINKING?
I'M ON A SECRET MISSION... I'M WORKING FOR CAP.
CAP WHO?
CAPTAIN AMERICA.
NO. YOU AREN'T.
I KNOW HOW SHADY IT ALL LOOKS, BUT I AM.
CAP WOULDN'T LET THIS HAPPEN. YOU KILLED PEOPLE, CLINT.
NO, I DIDN'T! THE STORIES ARE GETTING OUT OF CONTROL. I MESSED UP SOME VERY BAD DUDES, BUT I WOULDN'T KILL ANYONE! YOU KNOW THAT--
IT LOOKS BAD. WHERE'S ALL THE MONEY GOING?
I...I CAN'T TELL YOU. YOU JUST HAVE TO TRUST ME. AND CAP.
I DON'T.
ONE LAST CARD I CAN PLAY.
SPIDEY, I'M BEGGING YOU TO TRUST ME... AS MY FRIEND. PLEASE.
...OKAY, CLINT.
THANKS, SPIDEY. REALLY.
I HAVE TO RUN.
IT WORKED...I'M A PIECE OF @#$%.

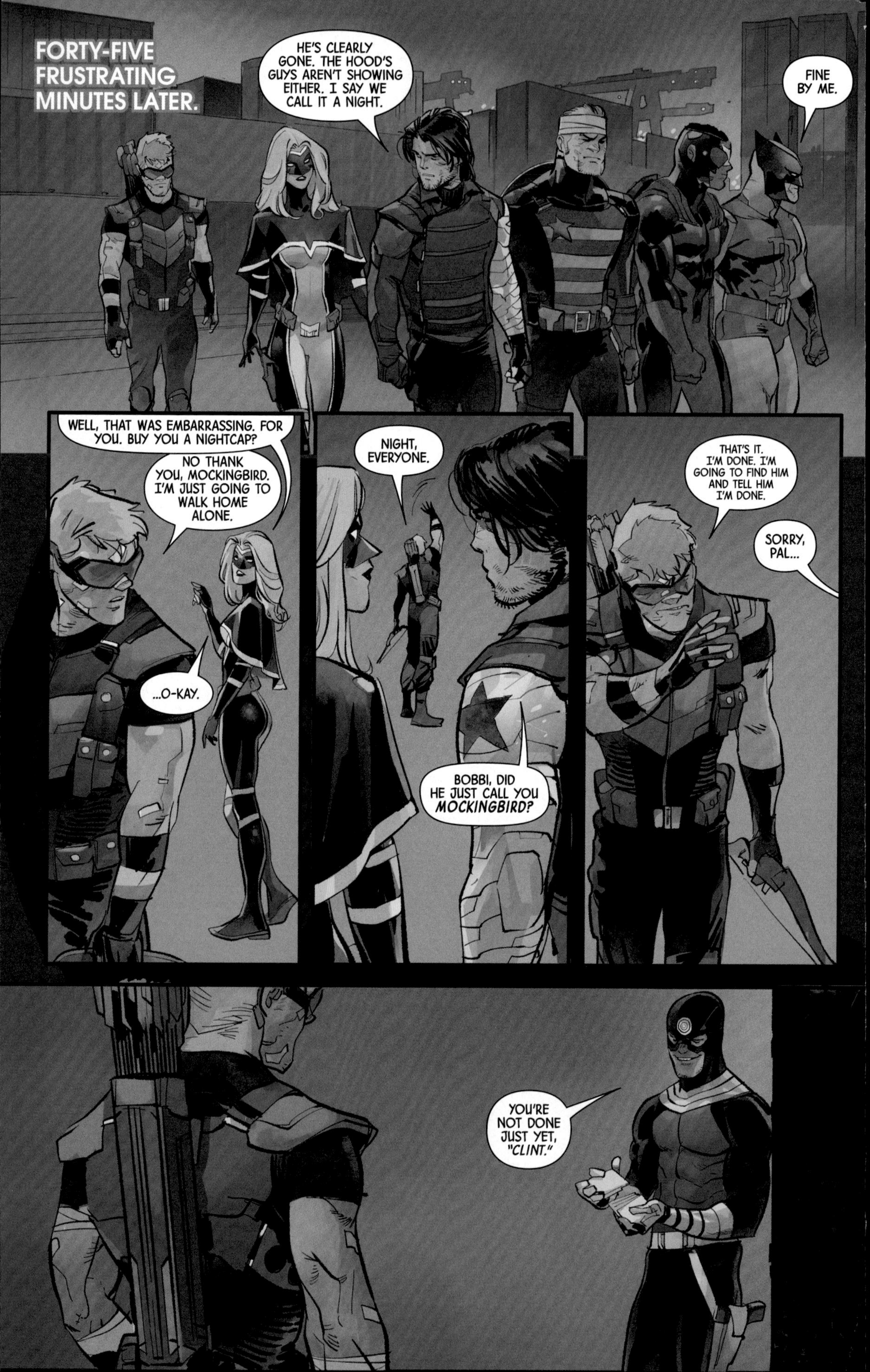
FORTY-FIVE FRUSTRATING MINUTES LATER.
HE'S CLEARLY GONE. THE HOOD'S GUYS AREN'T SHOWING EITHER. I SAY WE CALL IT A NIGHT.
FINE BY ME.
WELL, THAT WAS EMBARRASSING. FOR YOU. BUY YOU A NIGHTCAP?
NO THANK YOU, MOCKINGBIRD. I'M JUST GOING TO WALK HOME ALONE.
...O-KAY.
NIGHT, EVERYONE.
BOBBI, DID HE JUST CALL YOU *MOCKINGBIRD?*
THAT'S IT. I'M DONE. I'M GOING TO FIND HIM AND TELL HIM I'M DONE.
SORRY, PAL...
YOU'RE NOT DONE JUST YET, *"CLINT."*

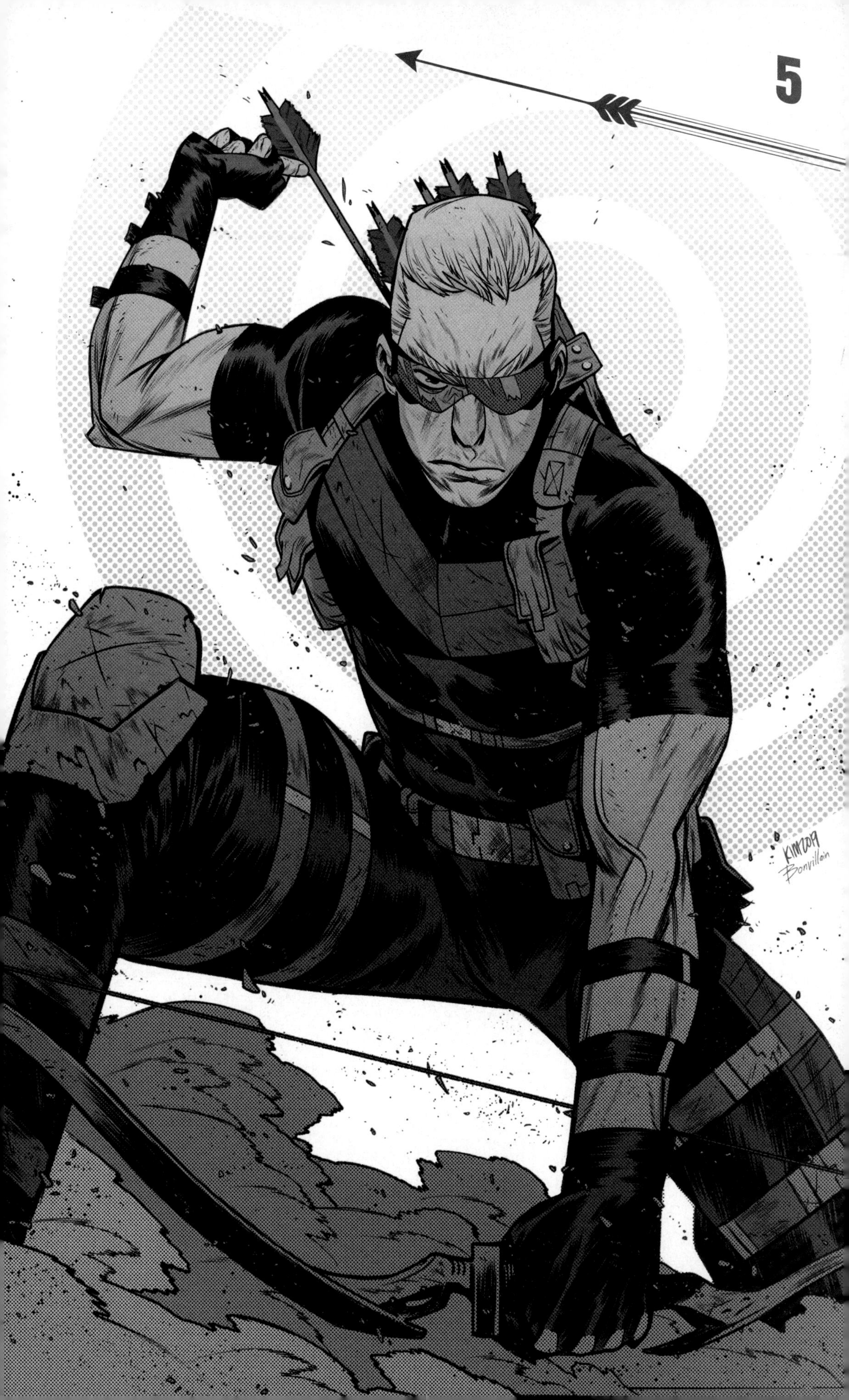
5

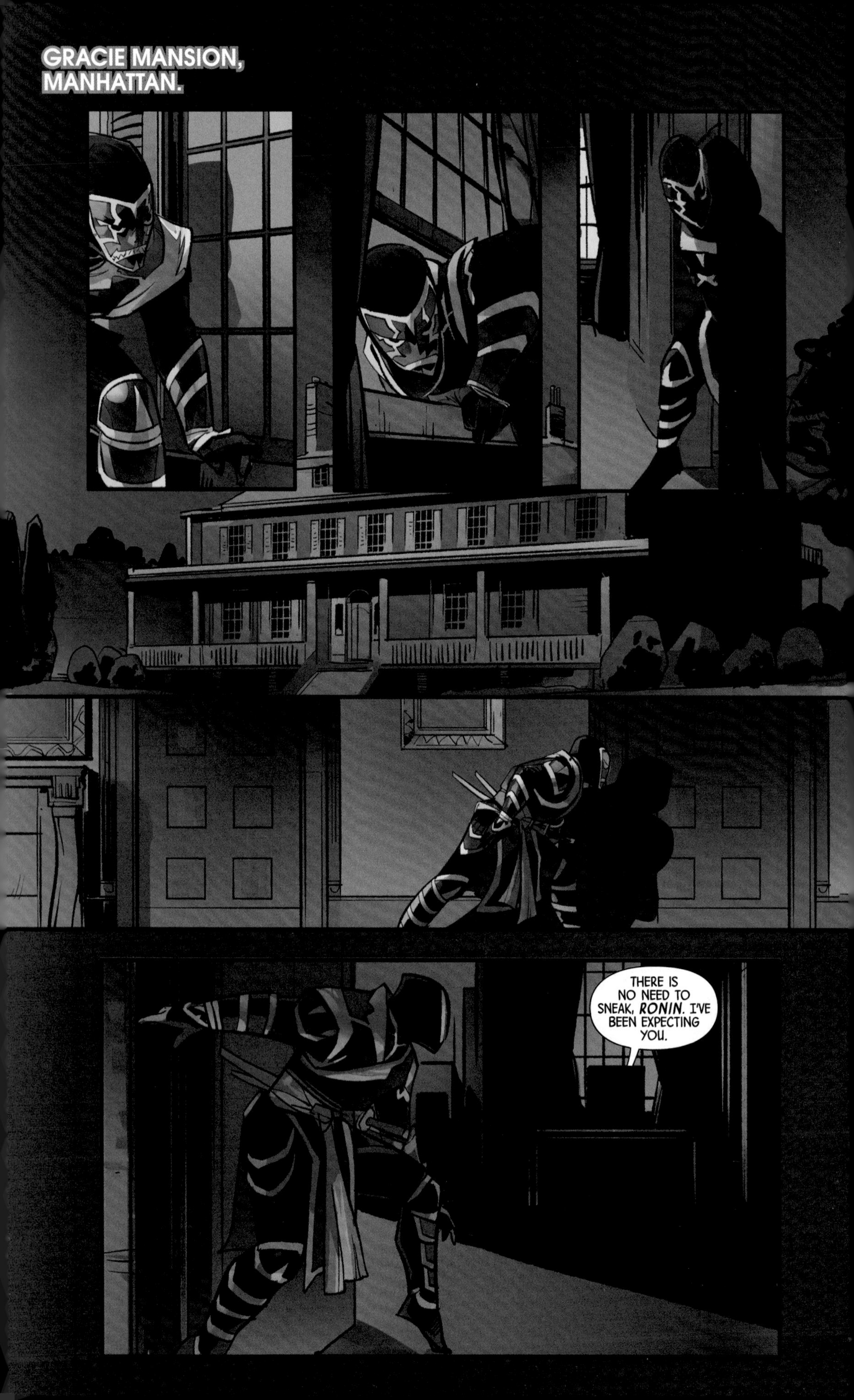
GRACIE MANSION, MANHATTAN.
THERE IS NO NEED TO SNEAK, RONIN. I'VE BEEN EXPECTING YOU.

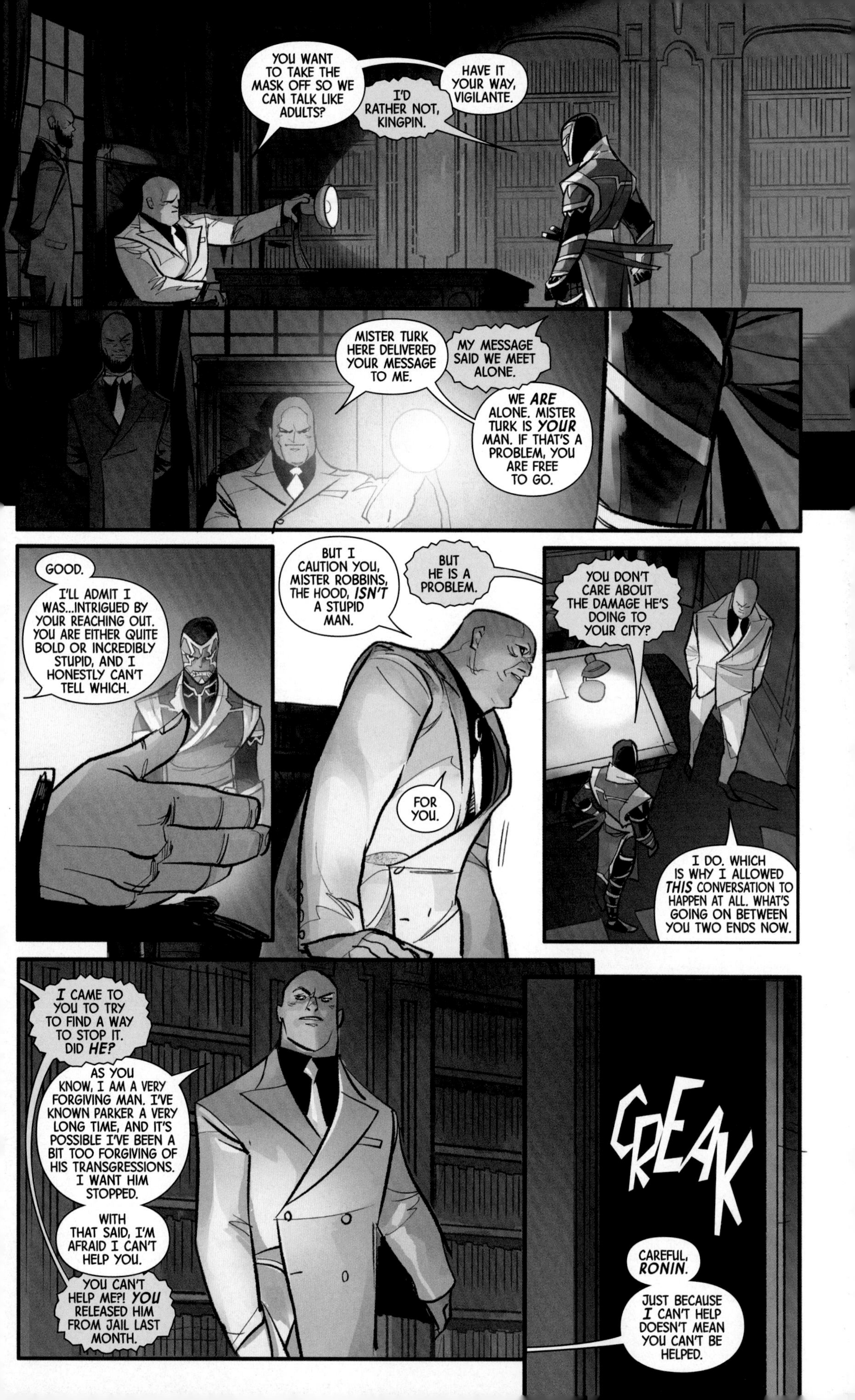

YOU WANT TO TAKE THE MASK OFF SO WE CAN TALK LIKE ADULTS?
I'D RATHER NOT, KINGPIN.
HAVE IT YOUR WAY, VIGILANTE.
MISTER TURK HERE DELIVERED YOUR MESSAGE TO ME.
MY MESSAGE SAID WE MEET ALONE.
WE ARE ALONE. MISTER TURK IS YOUR MAN. IF THAT'S A PROBLEM, YOU ARE FREE TO GO.
GOOD.
I'LL ADMIT I WAS...INTRIGUED BY YOUR REACHING OUT. YOU ARE EITHER QUITE BOLD OR INCREDIBLY STUPID, AND I HONESTLY CAN'T TELL WHICH.
BUT I CAUTION YOU, MISTER ROBBINS, THE HOOD, ISN'T A STUPID MAN.
BUT HE IS A PROBLEM.
FOR YOU.
YOU DON'T CARE ABOUT THE DAMAGE HE'S DOING TO YOUR CITY?
I DO. WHICH IS WHY I ALLOWED THIS CONVERSATION TO HAPPEN AT ALL. WHAT'S GOING ON BETWEEN YOU TWO ENDS NOW.
I CAME TO YOU TO TRY TO FIND A WAY TO STOP IT. DID HE?
AS YOU KNOW, I AM A VERY FORGIVING MAN. I'VE KNOWN PARKER A VERY LONG TIME, AND IT'S POSSIBLE I'VE BEEN A BIT TOO FORGIVING OF HIS TRANSGRESSIONS. I WANT HIM STOPPED.
WITH THAT SAID, I'M AFRAID I CAN'T HELP YOU.
YOU CAN'T HELP ME?! YOU RELEASED HIM FROM JAIL LAST MONTH.
CREAK
CAREFUL, RONIN.
JUST BECAUSE I CAN'T HELP DOESN'T MEAN YOU CAN'T BE HELPED.

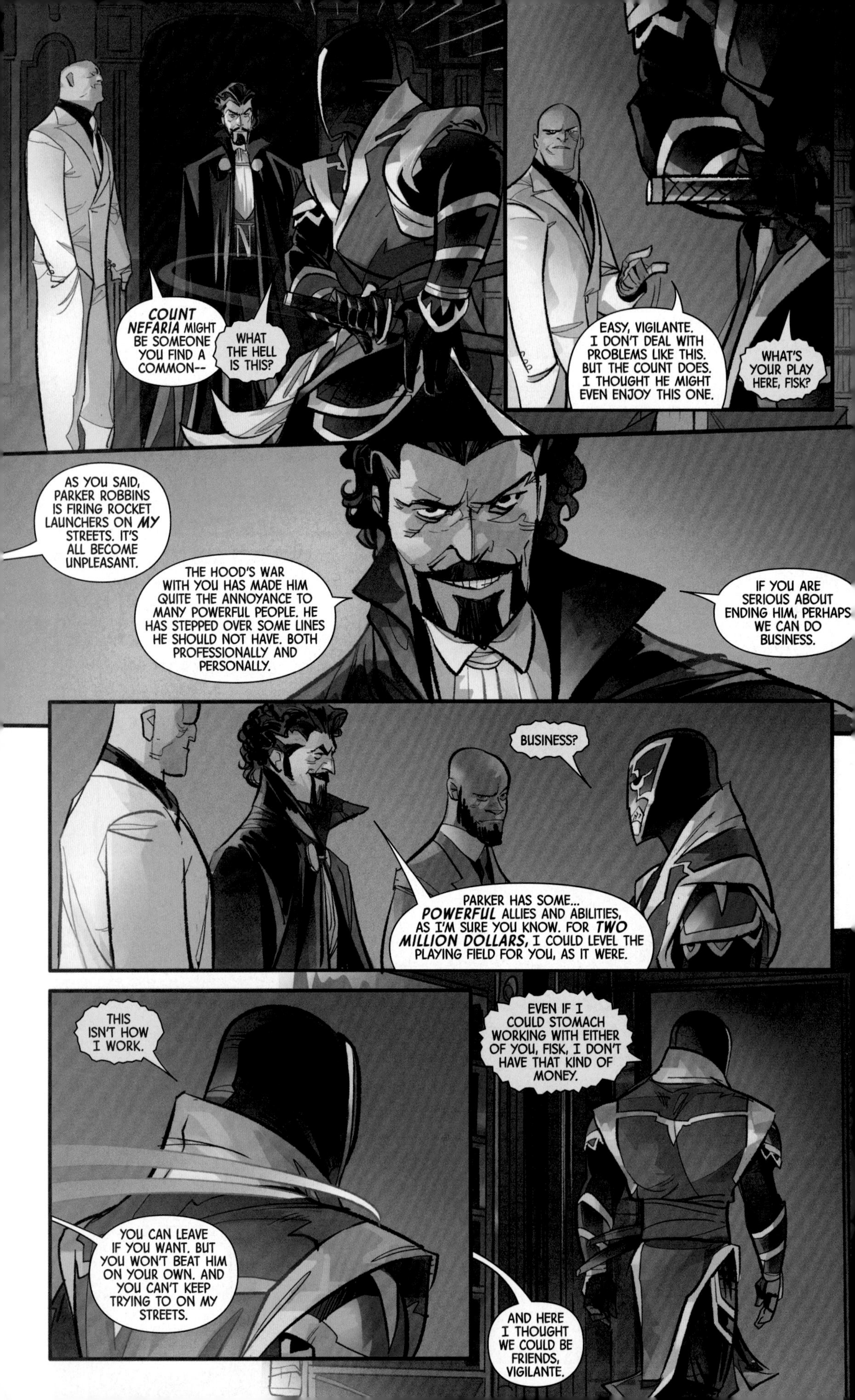

COUNT NEFARIA MIGHT BE SOMEONE YOU FIND A COMMON--
WHAT THE HELL IS THIS?
EASY, VIGILANTE. I DON'T DEAL WITH PROBLEMS LIKE THIS. BUT THE COUNT DOES. I THOUGHT HE MIGHT EVEN ENJOY THIS ONE.
WHAT'S YOUR PLAY HERE, FISK?
AS YOU SAID, PARKER ROBBINS IS FIRING ROCKET LAUNCHERS ON MY STREETS. IT'S ALL BECOME UNPLEASANT.
THE HOOD'S WAR WITH YOU HAS MADE HIM QUITE THE ANNOYANCE TO MANY POWERFUL PEOPLE. HE HAS STEPPED OVER SOME LINES HE SHOULD NOT HAVE. BOTH PROFESSIONALLY AND PERSONALLY.
IF YOU ARE SERIOUS ABOUT ENDING HIM, PERHAPS WE CAN DO BUSINESS.
BUSINESS?
PARKER HAS SOME... POWERFUL ALLIES AND ABILITIES, AS I'M SURE YOU KNOW. FOR TWO MILLION DOLLARS, I COULD LEVEL THE PLAYING FIELD FOR YOU, AS IT WERE.
THIS ISN'T HOW I WORK.
EVEN IF I COULD STOMACH WORKING WITH EITHER OF YOU, FISK, I DON'T HAVE THAT KIND OF MONEY.
YOU CAN LEAVE IF YOU WANT. BUT YOU WON'T BEAT HIM ON YOUR OWN. AND YOU CAN'T KEEP TRYING TO ON MY STREETS.
AND HERE I THOUGHT WE COULD BE FRIENDS, VIGILANTE.

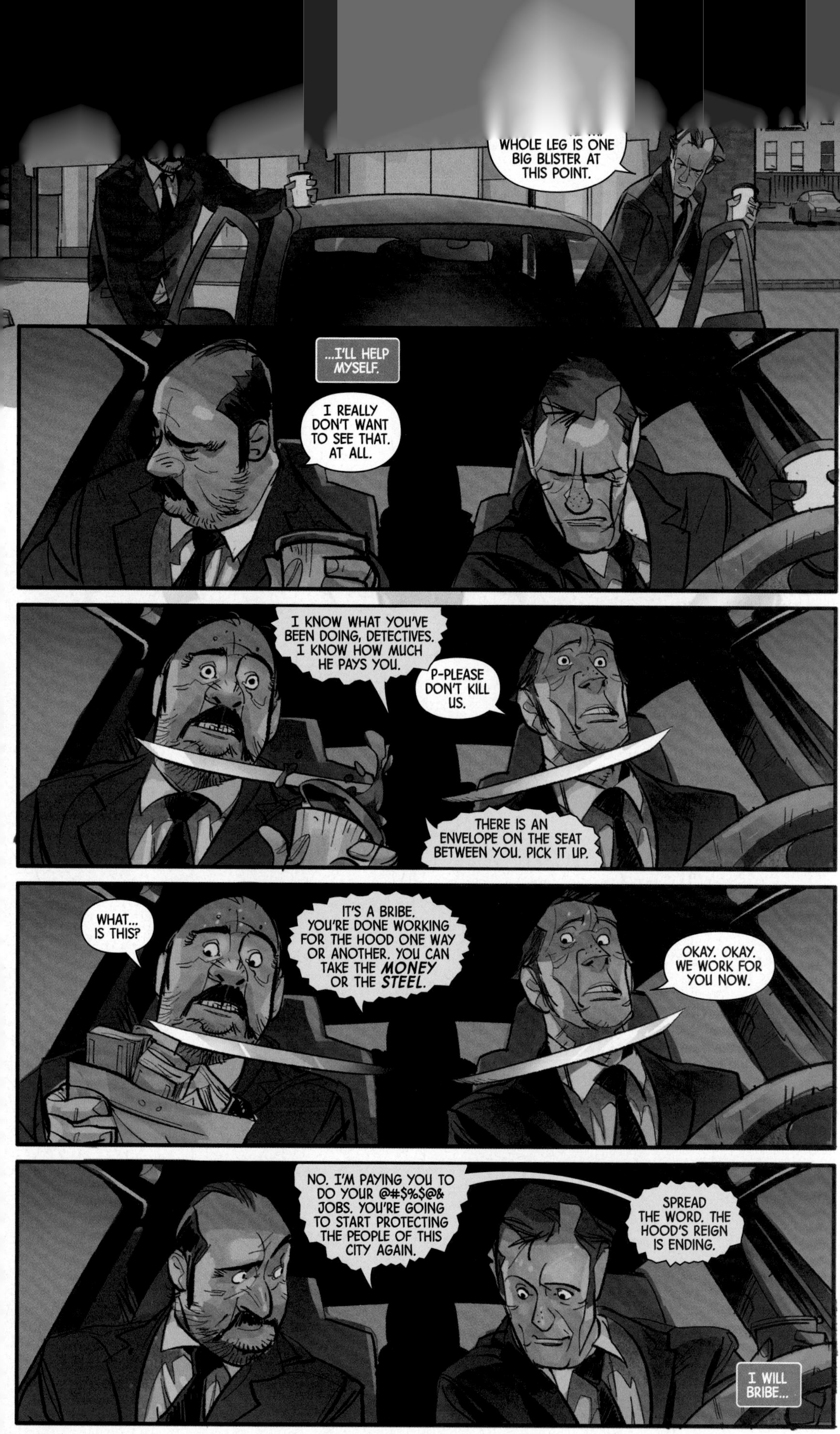
WHOLE LEG IS ONE BIG BLISTER AT THIS POINT.
...I'LL HELP MYSELF.
I REALLY DON'T WANT TO SEE THAT. AT ALL.
I KNOW WHAT YOU'VE BEEN DOING, DETECTIVES. I KNOW HOW MUCH HE PAYS YOU.
P-PLEASE DON'T KILL US.
THERE IS AN ENVELOPE ON THE SEAT BETWEEN YOU. PICK IT UP.
WHAT... IS THIS?
IT'S A BRIBE. YOU'RE DONE WORKING FOR THE HOOD ONE WAY OR ANOTHER. YOU CAN TAKE THE MONEY OR THE STEEL.
OKAY. OKAY. WE WORK FOR YOU NOW.
NO. I'M PAYING YOU TO DO YOUR @#$%$@& JOBS. YOU'RE GOING TO START PROTECTING THE PEOPLE OF THIS CITY AGAIN.
SPREAD THE WORD. THE HOOD'S REIGN IS ENDING.
I WILL BRIBE...

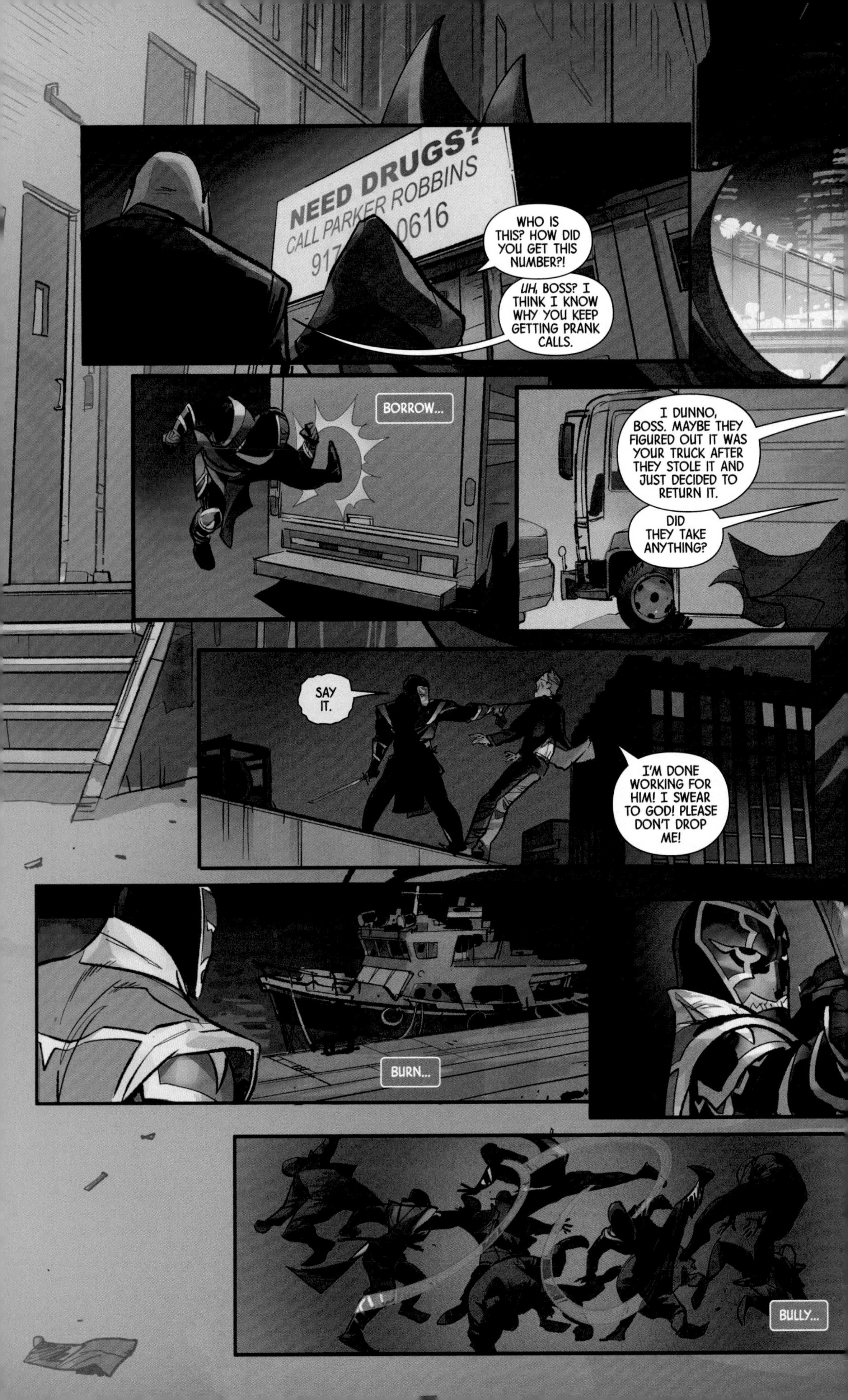

NEED DRUGS?
CALL PARKER ROBBINS
917 0616
WHO IS THIS? HOW DID YOU GET THIS NUMBER?!
UH, BOSS? I THINK I KNOW WHY YOU KEEP GETTING PRANK CALLS.
BORROW...
I DUNNO, BOSS. MAYBE THEY FIGURED OUT IT WAS YOUR TRUCK AFTER THEY STOLE IT AND JUST DECIDED TO RETURN IT.
DID THEY TAKE ANYTHING?
SAY IT.
I'M DONE WORKING FOR HIM! I SWEAR TO GOD! PLEASE DON'T DROP ME!
BURN...
BULLY...

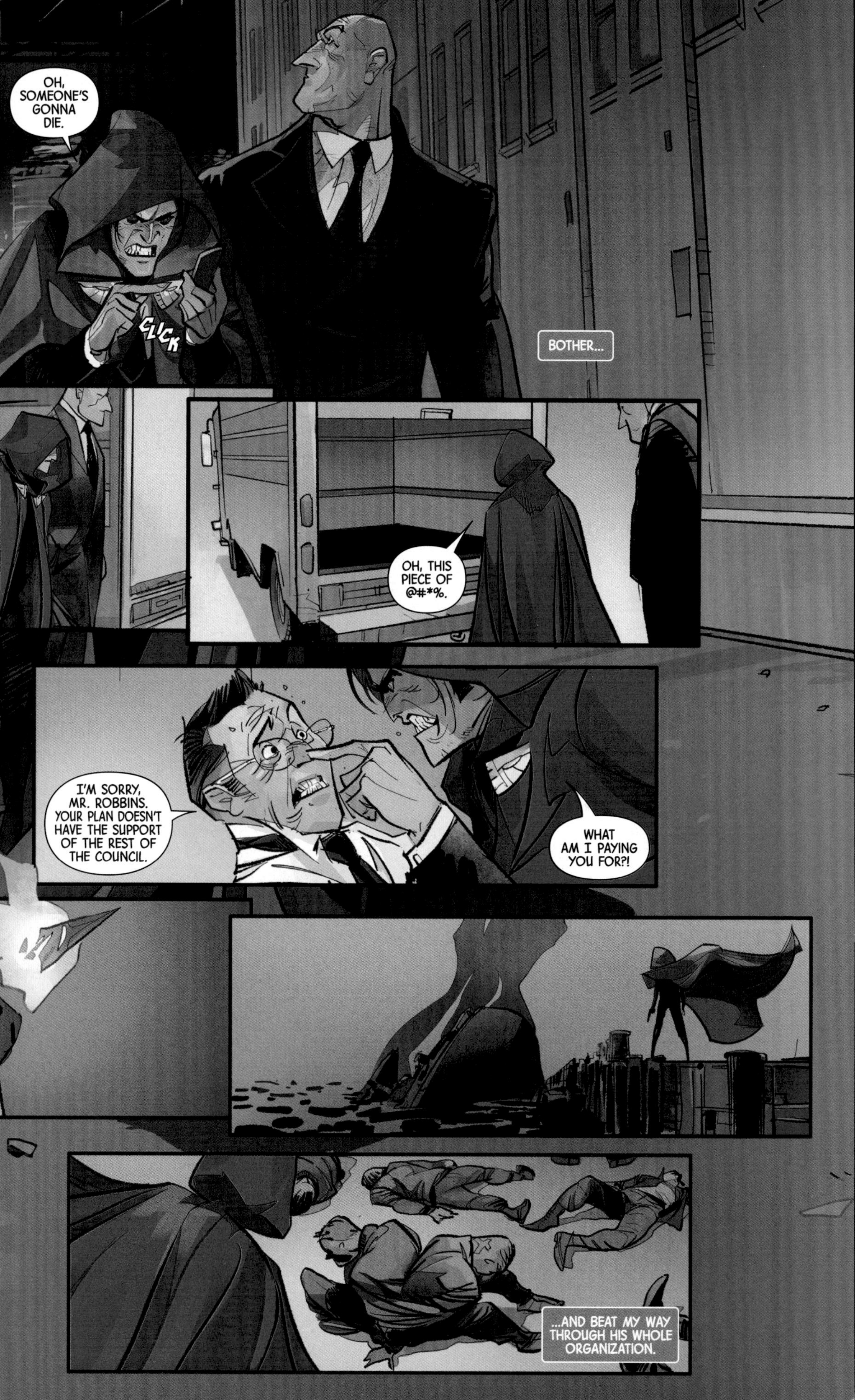
OH, SOMEONE'S GONNA DIE.
CLICK
BOTHER...
OH, THIS PIECE OF @#*%.
I'M SORRY, MR. ROBBINS. YOUR PLAN DOESN'T HAVE THE SUPPORT OF THE REST OF THE COUNCIL.
WHAT AM I PAYING YOU FOR?!
...AND BEAT MY WAY THROUGH HIS WHOLE ORGANIZATION.

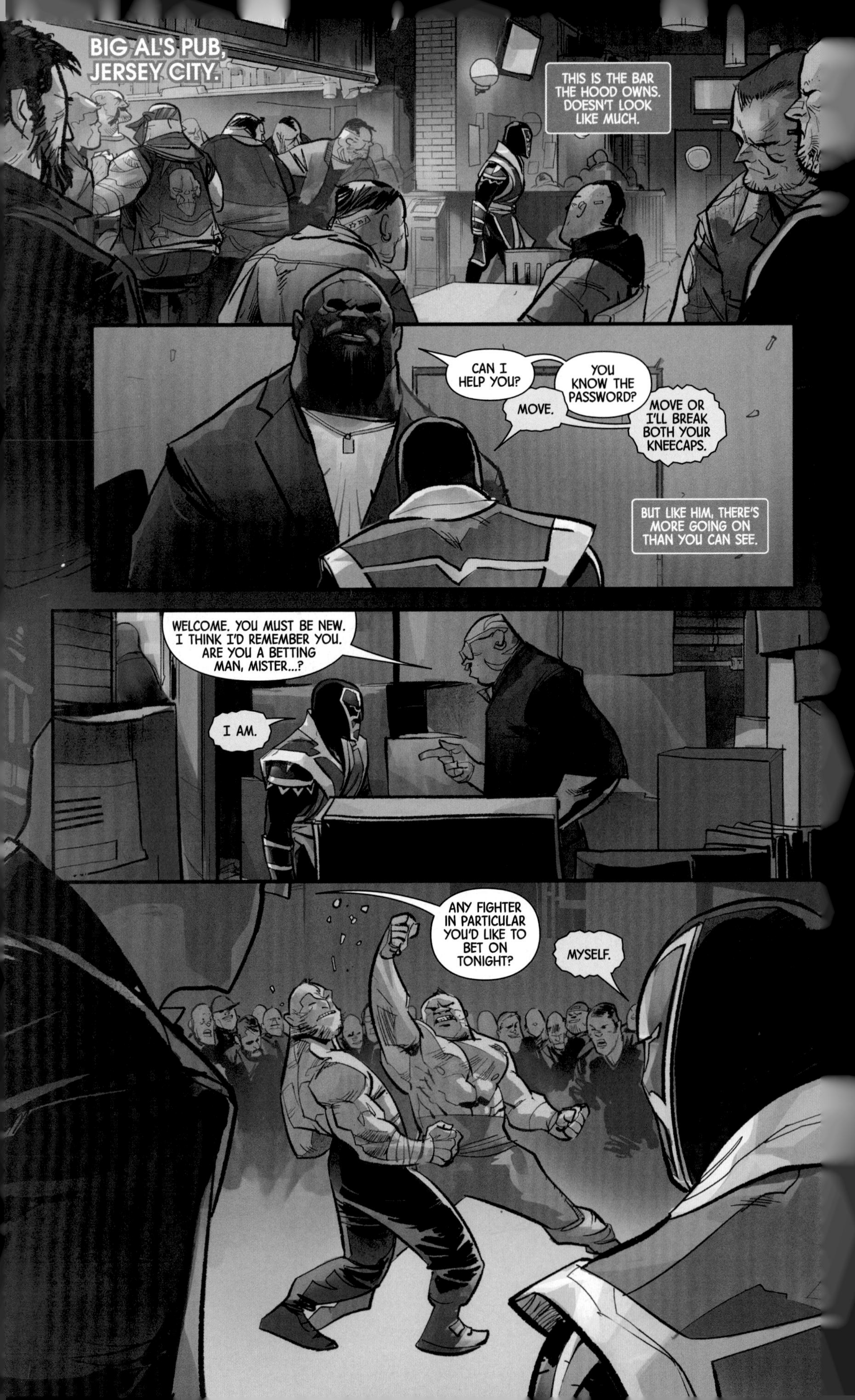
BIG AL'S PUB, JERSEY CITY.
THIS IS THE BAR THE HOOD OWNS. DOESN'T LOOK LIKE MUCH.
CAN I HELP YOU?
MOVE.
YOU KNOW THE PASSWORD?
MOVE OR I'LL BREAK BOTH YOUR KNEECAPS.
BUT LIKE HIM, THERE'S MORE GOING ON THAN YOU CAN SEE.
WELCOME. YOU MUST BE NEW. I THINK I'D REMEMBER YOU. ARE YOU A BETTING MAN, MISTER...?
I AM.
ANY FIGHTER IN PARTICULAR YOU'D LIKE TO BET ON TONIGHT?
MYSELF.

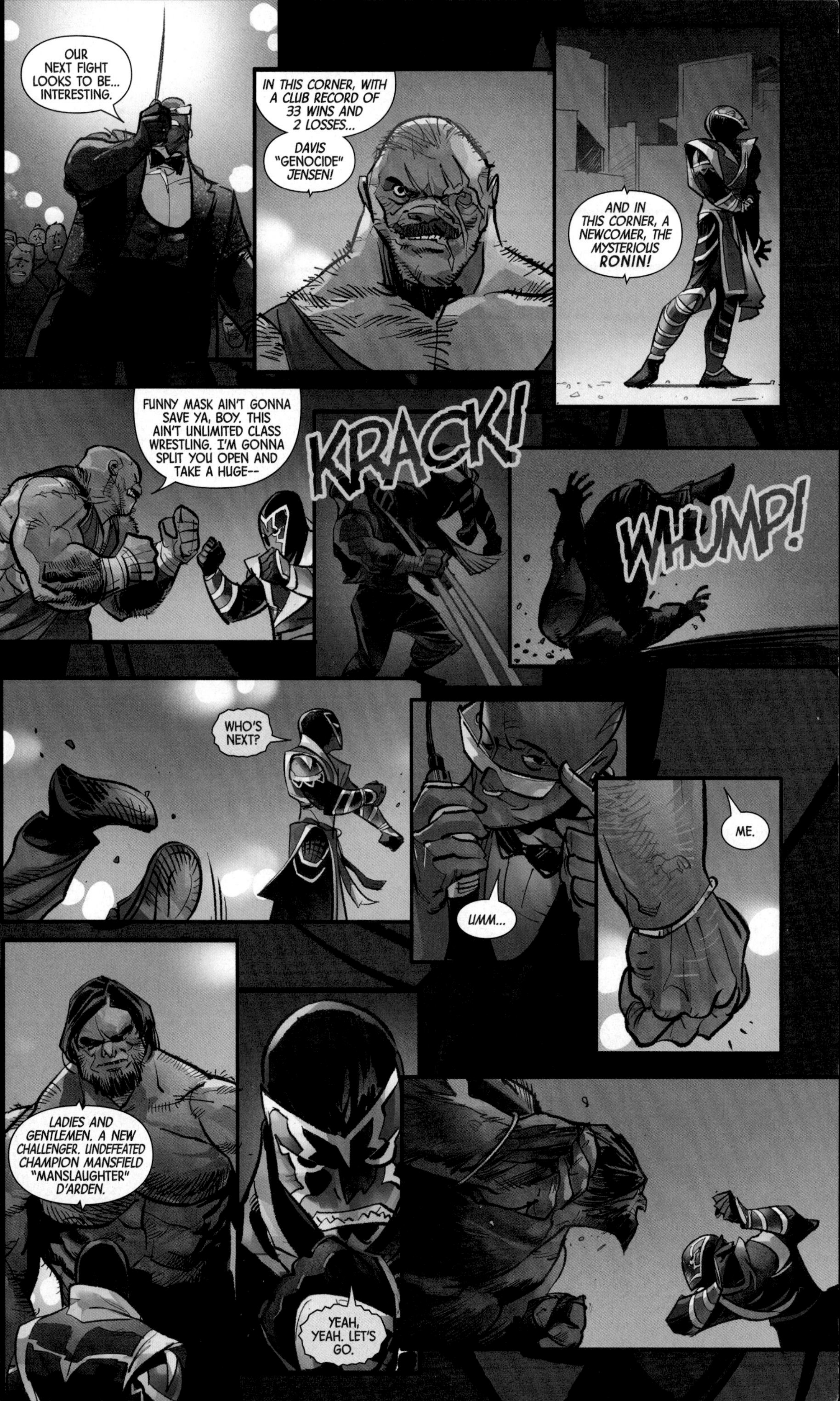
OUR NEXT FIGHT LOOKS TO BE... INTERESTING.
IN THIS CORNER, WITH A CLUB RECORD OF 33 WINS AND 2 LOSSES...
DAVIS "GENOCIDE" JENSEN!
AND IN THIS CORNER, A NEWCOMER, THE MYSTERIOUS RONIN!
FUNNY MASK AIN'T GONNA SAVE YA, BOY. THIS AIN'T UNLIMITED CLASS WRESTLING. I'M GONNA SPLIT YOU OPEN AND TAKE A HUGE--
KRACK!
WHUMP!
WHO'S NEXT?
UMM...
ME.
LADIES AND GENTLEMEN. A NEW CHALLENGER. UNDEFEATED CHAMPION MANSFIELD "MANSLAUGHTER" D'ARDEN.
YEAH, YEAH. LET'S GO.

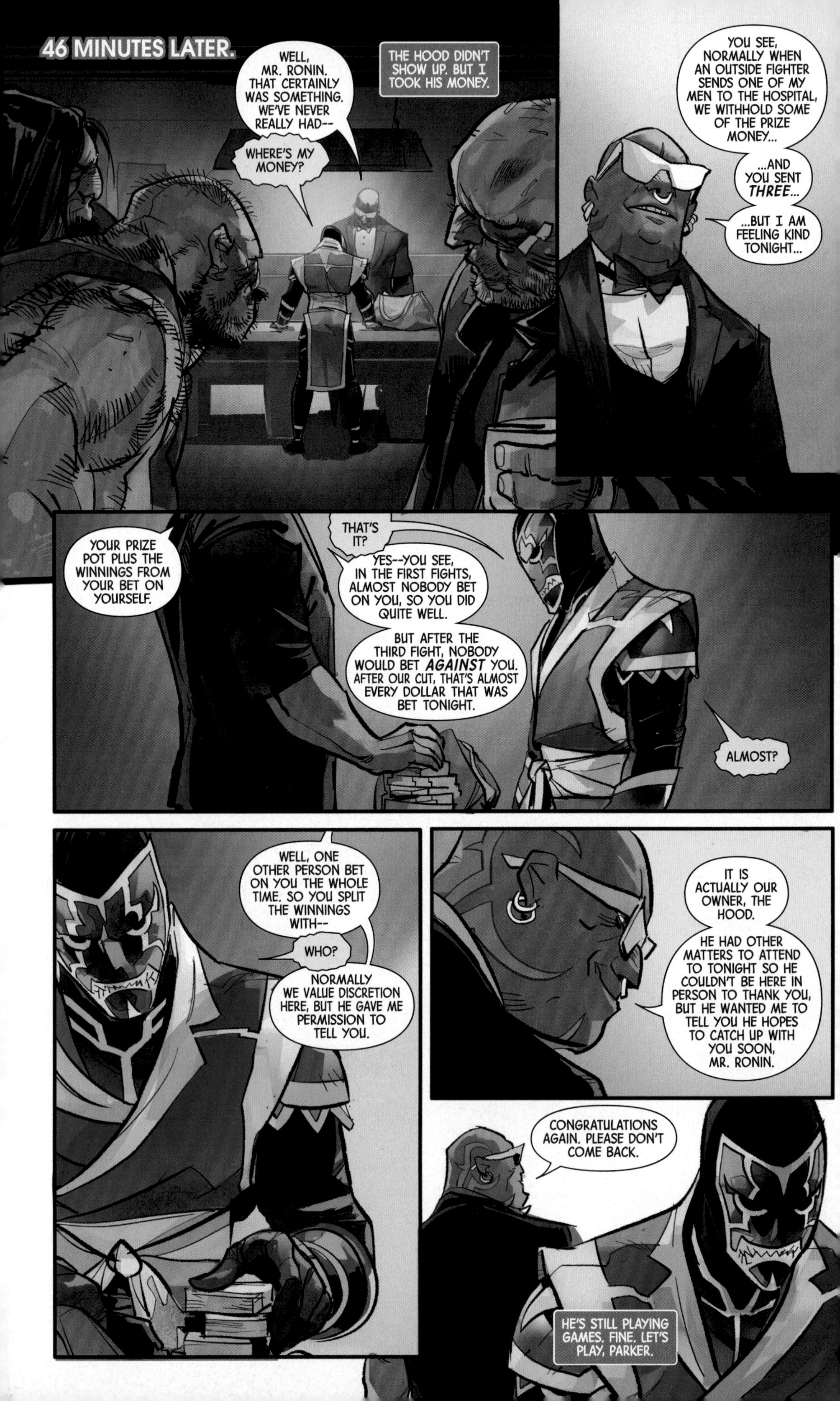
46 MINUTES LATER.
WELL, MR. RONIN. THAT CERTAINLY WAS SOMETHING. WE'VE NEVER REALLY HAD--
WHERE'S MY MONEY?
THE HOOD DIDN'T SHOW UP. BUT I TOOK HIS MONEY.
YOU SEE, NORMALLY WHEN AN OUTSIDE FIGHTER SENDS ONE OF MY MEN TO THE HOSPITAL, WE WITHHOLD SOME OF THE PRIZE MONEY...
...AND YOU SENT THREE...
...BUT I AM FEELING KIND TONIGHT...
YOUR PRIZE POT PLUS THE WINNINGS FROM YOUR BET ON YOURSELF.
THAT'S IT?
YES--YOU SEE, IN THE FIRST FIGHTS, ALMOST NOBODY BET ON YOU, SO YOU DID QUITE WELL.
BUT AFTER THE THIRD FIGHT, NOBODY WOULD BET AGAINST YOU. AFTER OUR CUT, THAT'S ALMOST EVERY DOLLAR THAT WAS BET TONIGHT.
ALMOST?
WELL, ONE OTHER PERSON BET ON YOU THE WHOLE TIME. SO YOU SPLIT THE WINNINGS WITH--
WHO?
NORMALLY WE VALUE DISCRETION HERE, BUT HE GAVE ME PERMISSION TO TELL YOU.
IT IS ACTUALLY OUR OWNER, THE HOOD.
HE HAD OTHER MATTERS TO ATTEND TO TONIGHT SO HE COULDN'T BE HERE IN PERSON TO THANK YOU, BUT HE WANTED ME TO TELL YOU HE HOPES TO CATCH UP WITH YOU SOON, MR. RONIN.
CONGRATULATIONS AGAIN. PLEASE DON'T COME BACK.
HE'S STILL PLAYING GAMES. FINE. LET'S PLAY, PARKER.

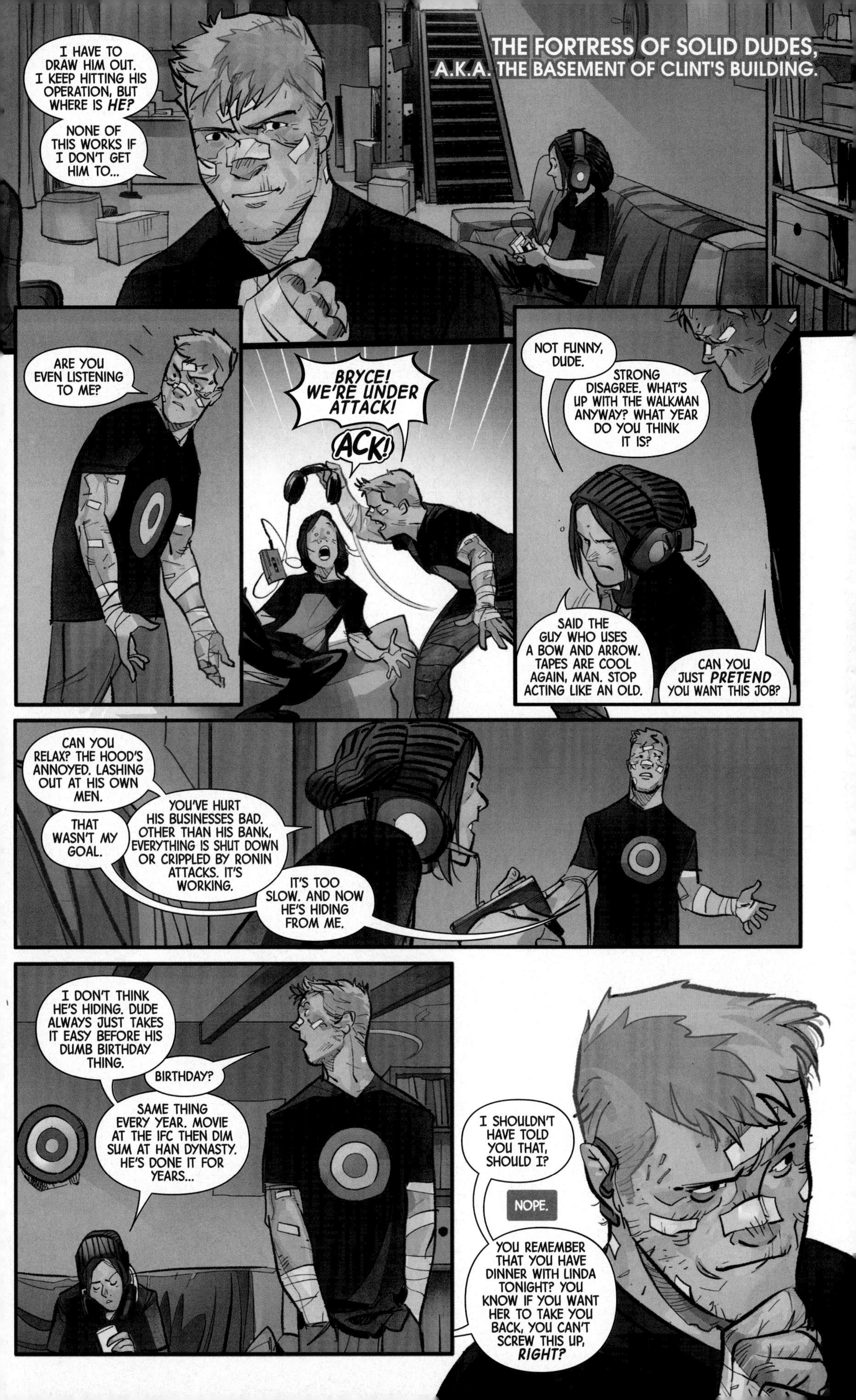
THE FORTRESS OF SOLID DUDES,
A.K.A. THE BASEMENT OF CLINT'S BUILDING.
I HAVE TO DRAW HIM OUT. I KEEP HITTING HIS OPERATION, BUT WHERE IS HE?
NONE OF THIS WORKS IF I DON'T GET HIM TO...
ARE YOU EVEN LISTENING TO ME?
BRYCE! WE'RE UNDER ATTACK!
ACK!
NOT FUNNY, DUDE.
STRONG DISAGREE. WHAT'S UP WITH THE WALKMAN ANYWAY? WHAT YEAR DO YOU THINK IT IS?
SAID THE GUY WHO USES A BOW AND ARROW. TAPES ARE COOL AGAIN, MAN. STOP ACTING LIKE AN OLD.
CAN YOU JUST PRETEND YOU WANT THIS JOB?
CAN YOU RELAX? THE HOOD'S ANNOYED. LASHING OUT AT HIS OWN MEN.
THAT WASN'T MY GOAL.
YOU'VE HURT HIS BUSINESSES BAD. OTHER THAN HIS BANK, EVERYTHING IS SHUT DOWN OR CRIPPLED BY RONIN ATTACKS. IT'S WORKING.
IT'S TOO SLOW. AND NOW HE'S HIDING FROM ME.
I DON'T THINK HE'S HIDING. DUDE ALWAYS JUST TAKES IT EASY BEFORE HIS DUMB BIRTHDAY THING.
BIRTHDAY?
SAME THING EVERY YEAR. MOVIE AT THE IFC THEN DIM SUM AT HAN DYNASTY. HE'S DONE IT FOR YEARS...
I SHOULDN'T HAVE TOLD YOU THAT, SHOULD I?
NOPE.
YOU REMEMBER THAT YOU HAVE DINNER WITH LINDA TONIGHT? YOU KNOW IF YOU WANT HER TO TAKE YOU BACK, YOU CAN'T SCREW THIS UP, RIGHT?

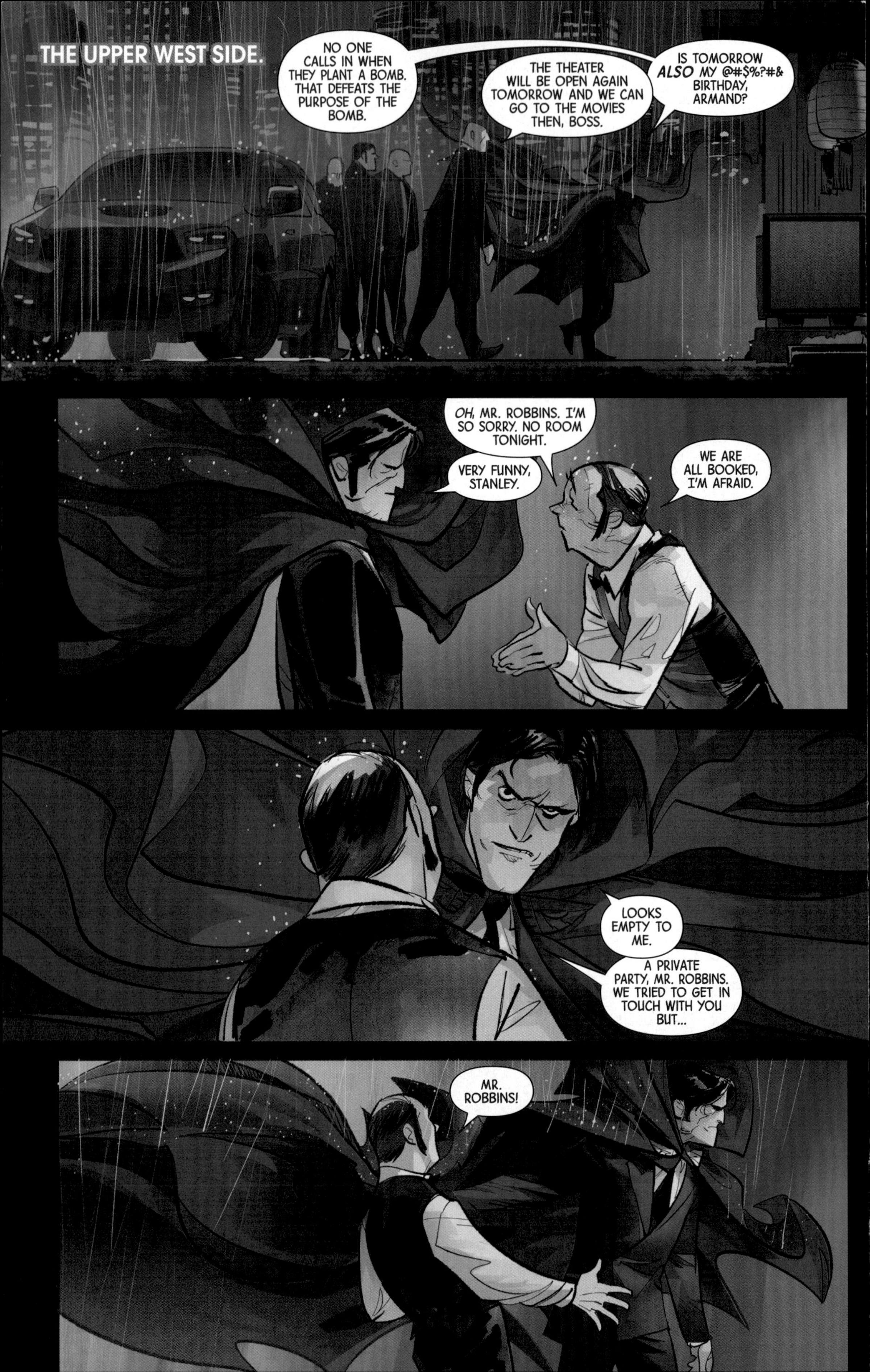
THE UPPER WEST SIDE.
NO ONE CALLS IN WHEN THEY PLANT A BOMB. THAT DEFEATS THE PURPOSE OF THE BOMB.
THE THEATER WILL BE OPEN AGAIN TOMORROW AND WE CAN GO TO THE MOVIES THEN, BOSS.
IS TOMORROW ALSO MY @#$%?#& BIRTHDAY, ARMAND?
OH, MR. ROBBINS. I'M SO SORRY. NO ROOM TONIGHT.
VERY FUNNY, STANLEY.
WE ARE ALL BOOKED, I'M AFRAID.
LOOKS EMPTY TO ME.
A PRIVATE PARTY, MR. ROBBINS. WE TRIED TO GET IN TOUCH WITH YOU BUT...
MR. ROBBINS!

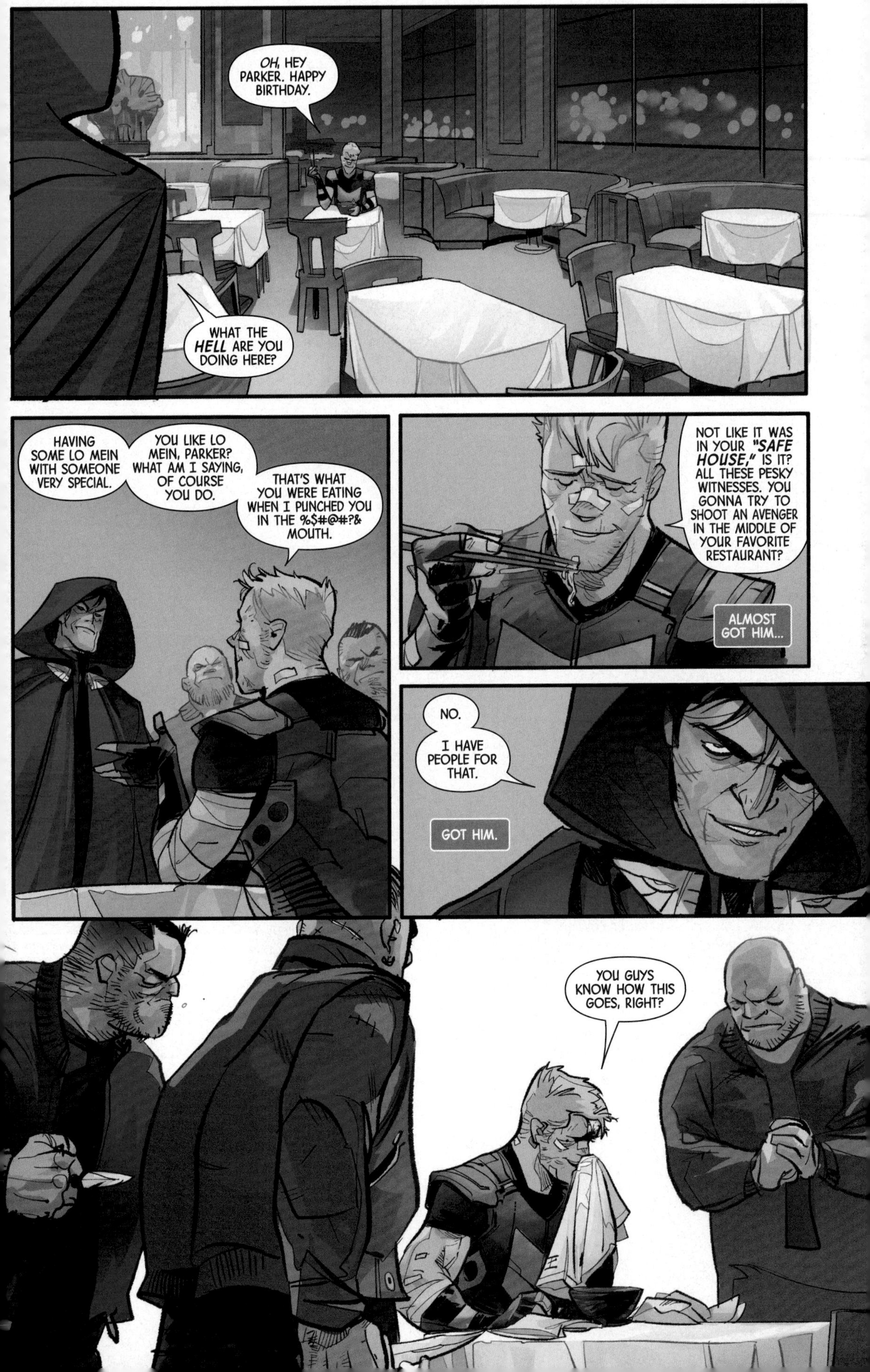
OH, HEY PARKER. HAPPY BIRTHDAY.
WHAT THE *HELL* ARE YOU DOING HERE?
HAVING SOME LO MEIN WITH SOMEONE VERY SPECIAL.
YOU LIKE LO MEIN, PARKER? WHAT AM I SAYING, OF COURSE YOU DO.
THAT'S WHAT YOU WERE EATING WHEN I PUNCHED YOU IN THE %$#@#?& MOUTH.
NOT LIKE IT WAS IN YOUR *"SAFE HOUSE,"* IS IT? ALL THESE PESKY WITNESSES. YOU GONNA TRY TO SHOOT AN AVENGER IN THE MIDDLE OF YOUR FAVORITE RESTAURANT?
ALMOST GOT HIM...
NO.
I HAVE PEOPLE FOR THAT.
GOT HIM.
YOU GUYS KNOW HOW THIS GOES, RIGHT?

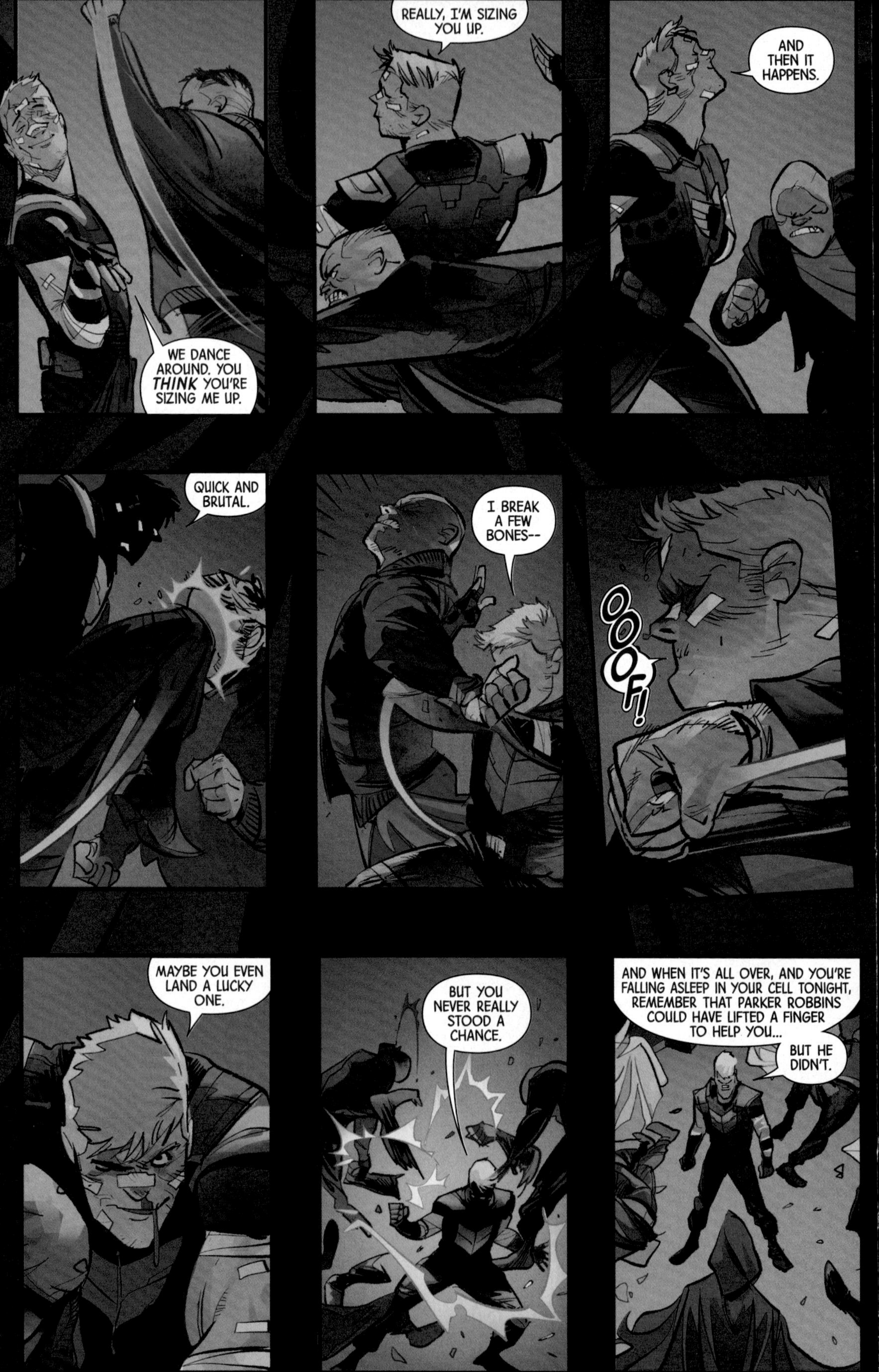
WE DANCE AROUND. YOU THINK YOU'RE SIZING ME UP.
REALLY, I'M SIZING YOU UP.
AND THEN IT HAPPENS.
QUICK AND BRUTAL.
I BREAK A FEW BONES--
OOOOF!
MAYBE YOU EVEN LAND A LUCKY ONE.
BUT YOU NEVER REALLY STOOD A CHANCE.
AND WHEN IT'S ALL OVER, AND YOU'RE FALLING ASLEEP IN YOUR CELL TONIGHT, REMEMBER THAT PARKER ROBBINS COULD HAVE LIFTED A FINGER TO HELP YOU...
BUT HE DIDN'T.

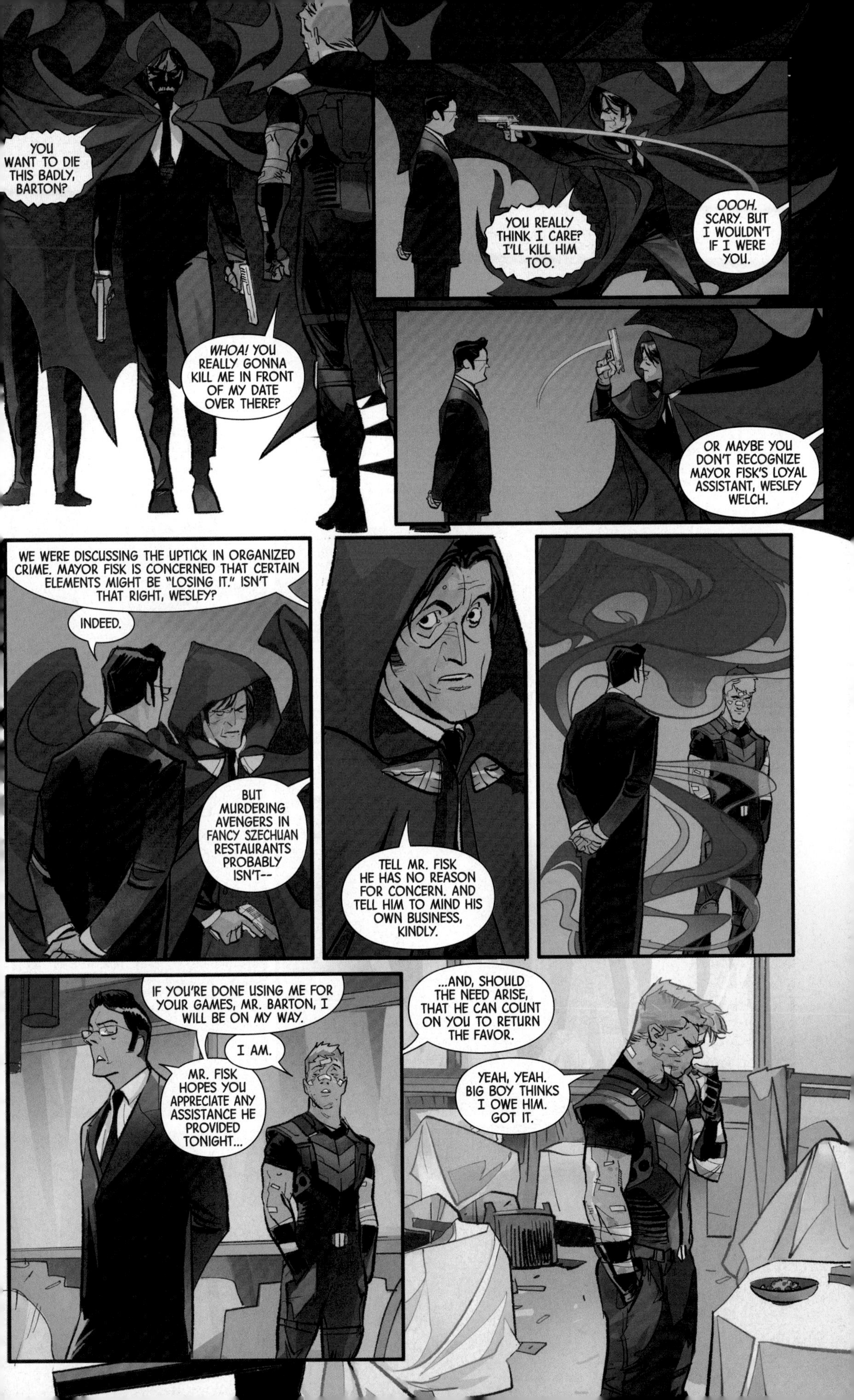

YOU WANT TO DIE THIS BADLY, BARTON?
WHOA! YOU REALLY GONNA KILL ME IN FRONT OF MY DATE OVER THERE?
YOU REALLY THINK I CARE? I'LL KILL HIM TOO.
OOOH. SCARY. BUT I WOULDN'T IF I WERE YOU.
OR MAYBE YOU DON'T RECOGNIZE MAYOR FISK'S LOYAL ASSISTANT, WESLEY WELCH.
WE WERE DISCUSSING THE UPTICK IN ORGANIZED CRIME. MAYOR FISK IS CONCERNED THAT CERTAIN ELEMENTS MIGHT BE "LOSING IT." ISN'T THAT RIGHT, WESLEY?
INDEED.
BUT MURDERING AVENGERS IN FANCY SZECHUAN RESTAURANTS PROBABLY ISN'T--
TELL MR. FISK HE HAS NO REASON FOR CONCERN. AND TELL HIM TO MIND HIS OWN BUSINESS, KINDLY.
IF YOU'RE DONE USING ME FOR YOUR GAMES, MR. BARTON, I WILL BE ON MY WAY.
I AM.
MR. FISK HOPES YOU APPRECIATE ANY ASSISTANCE HE PROVIDED TONIGHT...
...AND, SHOULD THE NEED ARISE, THAT HE CAN COUNT ON YOU TO RETURN THE FAVOR.
YEAH, YEAH. BIG BOY THINKS I OWE HIM. GOT IT.

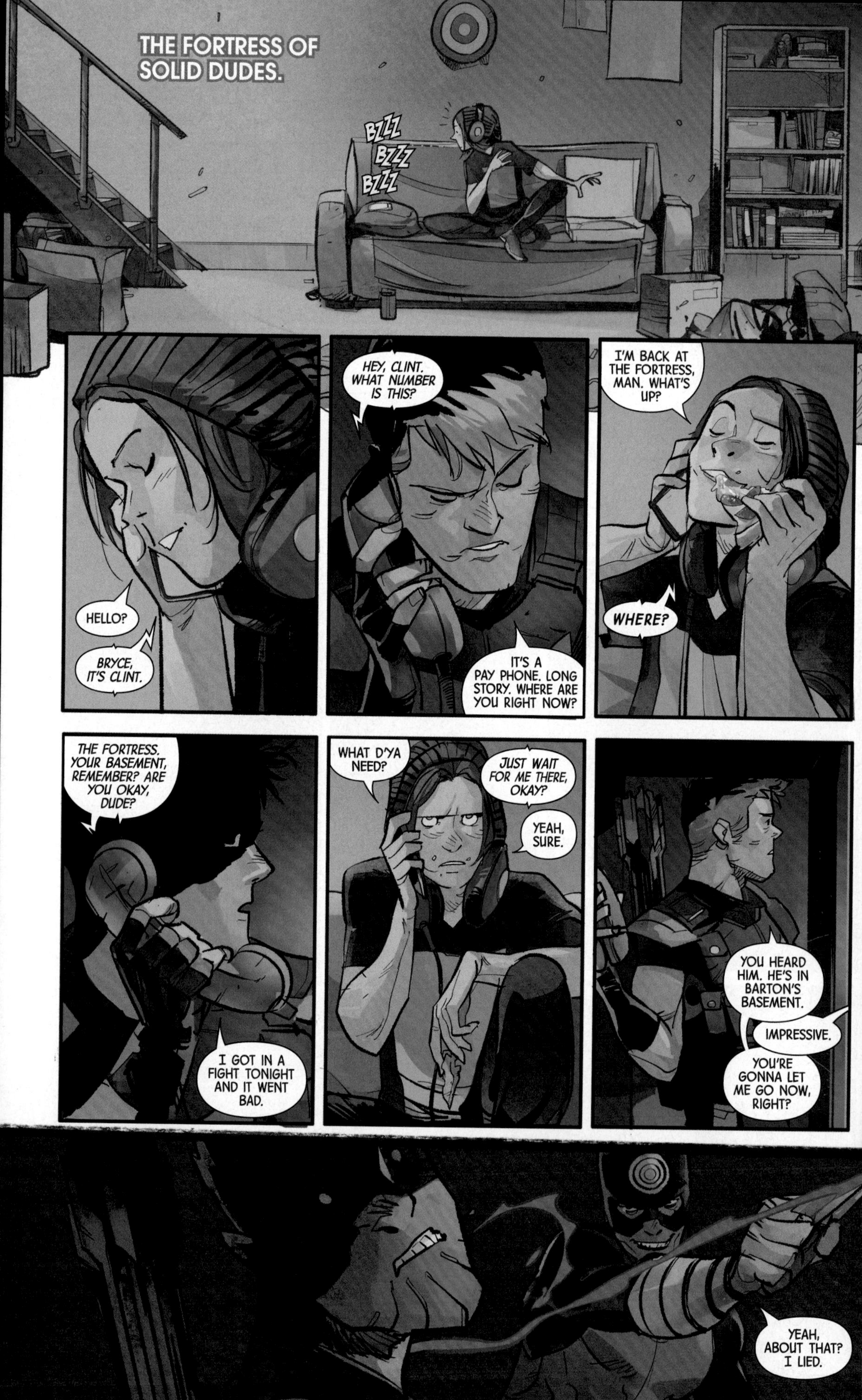
THE FORTRESS OF SOLID DUDES.
BZZZ
BZZZ
BZZZ
HELLO?
BRYCE, IT'S CLINT.
HEY, CLINT. WHAT NUMBER IS THIS?
IT'S A PAY PHONE. LONG STORY. WHERE ARE YOU RIGHT NOW?
I'M BACK AT THE FORTRESS, MAN. WHAT'S UP?
WHERE?
THE FORTRESS. YOUR BASEMENT, REMEMBER? ARE YOU OKAY, DUDE?
I GOT IN A FIGHT TONIGHT AND IT WENT BAD.
WHAT D'YA NEED?
JUST WAIT FOR ME THERE, OKAY?
YEAH, SURE.
YOU HEARD HIM. HE'S IN BARTON'S BASEMENT.
IMPRESSIVE.
YOU'RE GONNA LET ME GO NOW, RIGHT?
YEAH, ABOUT THAT? I LIED.

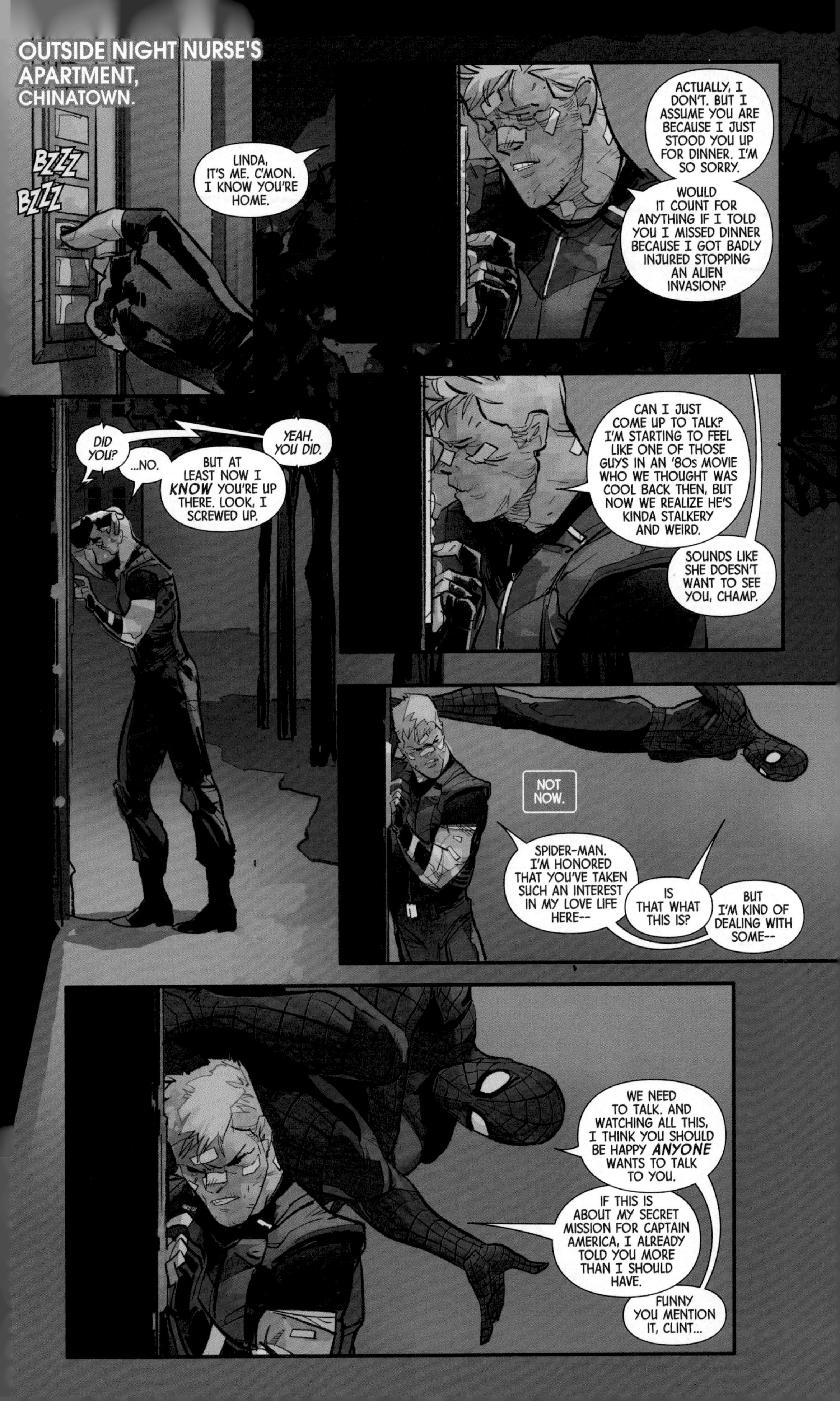

OUTSIDE NIGHT NURSE'S APARTMENT, CHINATOWN.
BZZZ BZZZ
LINDA, IT'S ME. C'MON. I KNOW YOU'RE HOME.
ACTUALLY, I DON'T. BUT I ASSUME YOU ARE BECAUSE I JUST STOOD YOU UP FOR DINNER. I'M SO SORRY.
WOULD IT COUNT FOR ANYTHING IF I TOLD YOU I MISSED DINNER BECAUSE I GOT BADLY INJURED STOPPING AN ALIEN INVASION?
DID YOU?
...NO.
YEAH. YOU DID.
BUT AT LEAST NOW I **KNOW** YOU'RE UP THERE. LOOK, I SCREWED UP.
CAN I JUST COME UP TO TALK? I'M STARTING TO FEEL LIKE ONE OF THOSE GUYS IN AN '80s MOVIE WHO WE THOUGHT WAS COOL BACK THEN, BUT NOW WE REALIZE HE'S KINDA STALKERY AND WEIRD.
SOUNDS LIKE SHE DOESN'T WANT TO SEE YOU, CHAMP.
NOT NOW.
SPIDER-MAN. I'M HONORED THAT YOU'VE TAKEN SUCH AN INTEREST IN MY LOVE LIFE HERE--
IS THAT WHAT THIS IS?
BUT I'M KIND OF DEALING WITH SOME--
WE NEED TO TALK. AND WATCHING ALL THIS, I THINK YOU SHOULD BE HAPPY **ANYONE** WANTS TO TALK TO YOU.
IF THIS IS ABOUT MY SECRET MISSION FOR CAPTAIN AMERICA, I ALREADY TOLD YOU MORE THAN I SHOULD HAVE.
FUNNY YOU MENTION IT, CLINT...

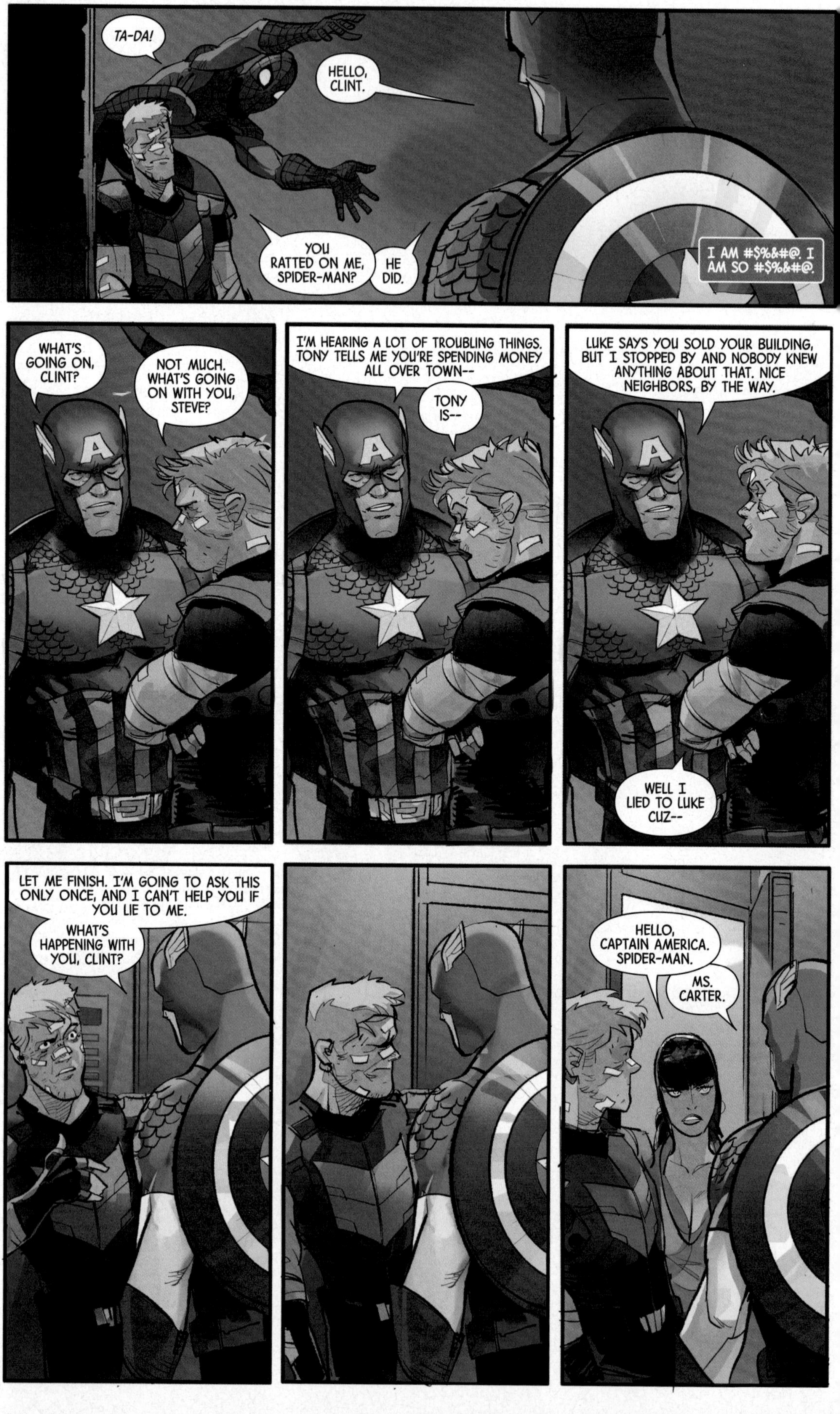
TA-DA!
HELLO, CLINT.
YOU RATTED ON ME, SPIDER-MAN?
HE DID.
I AM #$%&#@. I AM SO #$%&#@.
WHAT'S GOING ON, CLINT?
NOT MUCH. WHAT'S GOING ON WITH YOU, STEVE?
I'M HEARING A LOT OF TROUBLING THINGS. TONY TELLS ME YOU'RE SPENDING MONEY ALL OVER TOWN--
TONY IS--
LUKE SAYS YOU SOLD YOUR BUILDING, BUT I STOPPED BY AND NOBODY KNEW ANYTHING ABOUT THAT. NICE NEIGHBORS, BY THE WAY.
WELL I LIED TO LUKE CUZ--
LET ME FINISH. I'M GOING TO ASK THIS ONLY ONCE, AND I CAN'T HELP YOU IF YOU LIE TO ME.
WHAT'S HAPPENING WITH YOU, CLINT?
HELLO, CAPTAIN AMERICA. SPIDER-MAN.
MS. CARTER.

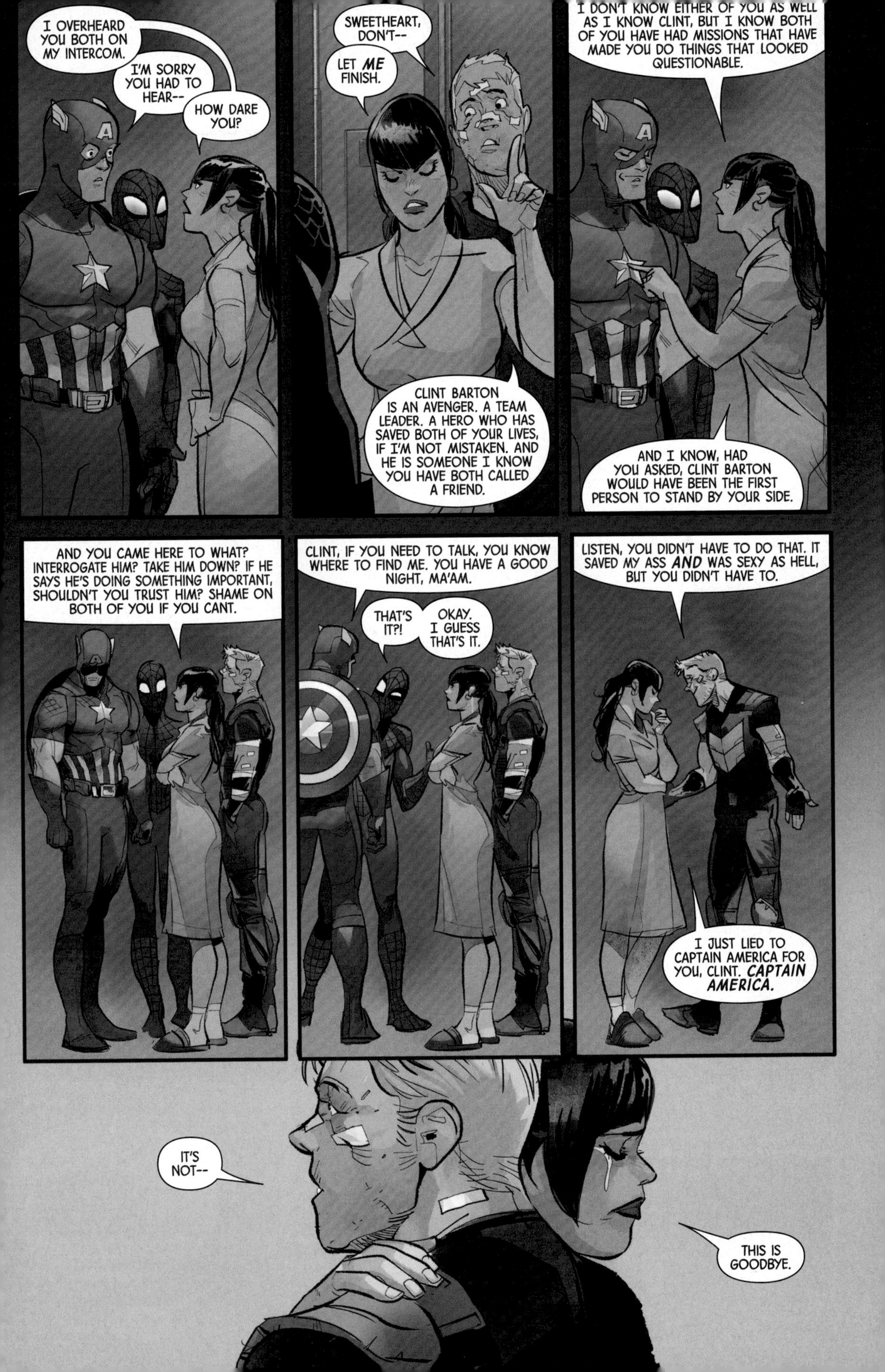
I OVERHEARD YOU BOTH ON MY INTERCOM.
I'M SORRY YOU HAD TO HEAR--
HOW DARE YOU?
SWEETHEART, DON'T--
LET ME FINISH.
CLINT BARTON IS AN AVENGER. A TEAM LEADER. A HERO WHO HAS SAVED BOTH OF YOUR LIVES, IF I'M NOT MISTAKEN. AND HE IS SOMEONE I KNOW YOU HAVE BOTH CALLED A FRIEND.
I DON'T KNOW EITHER OF YOU AS WELL AS I KNOW CLINT, BUT I KNOW BOTH OF YOU HAVE HAD MISSIONS THAT HAVE MADE YOU DO THINGS THAT LOOKED QUESTIONABLE.
AND I KNOW, HAD YOU ASKED, CLINT BARTON WOULD HAVE BEEN THE FIRST PERSON TO STAND BY YOUR SIDE.
AND YOU CAME HERE TO WHAT? INTERROGATE HIM? TAKE HIM DOWN? IF HE SAYS HE'S DOING SOMETHING IMPORTANT, SHOULDN'T YOU TRUST HIM? SHAME ON BOTH OF YOU IF YOU CANT.
CLINT, IF YOU NEED TO TALK, YOU KNOW WHERE TO FIND ME. YOU HAVE A GOOD NIGHT, MA'AM.
THAT'S IT?!
OKAY. I GUESS THAT'S IT.
LISTEN, YOU DIDN'T HAVE TO DO THAT. IT SAVED MY ASS AND WAS SEXY AS HELL, BUT YOU DIDN'T HAVE TO.
I JUST LIED TO CAPTAIN AMERICA FOR YOU, CLINT. CAPTAIN AMERICA.
IT'S NOT--
THIS IS GOODBYE.

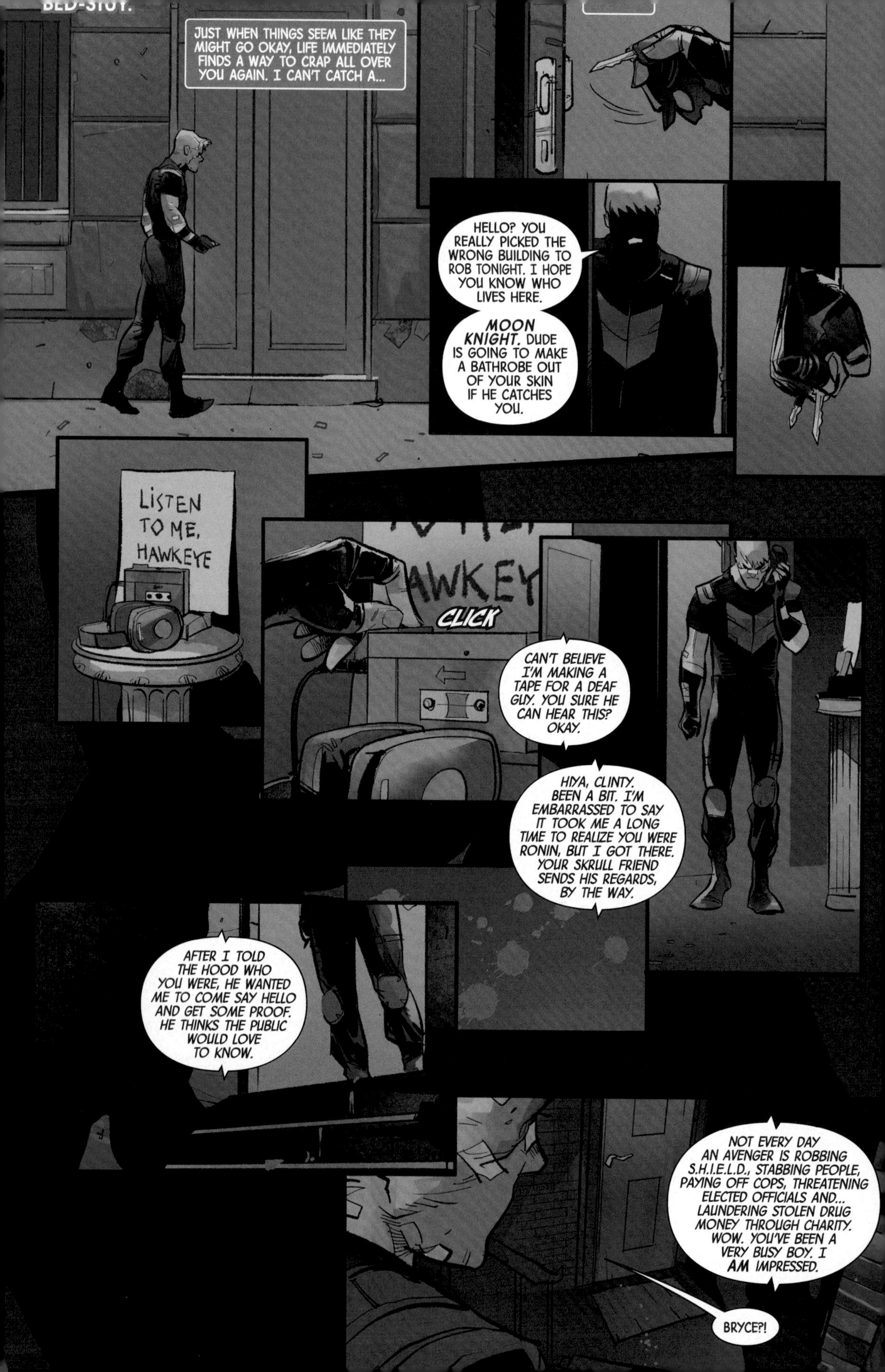
BED-STUY.
JUST WHEN THINGS SEEM LIKE THEY MIGHT GO OKAY, LIFE IMMEDIATELY FINDS A WAY TO CRAP ALL OVER YOU AGAIN. I CAN'T CATCH A...
HELLO? YOU REALLY PICKED THE WRONG BUILDING TO ROB TONIGHT. I HOPE YOU KNOW WHO LIVES HERE.
MOON KNIGHT. DUDE IS GOING TO MAKE A BATHROBE OUT OF YOUR SKIN IF HE CATCHES YOU.
LISTEN TO ME, HAWKEYE
CLICK
CAN'T BELIEVE I'M MAKING A TAPE FOR A DEAF GUY. YOU SURE HE CAN HEAR THIS? OKAY.
HIYA, CLINTY. BEEN A BIT. I'M EMBARRASSED TO SAY IT TOOK ME A LONG TIME TO REALIZE YOU WERE RONIN, BUT I GOT THERE. YOUR SKRULL FRIEND SENDS HIS REGARDS, BY THE WAY.
AFTER I TOLD THE HOOD WHO YOU WERE, HE WANTED ME TO COME SAY HELLO AND GET SOME PROOF. HE THINKS THE PUBLIC WOULD LOVE TO KNOW.
NOT EVERY DAY AN AVENGER IS ROBBING S.H.I.E.L.D., STABBING PEOPLE, PAYING OFF COPS, THREATENING ELECTED OFFICIALS AND... LAUNDERING STOLEN DRUG MONEY THROUGH CHARITY. WOW. YOU'VE BEEN A VERY BUSY BOY. I AM IMPRESSED.
BRYCE?!

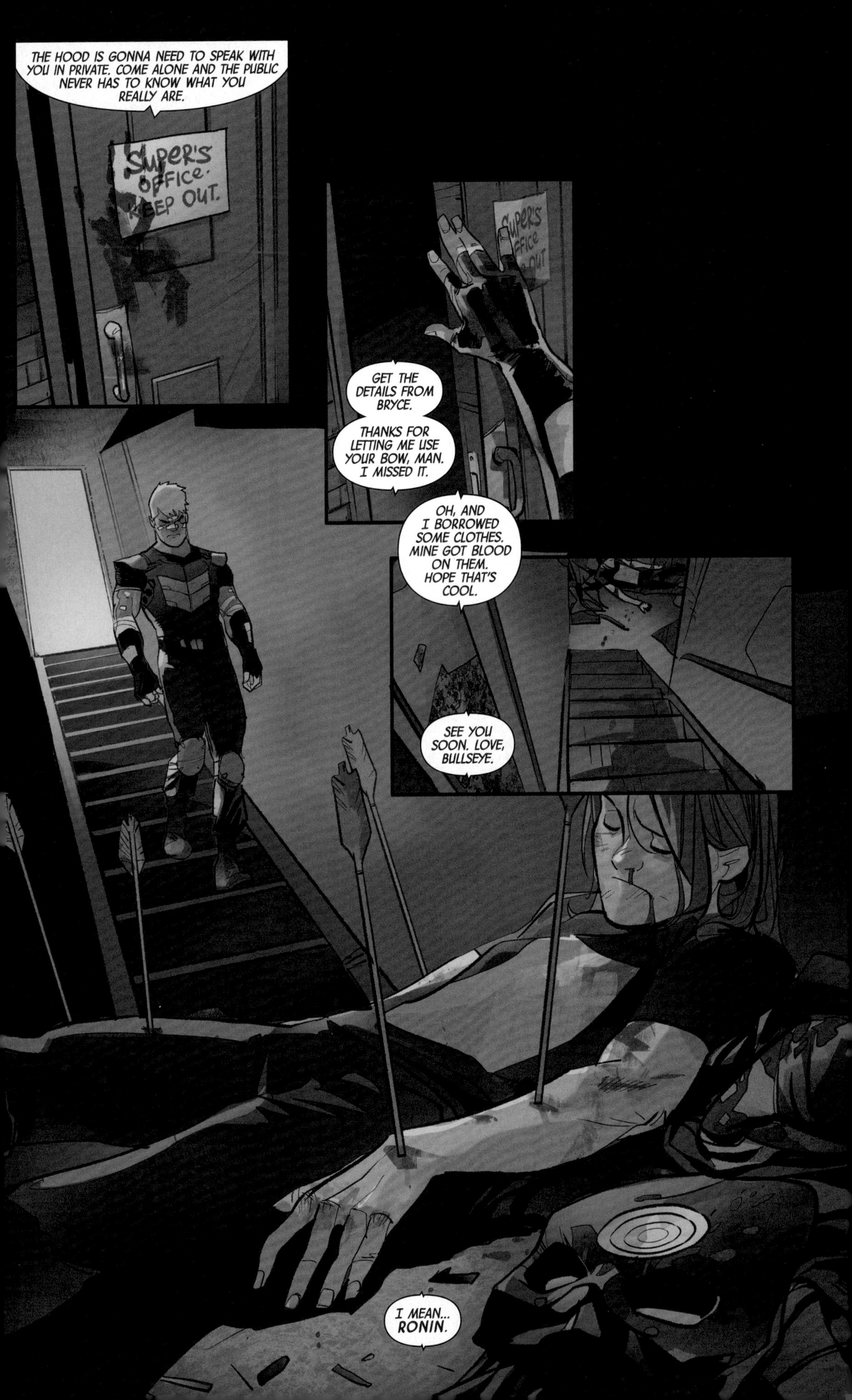
THE HOOD IS GONNA NEED TO SPEAK WITH YOU IN PRIVATE. COME ALONE AND THE PUBLIC NEVER HAS TO KNOW WHAT YOU REALLY ARE.
SUPER'S OFFICE. KEEP OUT.
GET THE DETAILS FROM BRYCE.
THANKS FOR LETTING ME USE YOUR BOW, MAN. I MISSED IT.
OH, AND I BORROWED SOME CLOTHES. MINE GOT BLOOD ON THEM. HOPE THAT'S COOL.
SEE YOU SOON. LOVE, BULLSEYE.
I MEAN... RONIN.

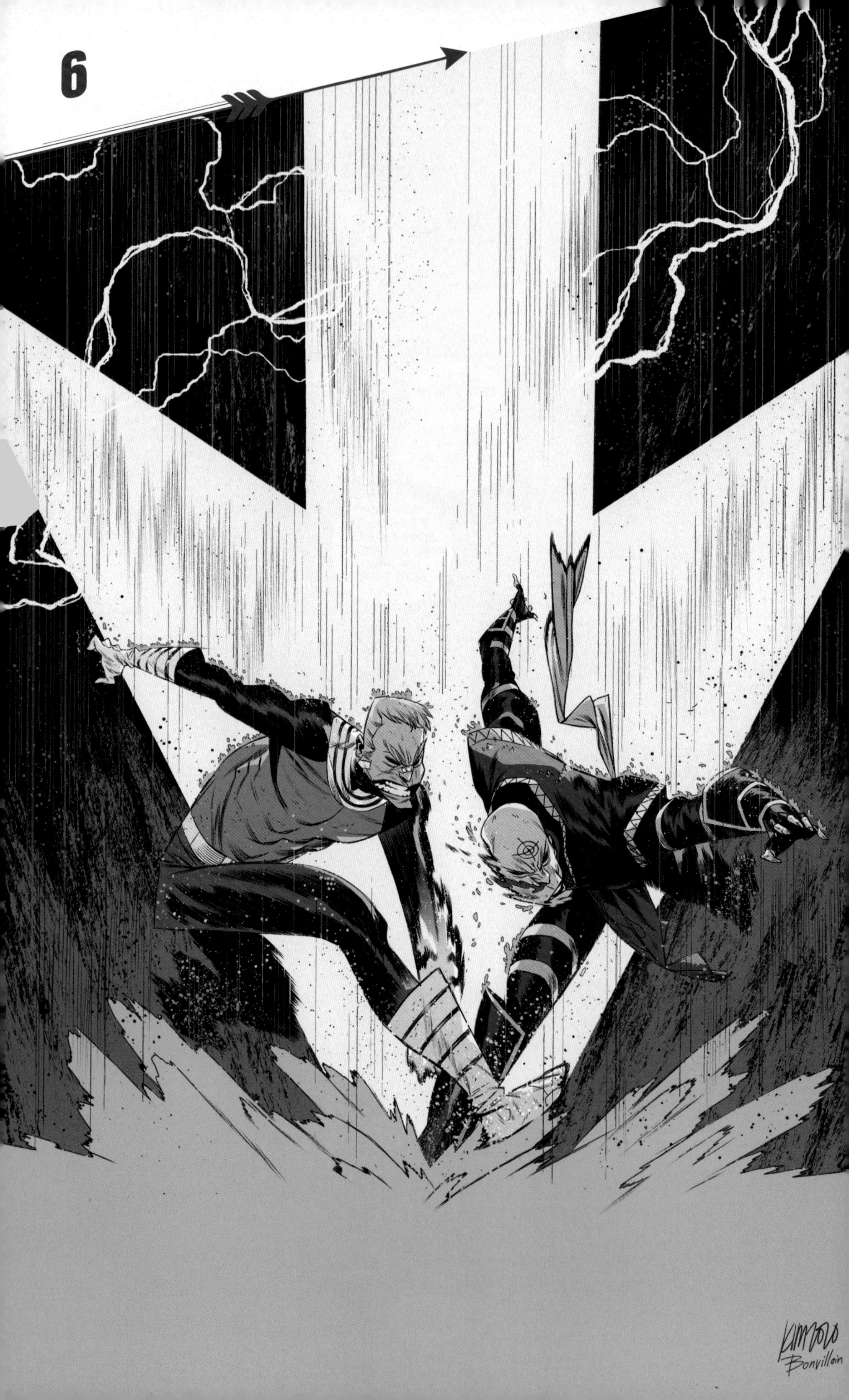
6

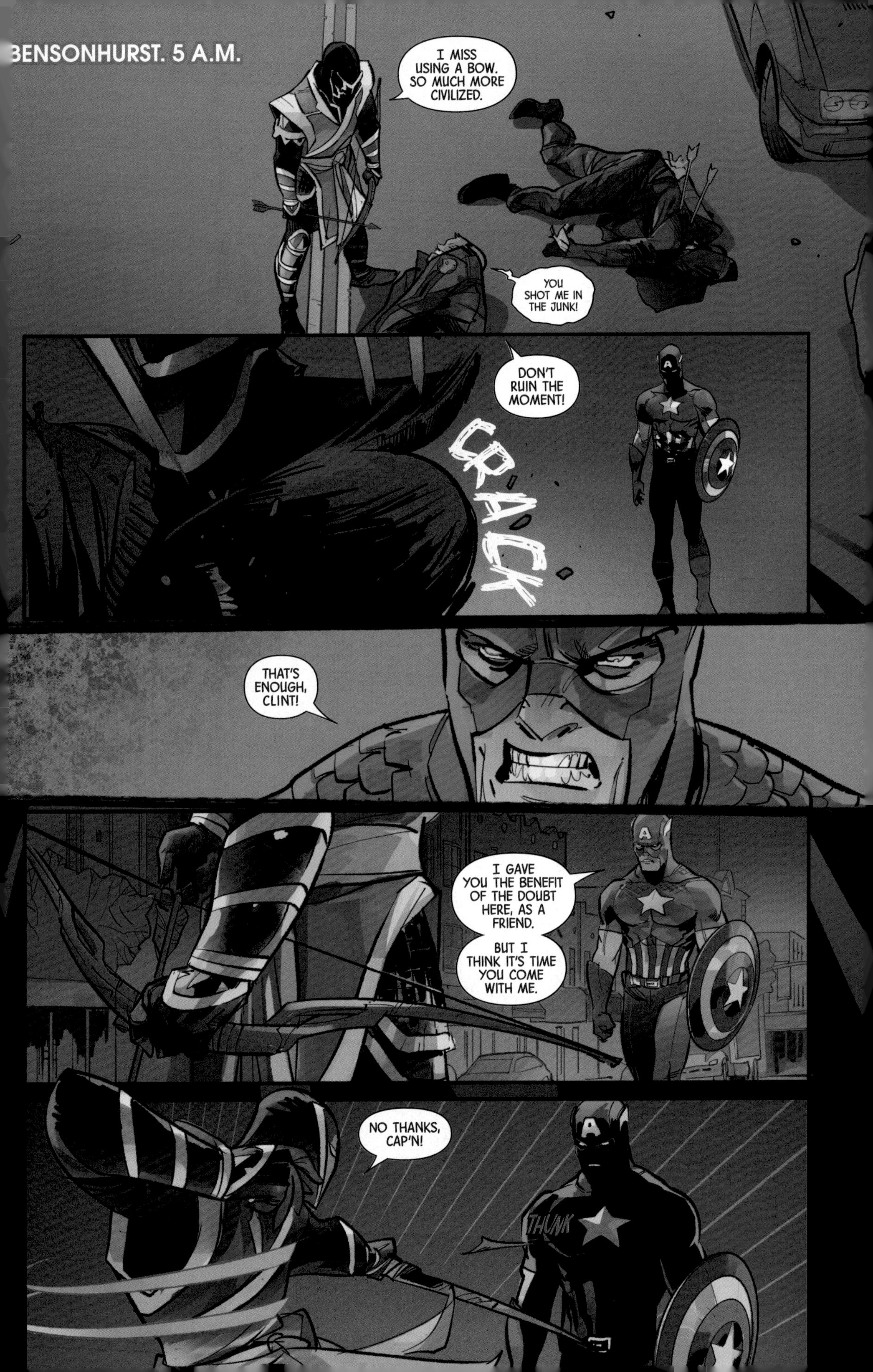
BENSONHURST. 5 A.M.
I MISS USING A BOW. SO MUCH MORE CIVILIZED.
YOU SHOT ME IN THE JUNK!
DON'T RUIN THE MOMENT!
CRACK
THAT'S ENOUGH, CLINT!
I GAVE YOU THE BENEFIT OF THE DOUBT HERE, AS A FRIEND.
BUT I THINK IT'S TIME YOU COME WITH ME.
NO THANKS, CAP'N!
THUNK

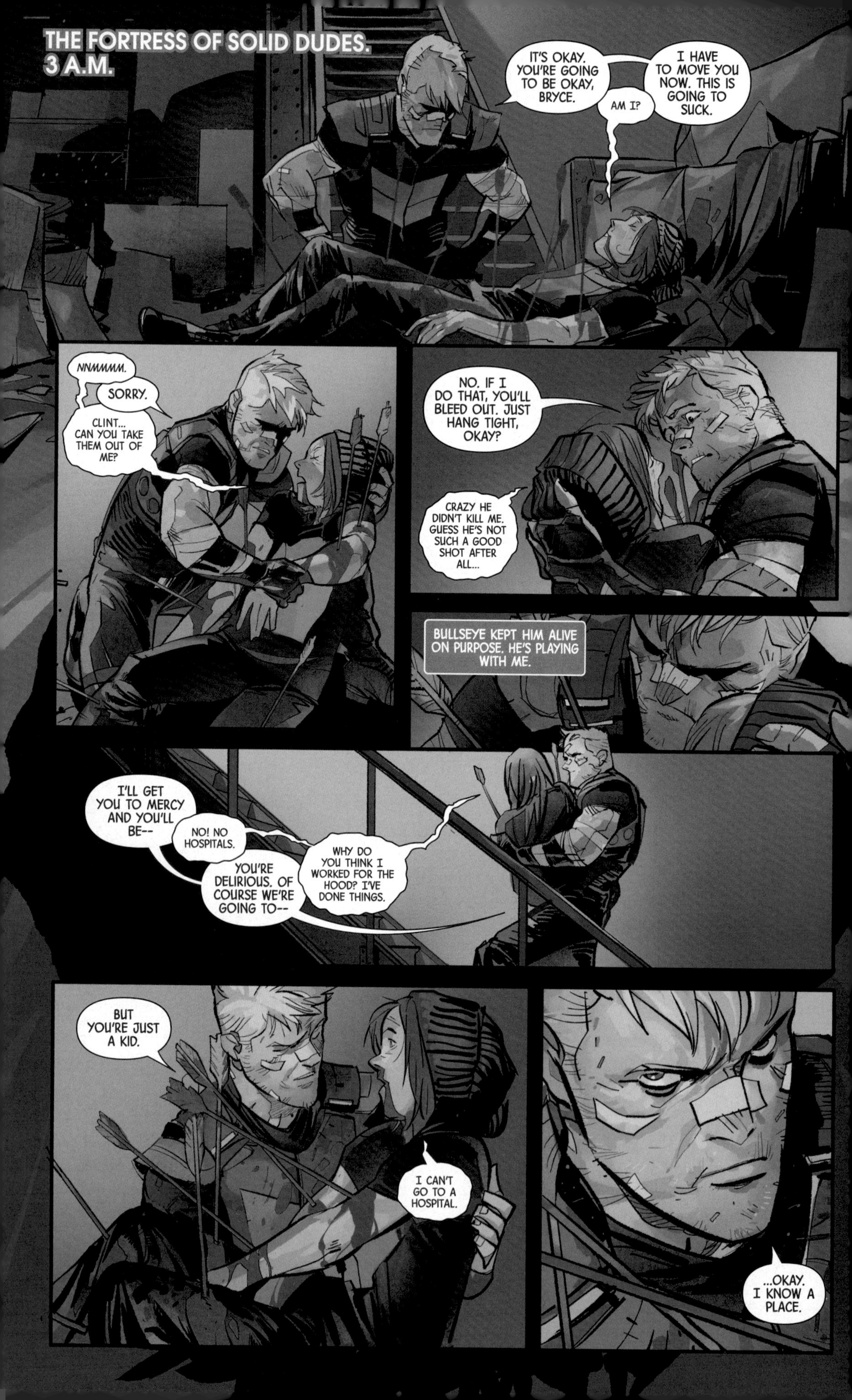
THE FORTRESS OF SOLID DUDES. 3 A.M.
IT'S OKAY. YOU'RE GOING TO BE OKAY, BRYCE.
AM I?
I HAVE TO MOVE YOU NOW. THIS IS GOING TO SUCK.
NNMMMM.
SORRY.
CLINT... CAN YOU TAKE THEM OUT OF ME?
NO. IF I DO THAT, YOU'LL BLEED OUT. JUST HANG TIGHT, OKAY?
CRAZY HE DIDN'T KILL ME. GUESS HE'S NOT SUCH A GOOD SHOT AFTER ALL...
BULLSEYE KEPT HIM ALIVE ON PURPOSE. HE'S PLAYING WITH ME.
I'LL GET YOU TO MERCY AND YOU'LL BE--
NO! NO HOSPITALS.
YOU'RE DELIRIOUS. OF COURSE WE'RE GOING TO--
WHY DO YOU THINK I WORKED FOR THE HOOD? I'VE DONE THINGS.
BUT YOU'RE JUST A KID.
I CAN'T GO TO A HOSPITAL.
...OKAY. I KNOW A PLACE.

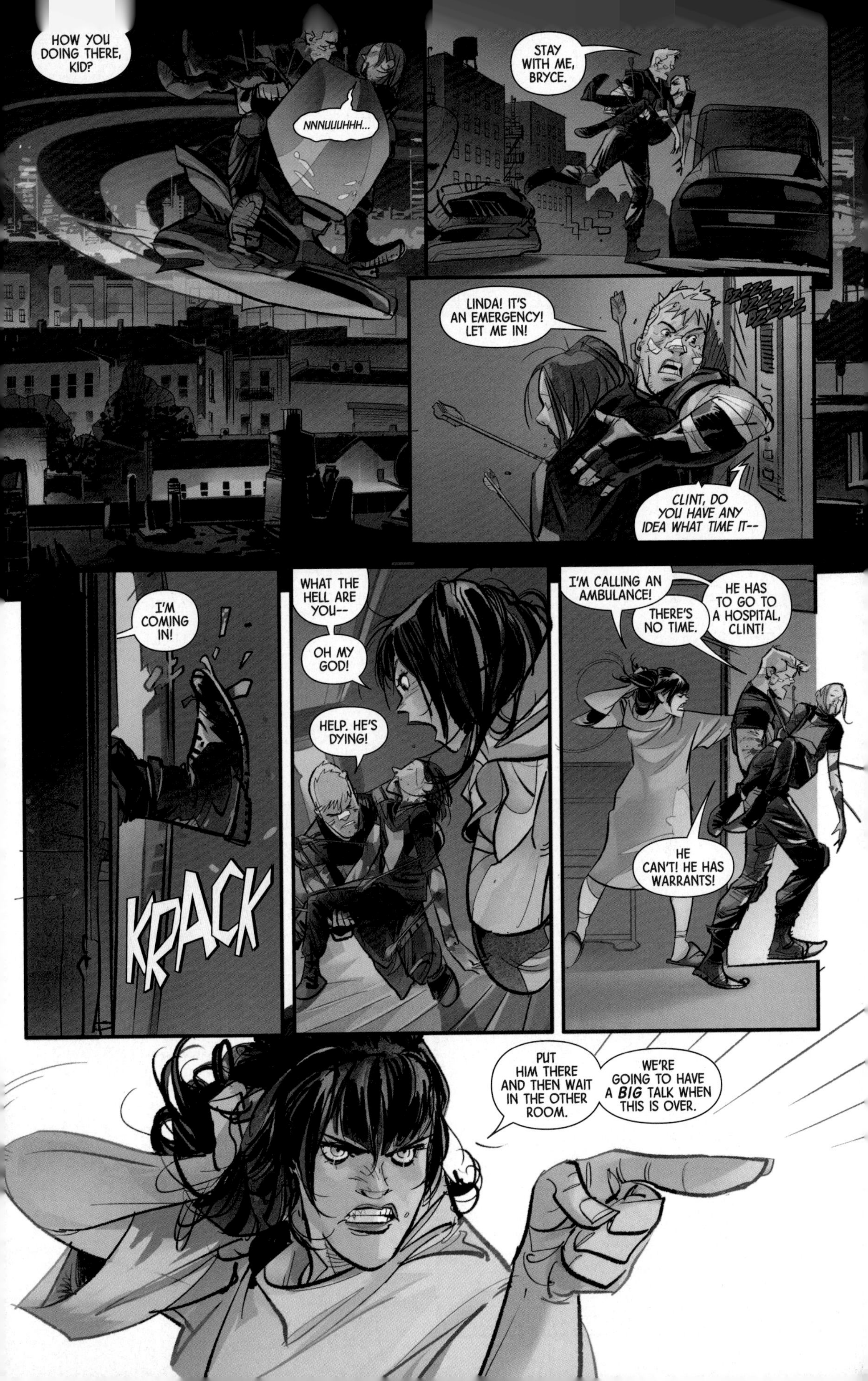
HOW YOU DOING THERE, KID?
NNNUUUHHH...
STAY WITH ME, BRYCE.
LINDA! IT'S AN EMERGENCY! LET ME IN!
BZZZZZ BZZZZZ BZZZZZ
CLINT, DO YOU HAVE ANY IDEA WHAT TIME IT--
I'M COMING IN!
KRACK
WHAT THE HELL ARE YOU--
OH MY GOD!
HELP. HE'S DYING!
I'M CALLING AN AMBULANCE!
THERE'S NO TIME.
HE HAS TO GO TO A HOSPITAL, CLINT!
HE CAN'T! HE HAS WARRANTS!
PUT HIM THERE AND THEN WAIT IN THE OTHER ROOM.
WE'RE GOING TO HAVE A BIG TALK WHEN THIS IS OVER.

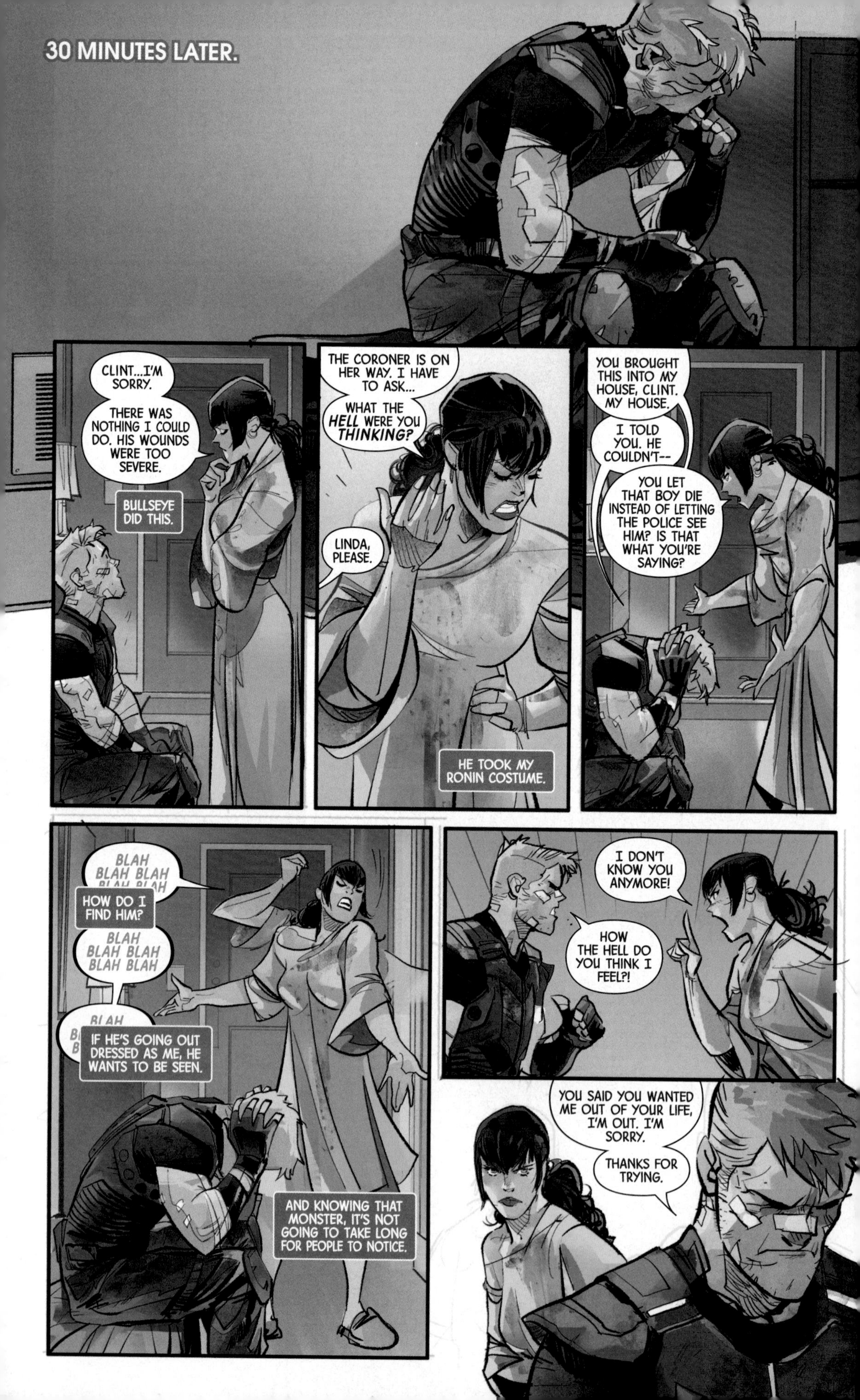
30 MINUTES LATER.
CLINT...I'M SORRY.
THERE WAS NOTHING I COULD DO. HIS WOUNDS WERE TOO SEVERE.
BULLSEYE DID THIS.
THE CORONER IS ON HER WAY. I HAVE TO ASK...
WHAT THE *HELL* WERE YOU *THINKING?*
LINDA, PLEASE.
HE TOOK MY RONIN COSTUME.
YOU BROUGHT THIS INTO MY HOUSE, CLINT. MY HOUSE.
I TOLD YOU. HE COULDN'T--
YOU LET THAT BOY DIE INSTEAD OF LETTING THE POLICE SEE HIM? IS THAT WHAT YOU'RE SAYING?
BLAH BLAH BLAH
HOW DO I FIND HIM?
BLAH BLAH BLAH BLAH BLAH
IF HE'S GOING OUT DRESSED AS ME, HE WANTS TO BE SEEN.
AND KNOWING THAT MONSTER, IT'S NOT GOING TO TAKE LONG FOR PEOPLE TO NOTICE.
I DON'T KNOW YOU ANYMORE!
HOW THE HELL DO YOU THINK I FEEL?!
YOU SAID YOU WANTED ME OUT OF YOUR LIFE, I'M OUT. I'M SORRY.
THANKS FOR TRYING.

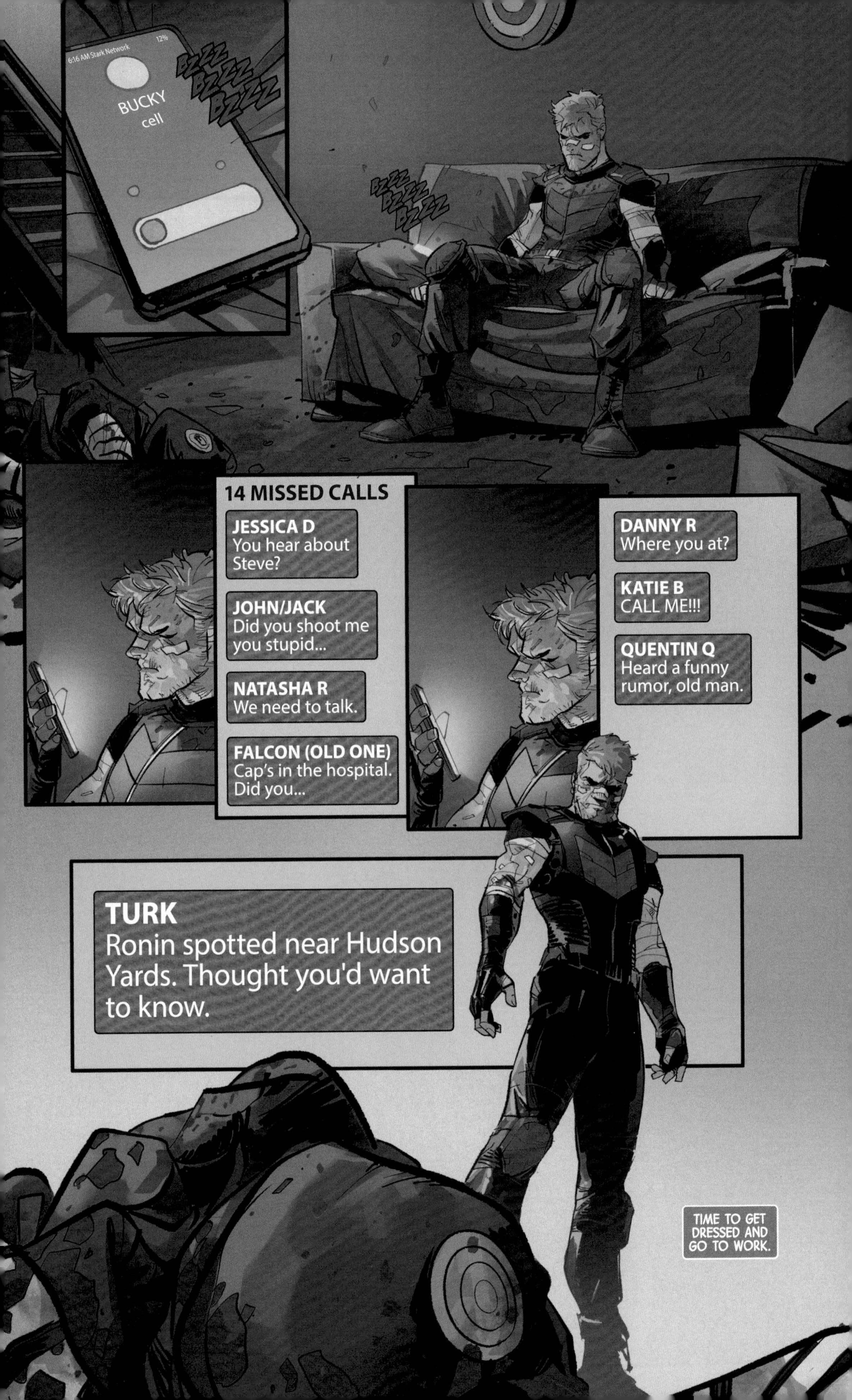
6:16 AM Stark Network
12%
BUCKY
cell
BZZZ BZZZ BZZZ
BZZZ BZZZ BZZZ
14 MISSED CALLS
JESSICA D
You hear about Steve?
JOHN/JACK
Did you shoot me you stupid...
NATASHA R
We need to talk.
FALCON (OLD ONE)
Cap's in the hospital. Did you...
DANNY R
Where you at?
KATIE B
CALL ME!!!
QUENTIN Q
Heard a funny rumor, old man.
TURK
Ronin spotted near Hudson Yards. Thought you'd want to know.
TIME TO GET DRESSED AND GO TO WORK.

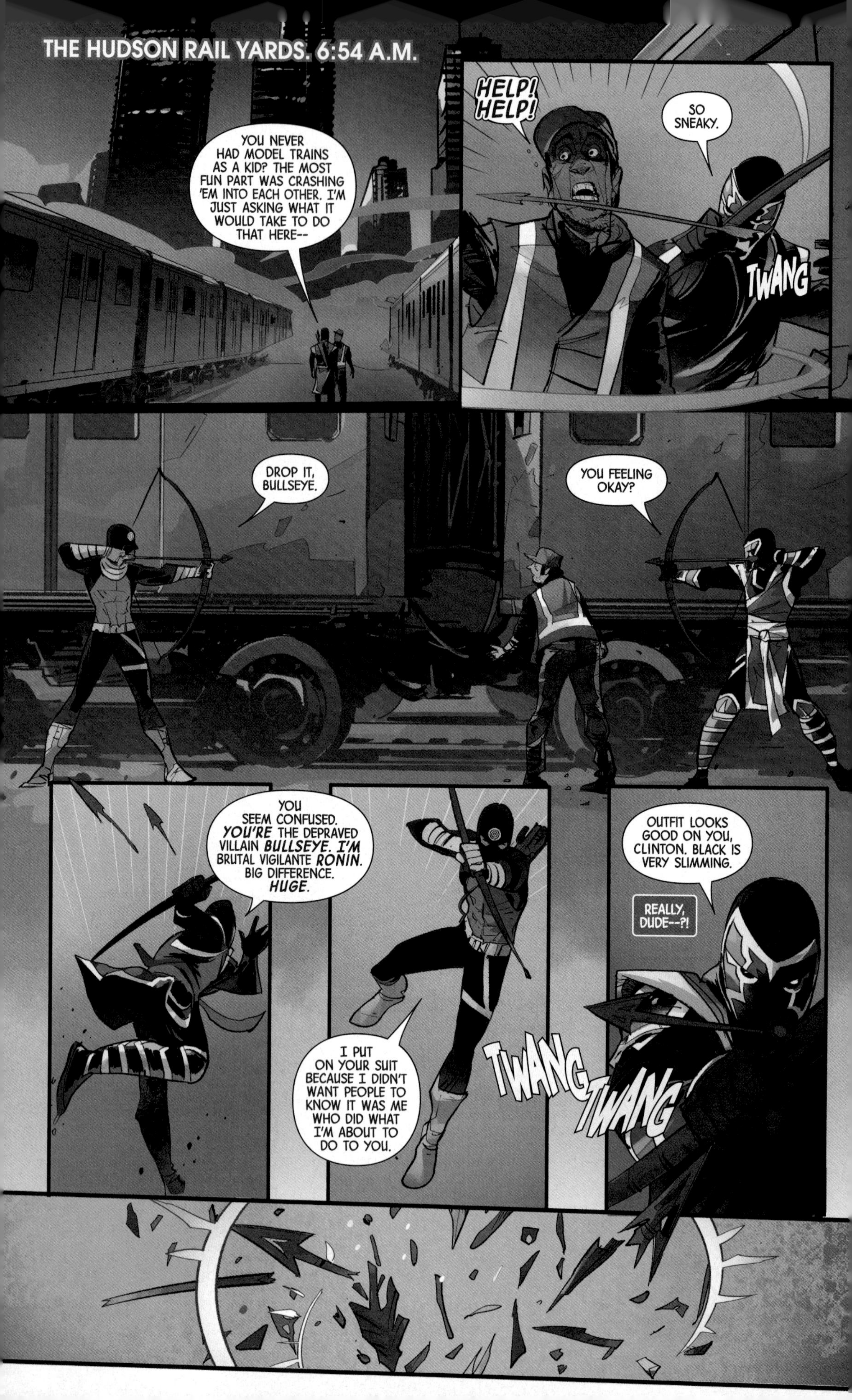
THE HUDSON RAIL YARDS. 6:54 A.M.
YOU NEVER HAD MODEL TRAINS AS A KID? THE MOST FUN PART WAS CRASHING 'EM INTO EACH OTHER. I'M JUST ASKING WHAT IT WOULD TAKE TO DO THAT HERE--
HELP! HELP!
SO SNEAKY.
TWANG
DROP IT, BULLSEYE.
YOU FEELING OKAY?
YOU SEEM CONFUSED. YOU'RE THE DEPRAVED VILLAIN BULLSEYE. I'M BRUTAL VIGILANTE RONIN. BIG DIFFERENCE. HUGE.
I PUT ON YOUR SUIT BECAUSE I DIDN'T WANT PEOPLE TO KNOW IT WAS ME WHO DID WHAT I'M ABOUT TO DO TO YOU.
OUTFIT LOOKS GOOD ON YOU, CLINTON. BLACK IS VERY SLIMMING.
REALLY, DUDE--?!
TWANG
TWANG

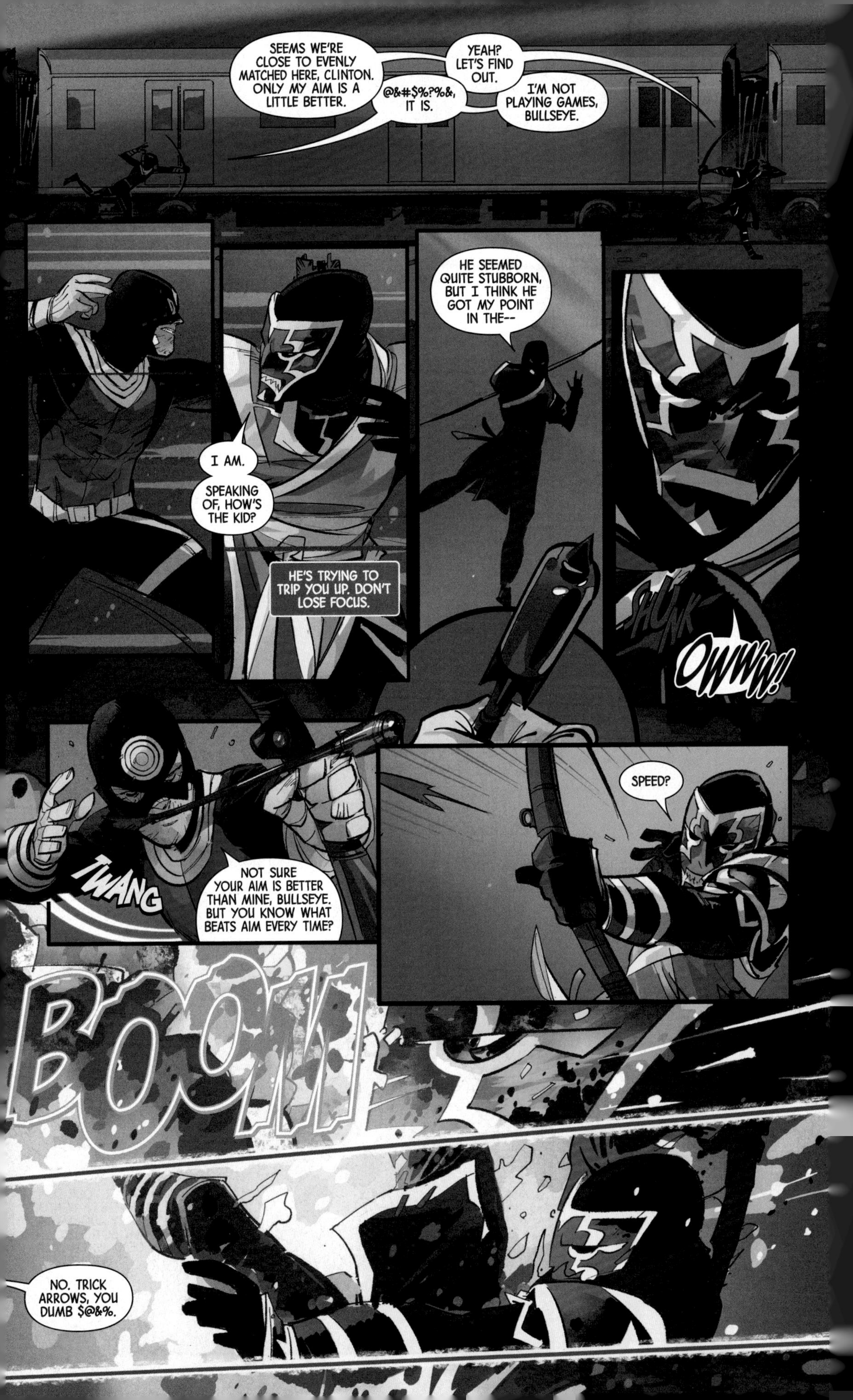
SEEMS WE'RE CLOSE TO EVENLY MATCHED HERE, CLINTON. ONLY MY AIM IS A LITTLE BETTER.
@&#$%?%&, IT IS.
YEAH? LET'S FIND OUT.
I'M NOT PLAYING GAMES, BULLSEYE.
I AM.
SPEAKING OF, HOW'S THE KID?
HE'S TRYING TO TRIP YOU UP. DON'T LOSE FOCUS.
HE SEEMED QUITE STUBBORN, BUT I THINK HE GOT MY POINT IN THE--
SHUNK
OWWW!
TWANG
NOT SURE YOUR AIM IS BETTER THAN MINE, BULLSEYE. BUT YOU KNOW WHAT BEATS AIM EVERY TIME?
SPEED?
BOOM
NO. TRICK ARROWS, YOU DUMB $@&%.

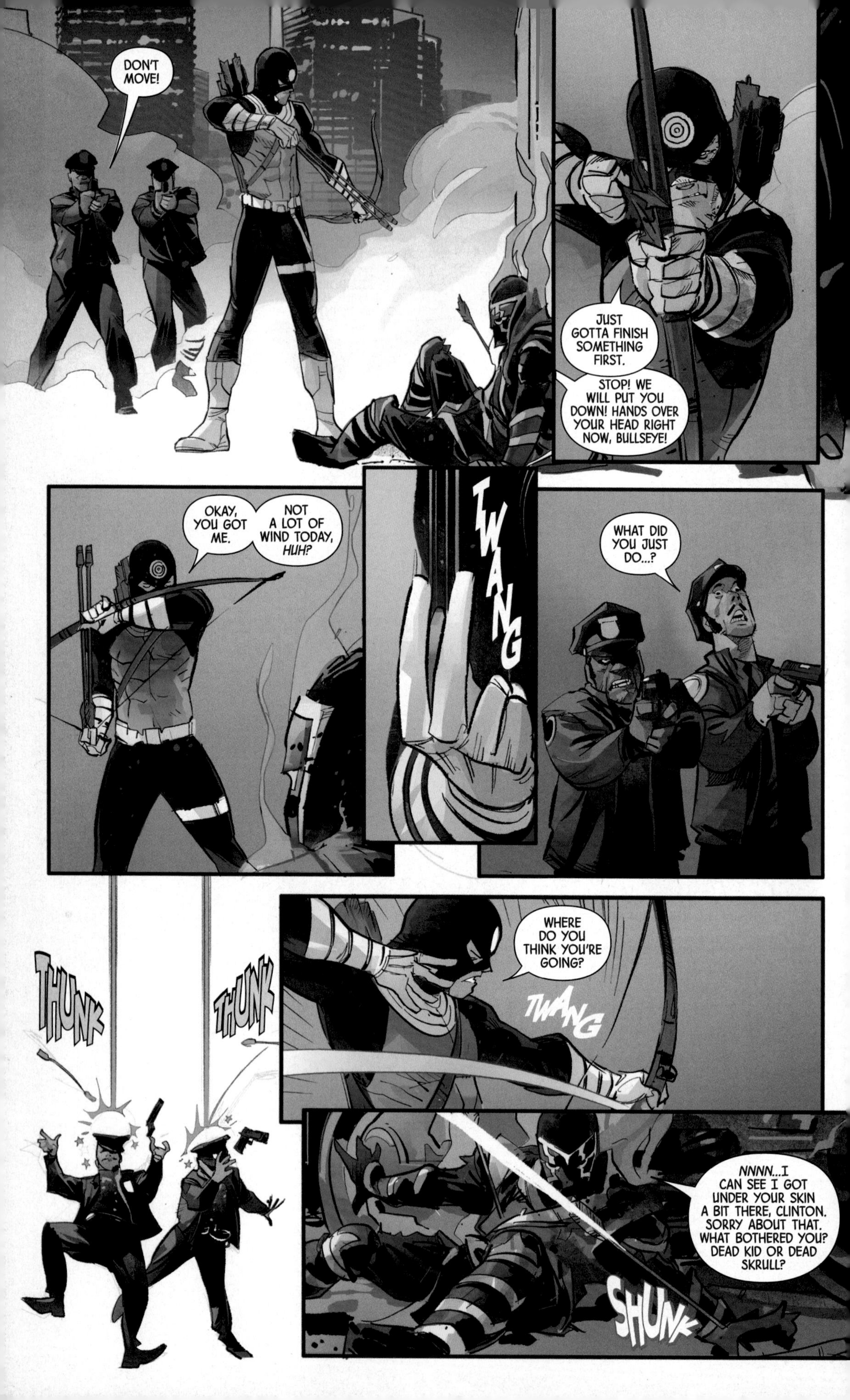
DON'T MOVE!
JUST GOTTA FINISH SOMETHING FIRST.
STOP! WE WILL PUT YOU DOWN! HANDS OVER YOUR HEAD RIGHT NOW, BULLSEYE!
OKAY, YOU GOT ME.
NOT A LOT OF WIND TODAY, *HUH?*
TWANG
WHAT DID YOU JUST DO...?
THUNK
THUNK
WHERE DO YOU THINK YOU'RE GOING?
TWANG
NNNN...I CAN SEE I GOT UNDER YOUR SKIN A BIT THERE, CLINTON. SORRY ABOUT THAT. WHAT BOTHERED YOU? DEAD KID OR DEAD SKRULL?
SHUNK

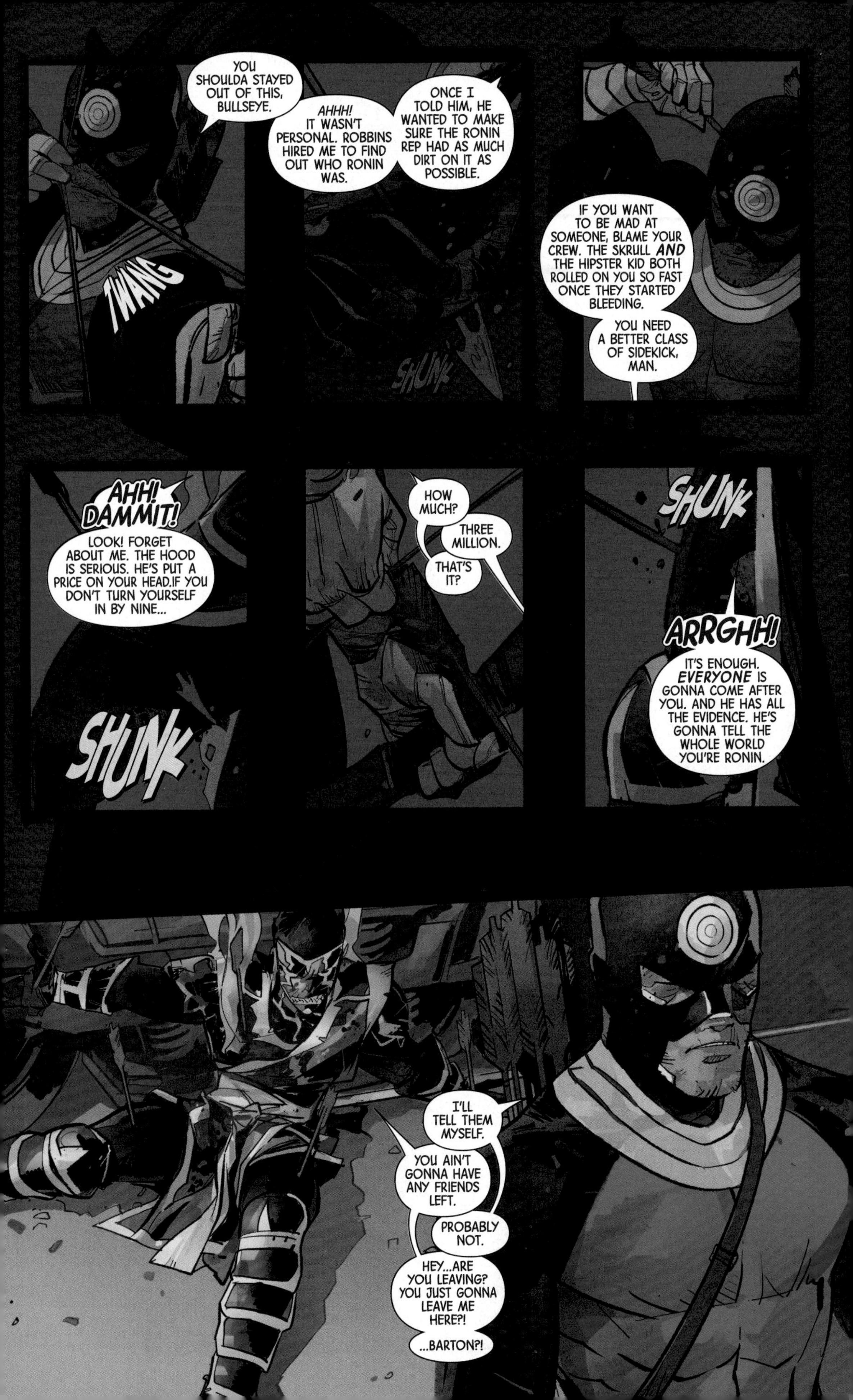

YOU SHOULDA STAYED OUT OF THIS, BULLSEYE.
TWANG
AHHH! IT WASN'T PERSONAL. ROBBINS HIRED ME TO FIND OUT WHO RONIN WAS.
ONCE I TOLD HIM, HE WANTED TO MAKE SURE THE RONIN REP HAD AS MUCH DIRT ON IT AS POSSIBLE.
SHUNK
IF YOU WANT TO BE MAD AT SOMEONE, BLAME YOUR CREW. THE SKRULL AND THE HIPSTER KID BOTH ROLLED ON YOU SO FAST ONCE THEY STARTED BLEEDING.
YOU NEED A BETTER CLASS OF SIDEKICK, MAN.
AHH! DAMMIT!
LOOK! FORGET ABOUT ME. THE HOOD IS SERIOUS. HE'S PUT A PRICE ON YOUR HEAD.IF YOU DON'T TURN YOURSELF IN BY NINE...
SHUNK
HOW MUCH?
THREE MILLION.
THAT'S IT?
SHUNK
ARRGHH!
IT'S ENOUGH. EVERYONE IS GONNA COME AFTER YOU. AND HE HAS ALL THE EVIDENCE. HE'S GONNA TELL THE WHOLE WORLD YOU'RE RONIN.
I'LL TELL THEM MYSELF.
YOU AIN'T GONNA HAVE ANY FRIENDS LEFT.
PROBABLY NOT.
HEY...ARE YOU LEAVING? YOU JUST GONNA LEAVE ME HERE?!
...BARTON?!

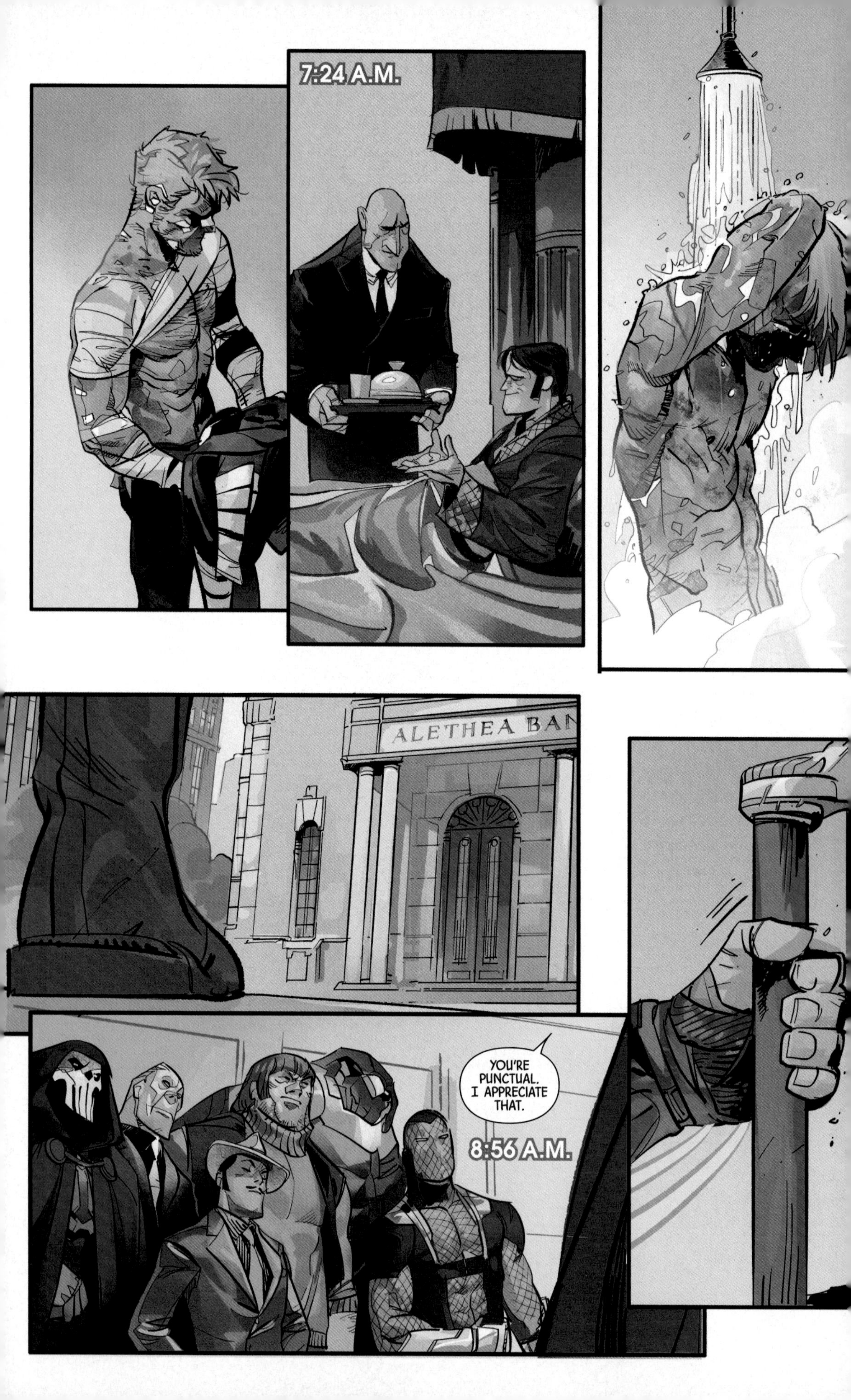
7:24 A.M.
ALETHEA BAN
YOU'RE PUNCTUAL. I APPRECIATE THAT.
8:56 A.M.

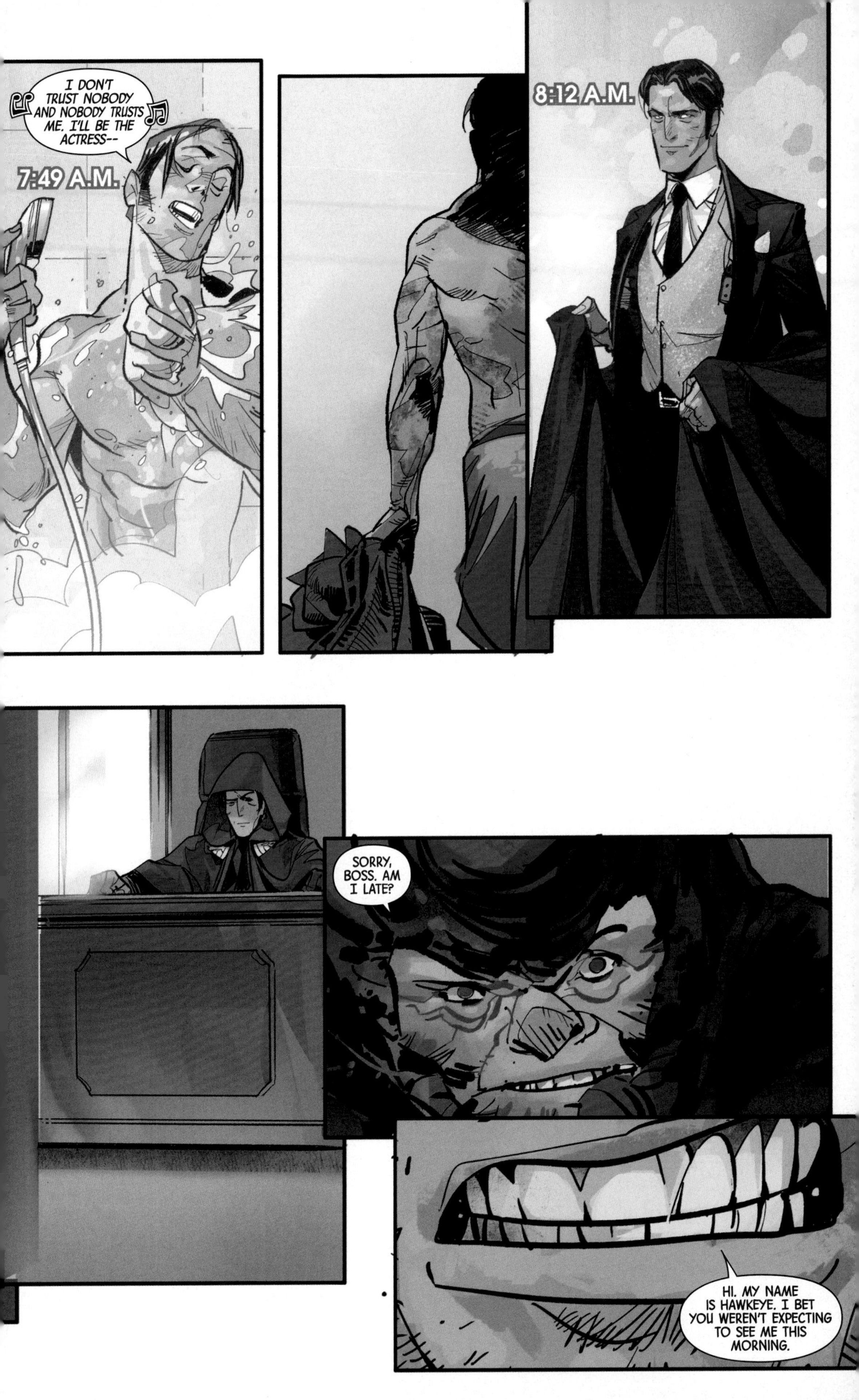
I DON'T TRUST NOBODY AND NOBODY TRUSTS ME. I'LL BE THE ACTRESS--
7:49 A.M.
8:12 A.M.
SORRY, BOSS. AM I LATE?
HI. MY NAME IS HAWKEYE. I BET YOU WEREN'T EXPECTING TO SEE ME THIS MORNING.

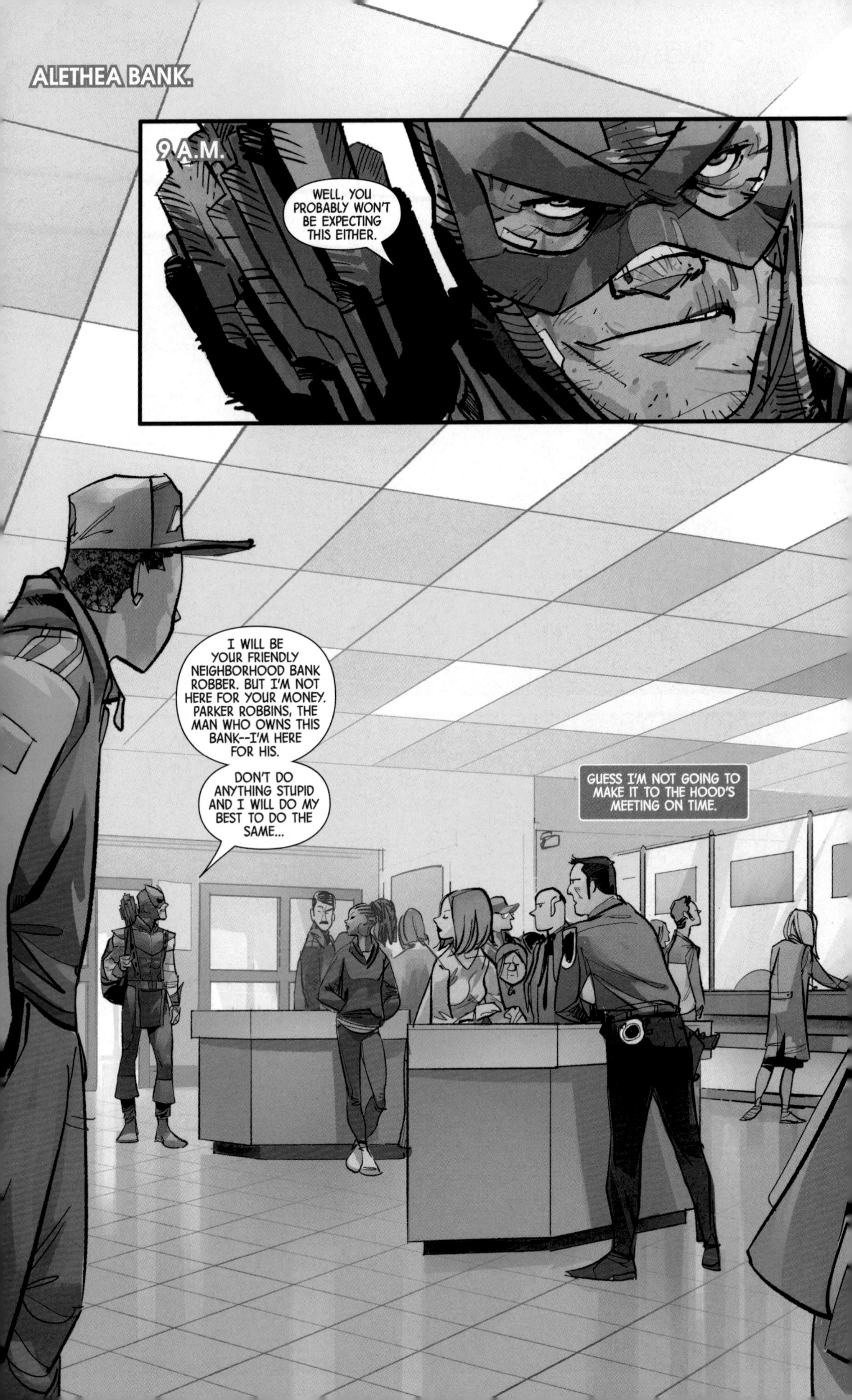
ALETHEA BANK.
9 A.M.
WELL, YOU PROBABLY WON'T BE EXPECTING THIS EITHER.
I WILL BE YOUR FRIENDLY NEIGHBORHOOD BANK ROBBER. BUT I'M NOT HERE FOR YOUR MONEY. PARKER ROBBINS, THE MAN WHO OWNS THIS BANK--I'M HERE FOR HIS.
DON'T DO ANYTHING STUPID AND I WILL DO MY BEST TO DO THE SAME...
GUESS I'M NOT GOING TO MAKE IT TO THE HOOD'S MEETING ON TIME.

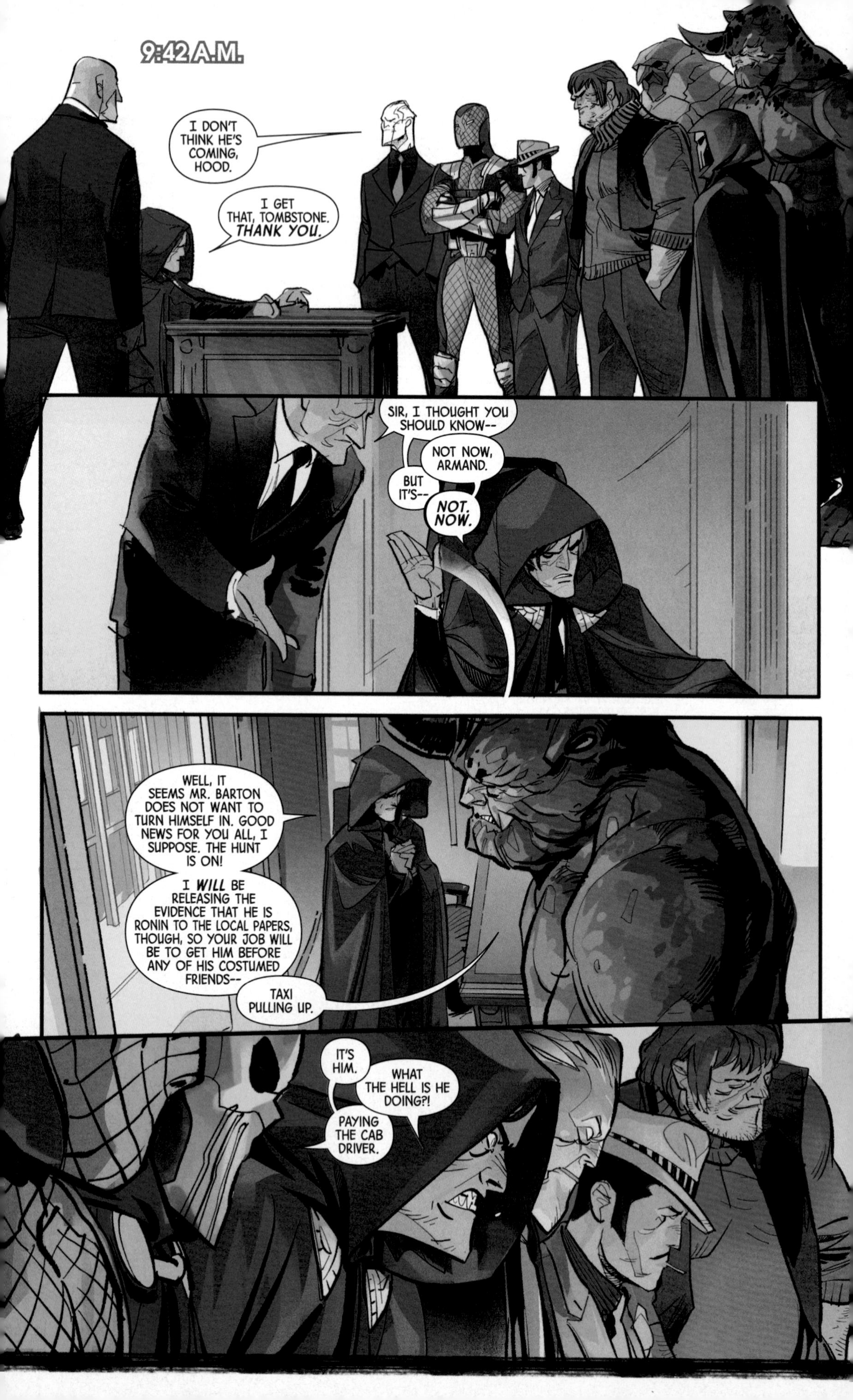
9:42 A.M.
I DON'T THINK HE'S COMING, HOOD.
I GET THAT, TOMBSTONE. THANK YOU.
SIR, I THOUGHT YOU SHOULD KNOW--
NOT NOW, ARMAND.
BUT IT'S--
NOT. NOW.
WELL, IT SEEMS MR. BARTON DOES NOT WANT TO TURN HIMSELF IN. GOOD NEWS FOR YOU ALL, I SUPPOSE. THE HUNT IS ON!
I WILL BE RELEASING THE EVIDENCE THAT HE IS RONIN TO THE LOCAL PAPERS, THOUGH, SO YOUR JOB WILL BE TO GET HIM BEFORE ANY OF HIS COSTUMED FRIENDS--
TAXI PULLING UP.
IT'S HIM.
WHAT THE HELL IS HE DOING?!
PAYING THE CAB DRIVER.

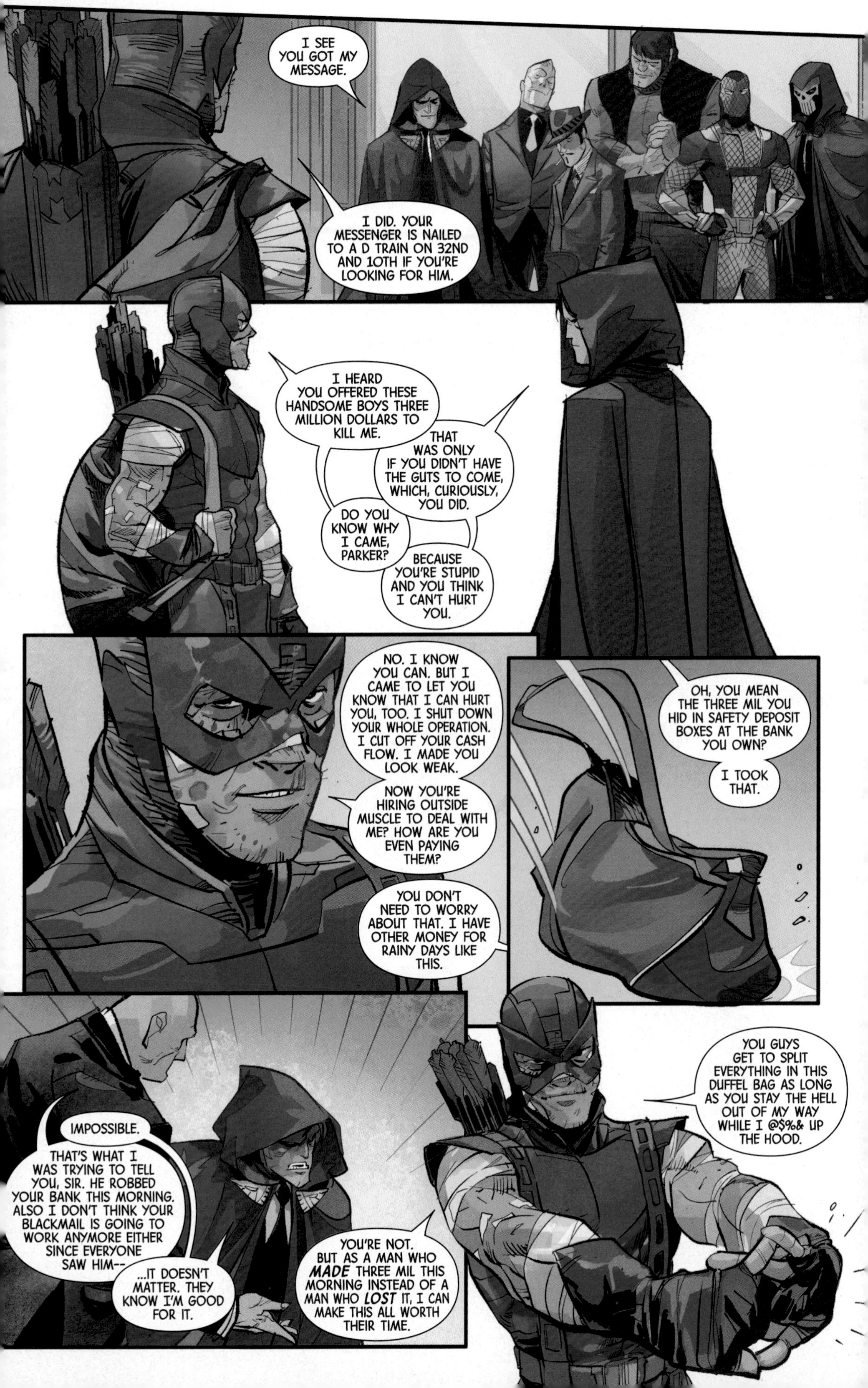
I SEE YOU GOT MY MESSAGE.
I DID. YOUR MESSENGER IS NAILED TO A D TRAIN ON 32ND AND 10TH IF YOU'RE LOOKING FOR HIM.
I HEARD YOU OFFERED THESE HANDSOME BOYS THREE MILLION DOLLARS TO KILL ME.
THAT WAS ONLY IF YOU DIDN'T HAVE THE GUTS TO COME, WHICH, CURIOUSLY, YOU DID.
DO YOU KNOW WHY I CAME, PARKER?
BECAUSE YOU'RE STUPID AND YOU THINK I CAN'T HURT YOU.
NO. I KNOW YOU CAN. BUT I CAME TO LET YOU KNOW THAT I CAN HURT YOU, TOO. I SHUT DOWN YOUR WHOLE OPERATION. I CUT OFF YOUR CASH FLOW. I MADE YOU LOOK WEAK.
NOW YOU'RE HIRING OUTSIDE MUSCLE TO DEAL WITH ME? HOW ARE YOU EVEN PAYING THEM?
YOU DON'T NEED TO WORRY ABOUT THAT. I HAVE OTHER MONEY FOR RAINY DAYS LIKE THIS.
OH, YOU MEAN THE THREE MIL YOU HID IN SAFETY DEPOSIT BOXES AT THE BANK YOU OWN?
I TOOK THAT.
YOU GUYS GET TO SPLIT EVERYTHING IN THIS DUFFEL BAG AS LONG AS YOU STAY THE HELL OUT OF MY WAY WHILE I @$%& UP THE HOOD.
IMPOSSIBLE.
THAT'S WHAT I WAS TRYING TO TELL YOU, SIR. HE ROBBED YOUR BANK THIS MORNING. ALSO I DON'T THINK YOUR BLACKMAIL IS GOING TO WORK ANYMORE EITHER SINCE EVERYONE SAW HIM--
...IT DOESN'T MATTER. THEY KNOW I'M GOOD FOR IT.
YOU'RE NOT. BUT AS A MAN WHO *MADE* THREE MIL THIS MORNING INSTEAD OF A MAN WHO *LOST* IT, I CAN MAKE THIS ALL WORTH THEIR TIME.

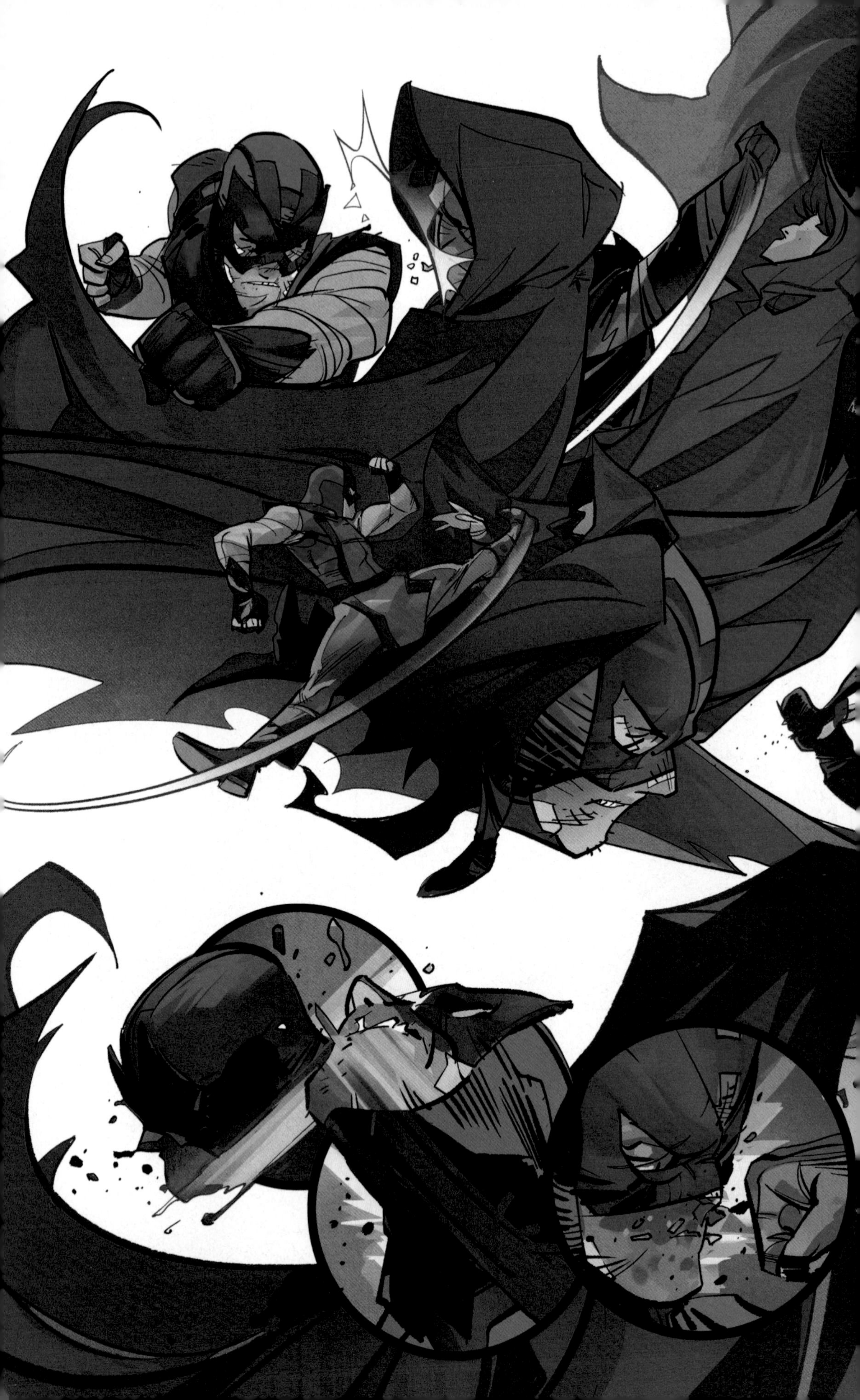

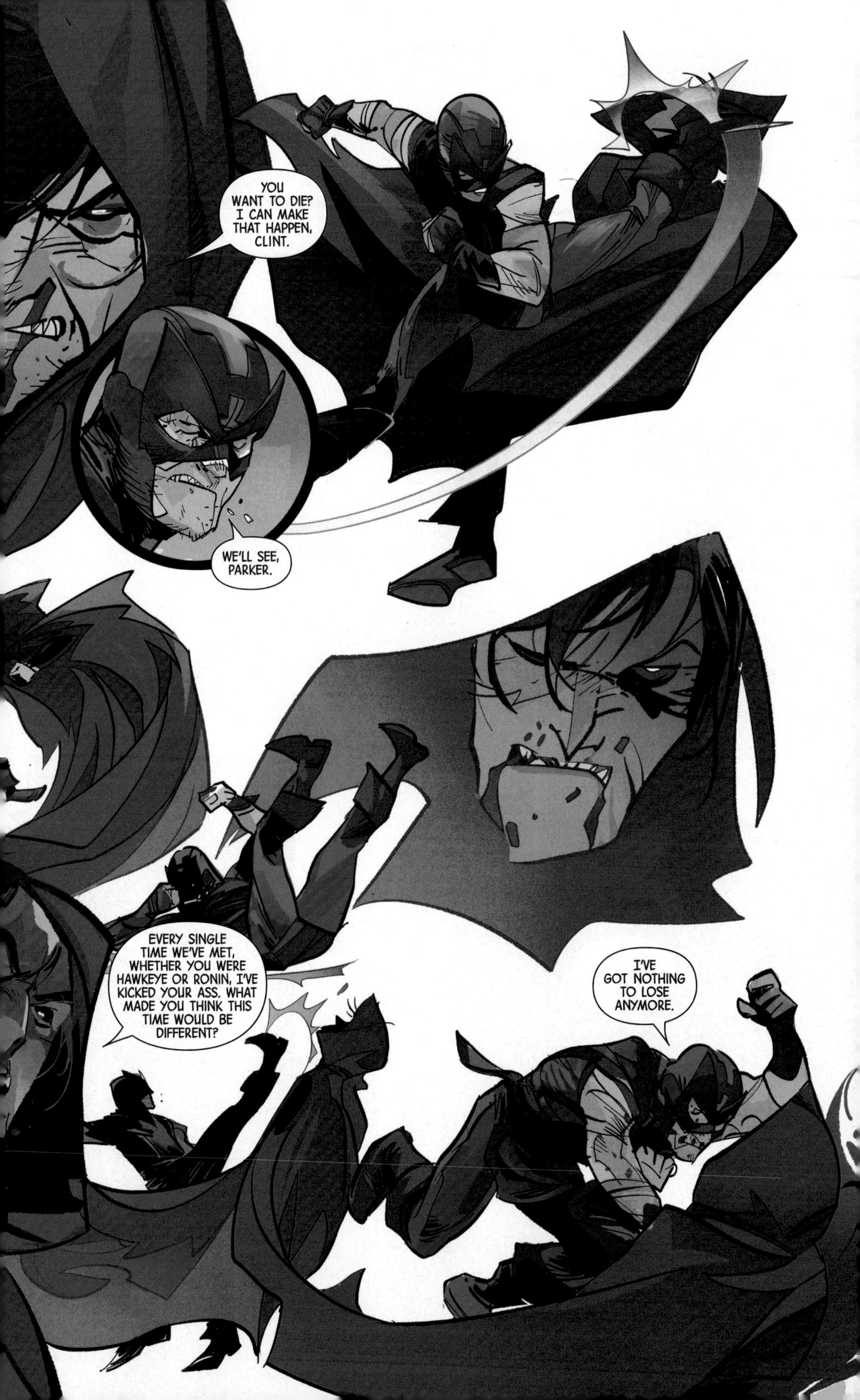
YOU WANT TO DIE? I CAN MAKE THAT HAPPEN, CLINT.
WE'LL SEE, PARKER.
EVERY SINGLE TIME WE'VE MET, WHETHER YOU WERE HAWKEYE OR RONIN, I'VE KICKED YOUR ASS. WHAT MADE YOU THINK THIS TIME WOULD BE DIFFERENT?
I'VE GOT NOTHING TO LOSE ANYMORE.

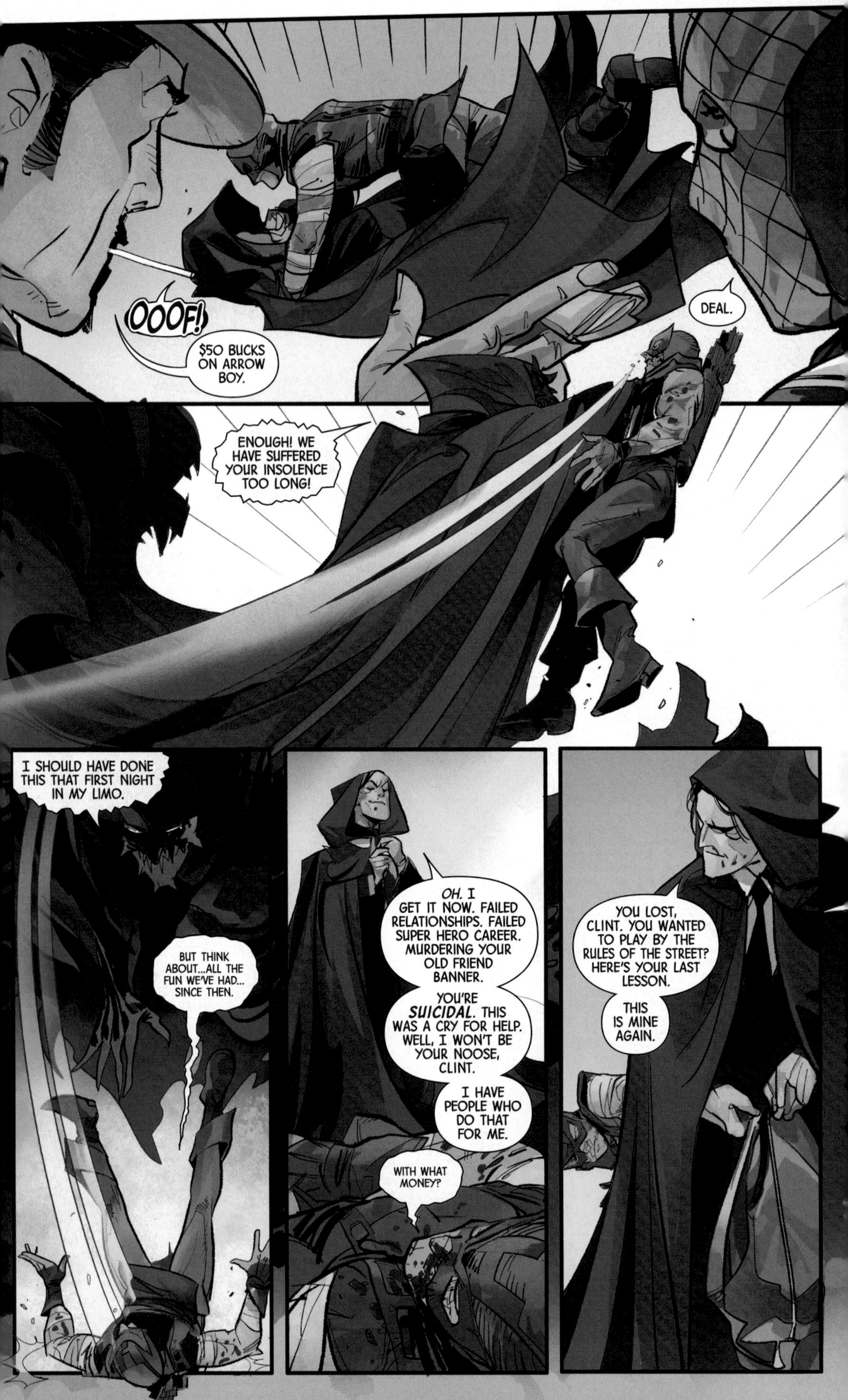

OOOF!
$50 BUCKS ON ARROW BOY.
DEAL.
ENOUGH! WE HAVE SUFFERED YOUR INSOLENCE TOO LONG!
I SHOULD HAVE DONE THIS THAT FIRST NIGHT IN MY LIMO.
BUT THINK ABOUT...ALL THE FUN WE'VE HAD... SINCE THEN.
OH. I GET IT NOW. FAILED RELATIONSHIPS. FAILED SUPER HERO CAREER. MURDERING YOUR OLD FRIEND BANNER.
YOU'RE SUICIDAL. THIS WAS A CRY FOR HELP. WELL, I WON'T BE YOUR NOOSE, CLINT.
I HAVE PEOPLE WHO DO THAT FOR ME.
WITH WHAT MONEY?
YOU LOST, CLINT. YOU WANTED TO PLAY BY THE RULES OF THE STREET? HERE'S YOUR LAST LESSON.
THIS IS MINE AGAIN.

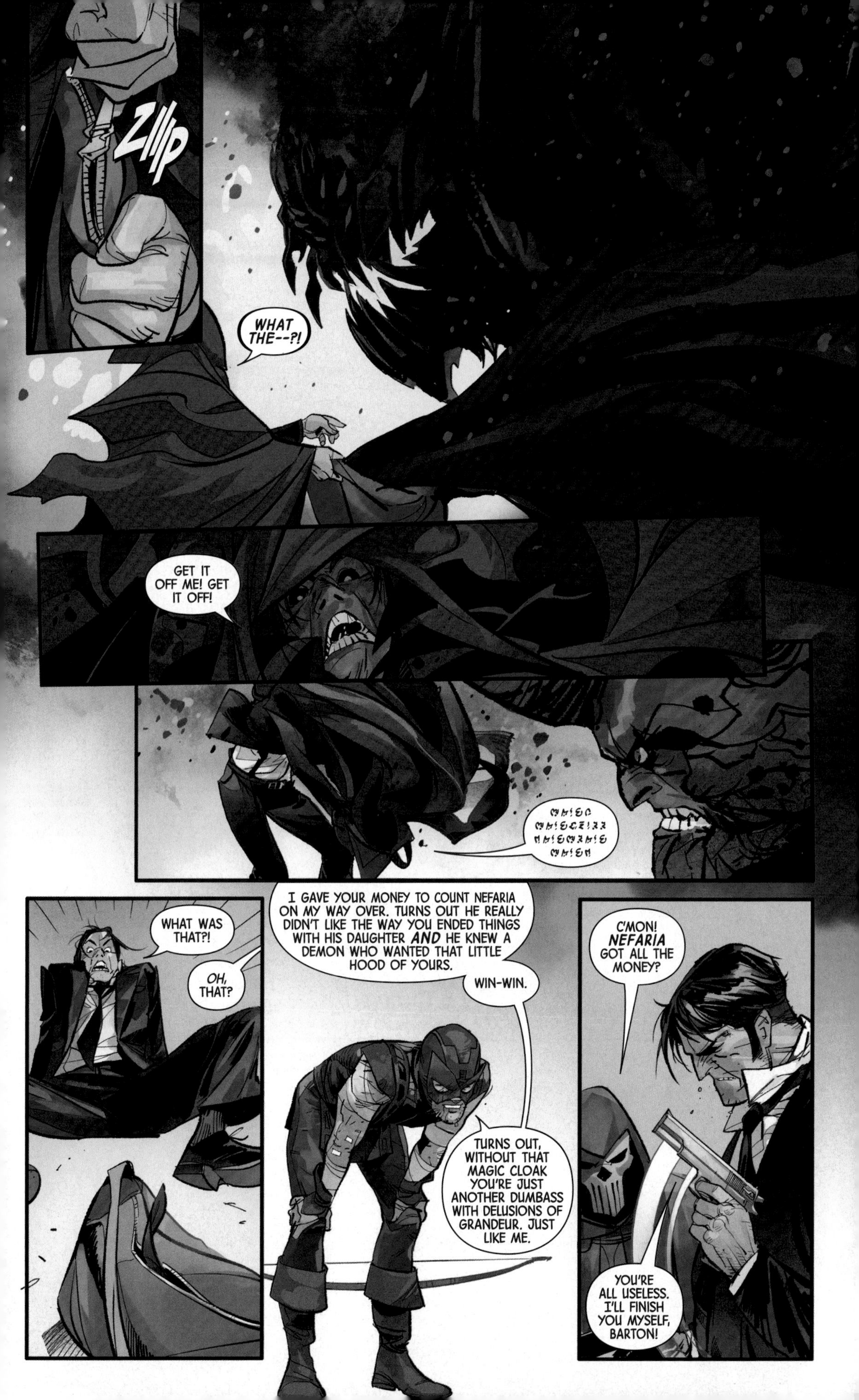
ZIIP
WHAT THE--?!
GET IT OFF ME! GET IT OFF!
WHAT WAS THAT?!
OH, THAT?
I GAVE YOUR MONEY TO COUNT NEFARIA ON MY WAY OVER. TURNS OUT HE REALLY DIDN'T LIKE THE WAY YOU ENDED THINGS WITH HIS DAUGHTER AND HE KNEW A DEMON WHO WANTED THAT LITTLE HOOD OF YOURS.
WIN-WIN.
TURNS OUT, WITHOUT THAT MAGIC CLOAK YOU'RE JUST ANOTHER DUMBASS WITH DELUSIONS OF GRANDEUR. JUST LIKE ME.
C'MON! NEFARIA GOT ALL THE MONEY?
YOU'RE ALL USELESS. I'LL FINISH YOU MYSELF, BARTON!

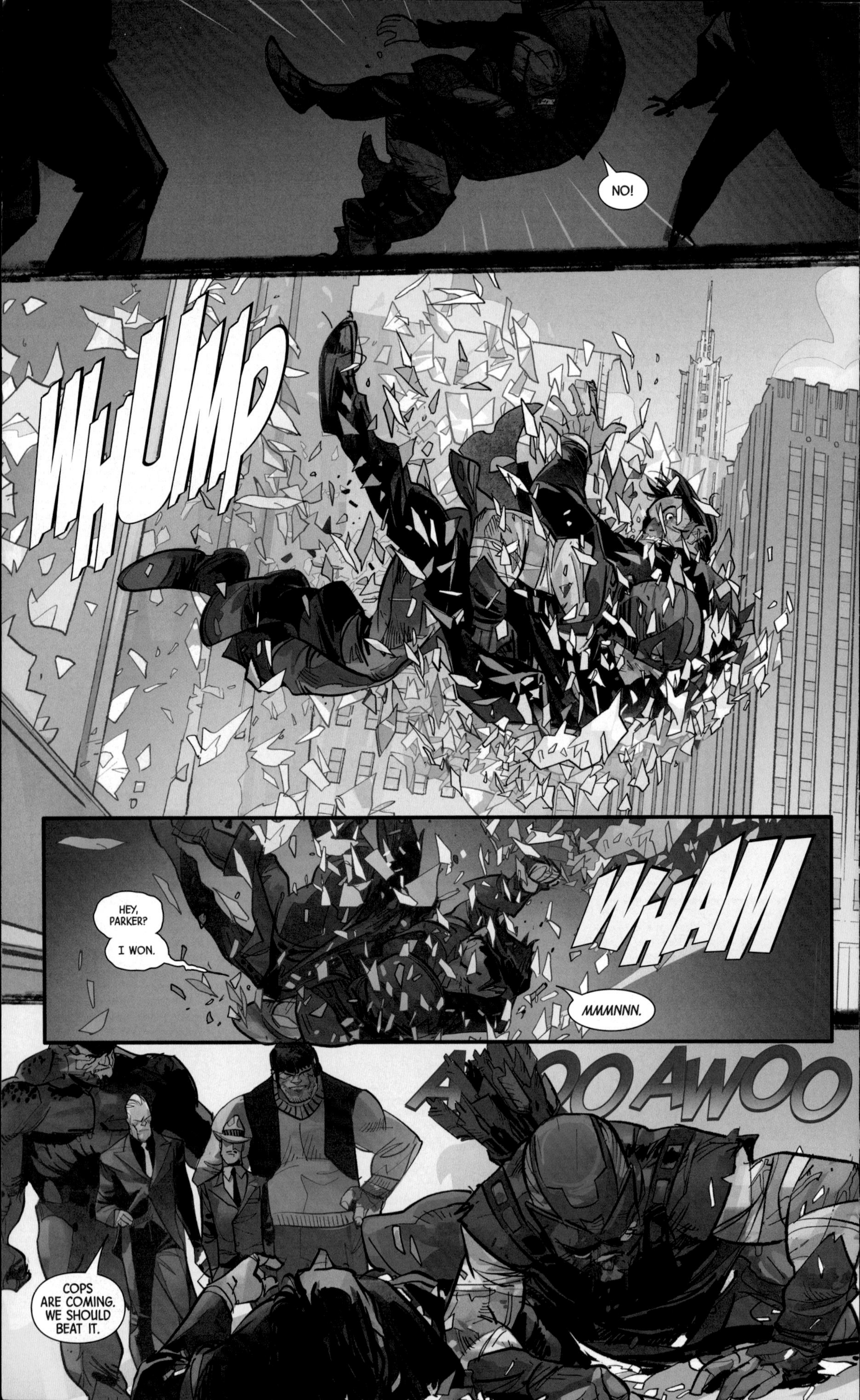
NO!
WHUMP
HEY, PARKER?
I WON.
WHAM
MMMNNN.
AWOO AWOO
COPS ARE COMING. WE SHOULD BEAT IT.

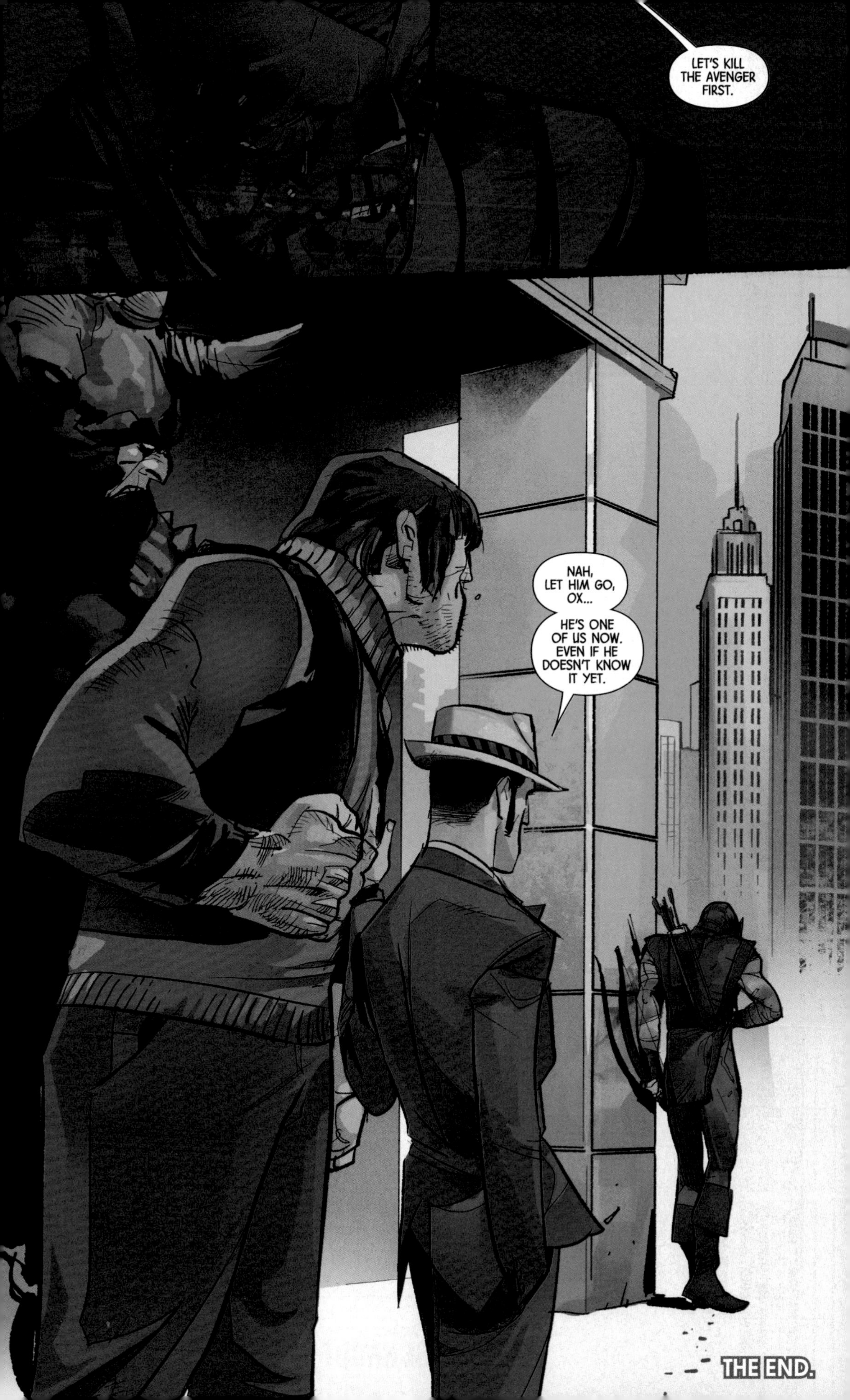
LET'S KILL THE AVENGER FIRST.
NAH, LET HIM GO, OX...
HE'S ONE OF US NOW. EVEN IF HE DOESN'T KNOW IT YET.
THE END.

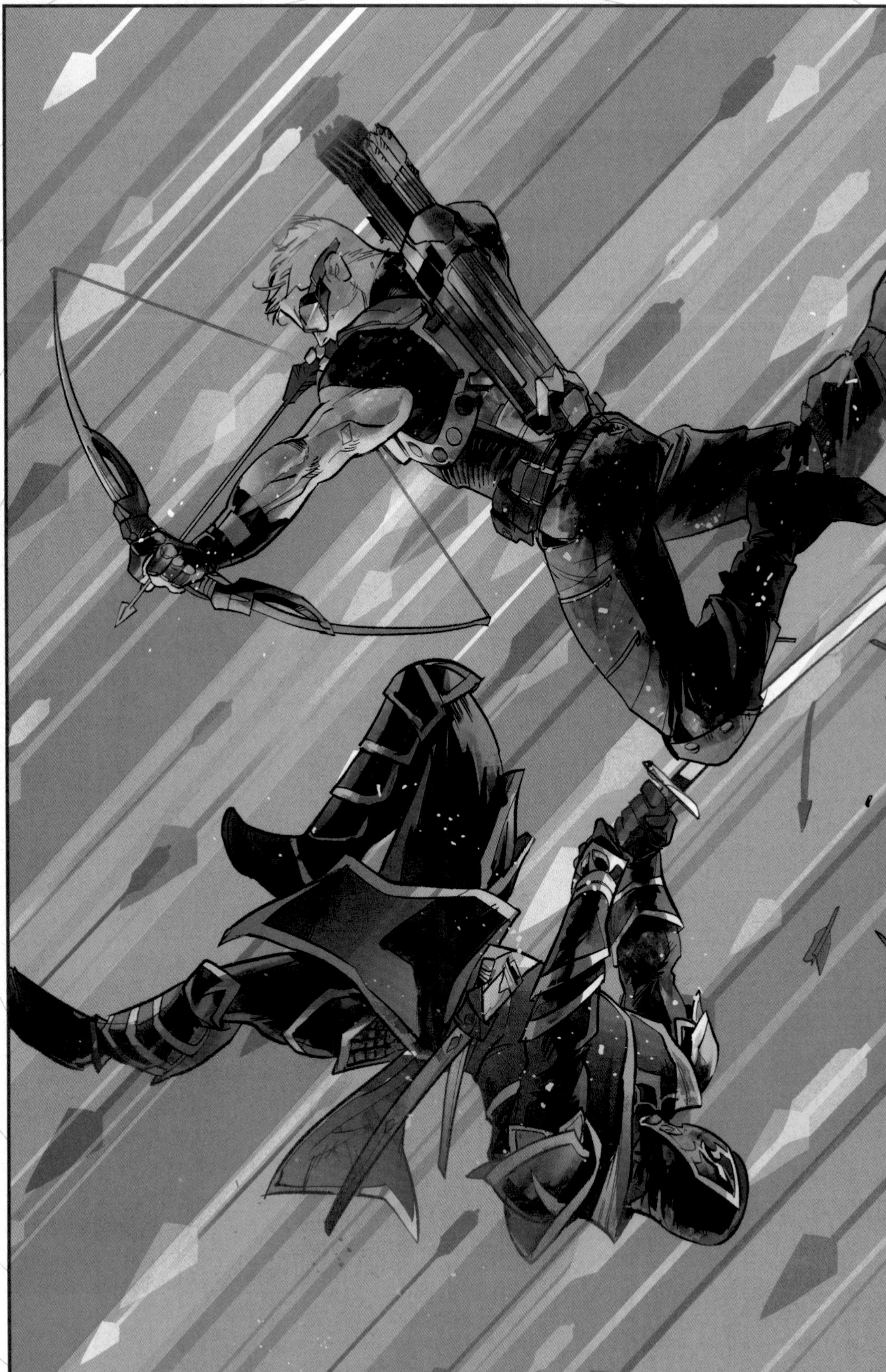

#1 VARIANT
OTTO SCHMIDT

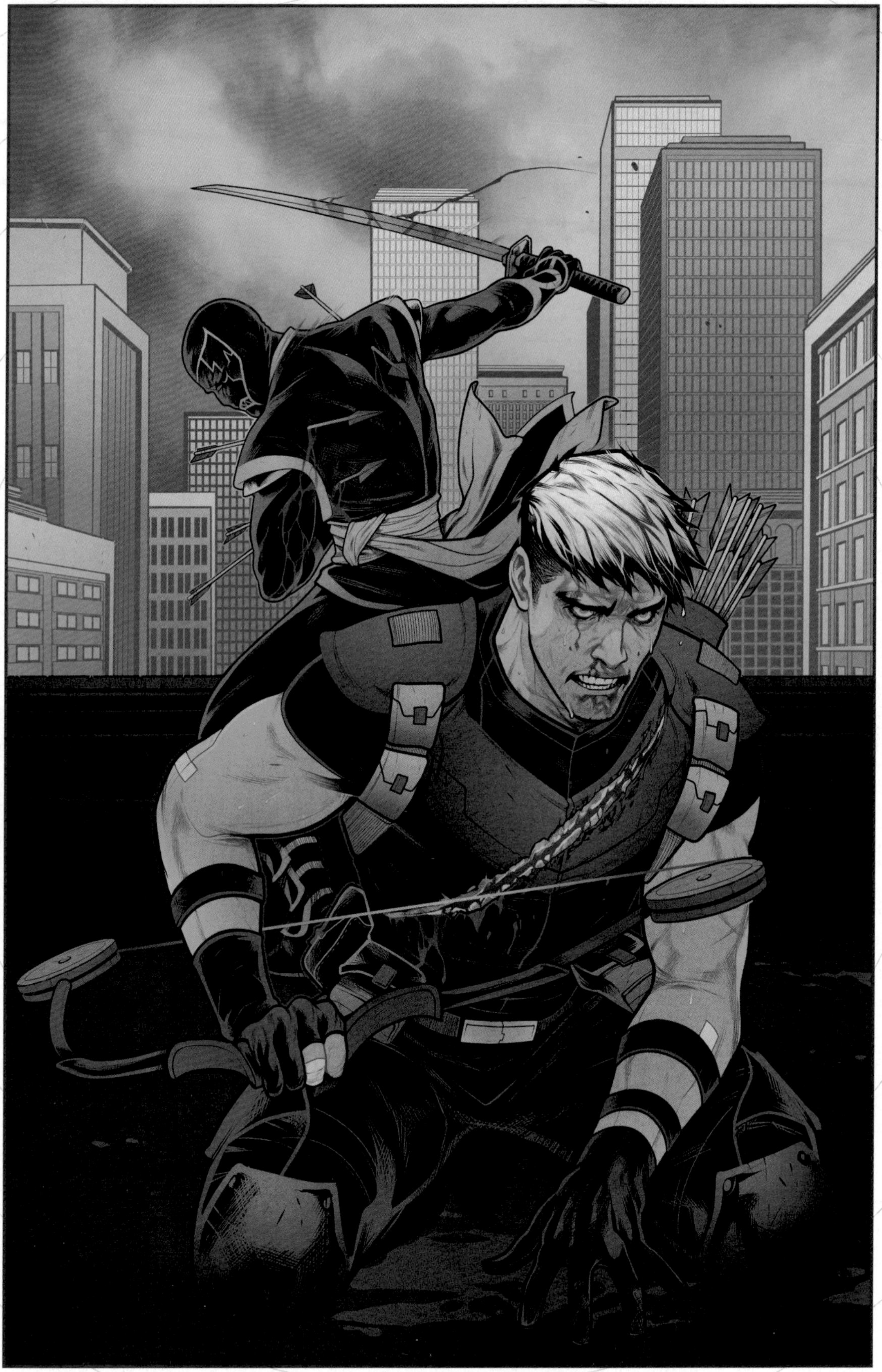

#1 VARIANT
ELIZABETH TORQUE

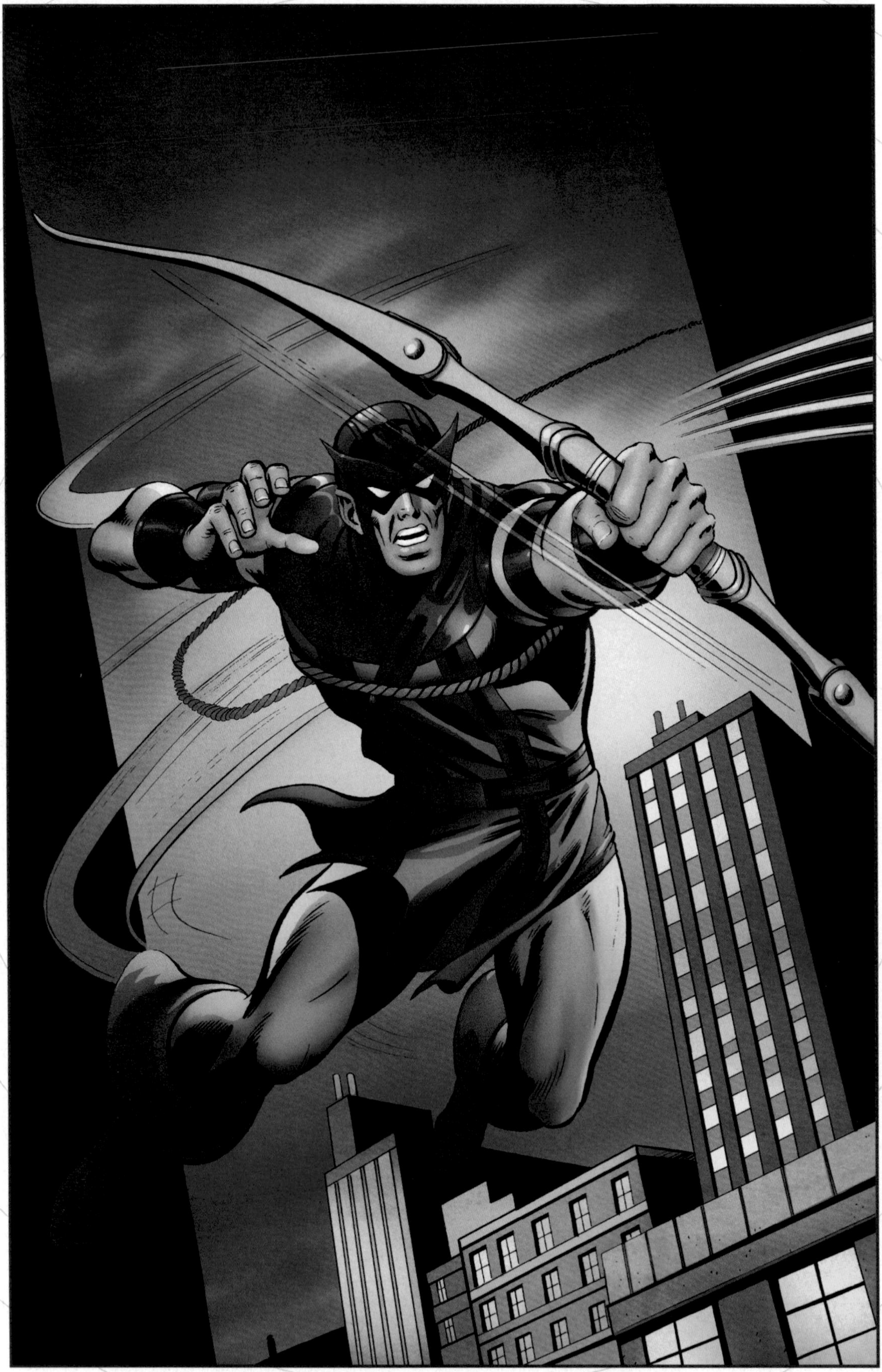

#1 HIDDEN GEM VARIANT
DAVE COCKRUM & JASON KEITH

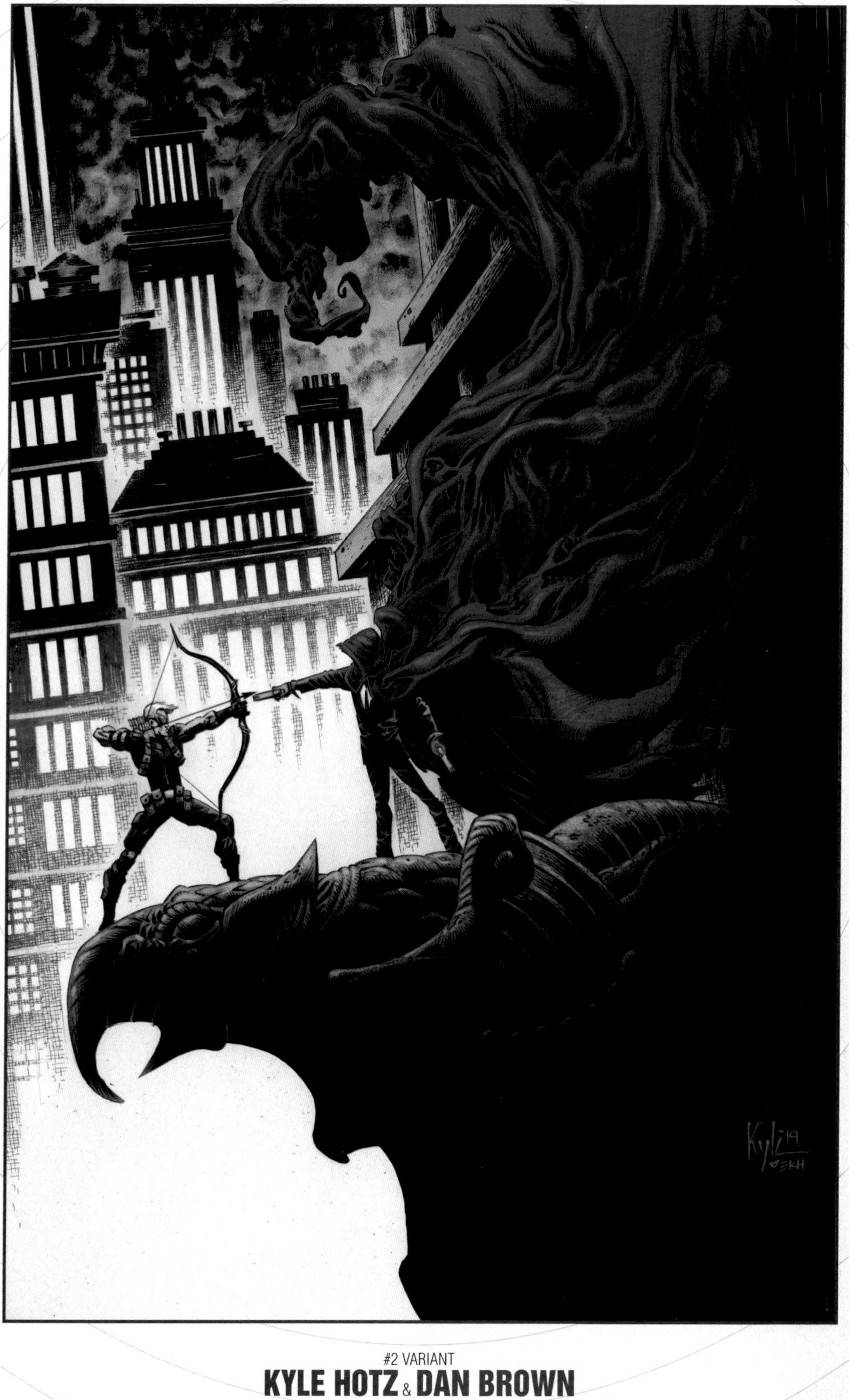

#2 VARIANT
KYLE HOTZ & DAN BROWN